Global Audit Leadership

Leaders across the globe have a common challenge they cannot ignore: CHANGE. This must be embraced and effectively managed to remain relevant and successful in a dynamic operating environment. Embracing change, including technological innovations, collaboration, and timely sharing of information, is paramount to the survival and success of everyone in an ever-changing environment.

In times of rapid change, organizations are often forced to adjust their strategic plans. Stakeholders usually need assistance to effectively manage the risks, unprecedented at times, and to capitalize on the opportunities that usually come with change. Change management must be effectively executed to assist in ensuring the viability of the organization.

This book provides advice and guidance to assist stakeholders in navigating the challenges and demands of change. It includes insights, measures, and tools that have contributed to my success as a leader in the internal audit profession for 27 years.

Security, Audit and Leadership Series

Series Editor: Dan Swanson, Dan Swanson and Associates, Ltd., Winnipeg, Manitoba, Canada

The **Security, Audit and Leadership Series** publishes leading-edge books on critical subjects facing security and audit executives as well as business leaders. Key topics addressed include Leadership, Cybersecurity, Security Leadership, Privacy, Strategic Risk Management, Auditing IT, Audit Management and Leadership

Auditing Information and Cyber Security Governance: A Controls-Based Approach
Robert E. Davis

The Security Leader's Communication Playbook: Bridging the Gap between Security and the Business
Jeffrey W. Brown

Modern Management and Leadership: Best Practice Essentials with CISO/CSO Applications
Mark Tarallo

Rising from the Mailroom to the Boardroom: Unique Insights for Governance, Risk, Compliance and Audit Leaders
Bruce Turner

Operational Auditing: Principles and Techniques for a Changing World, Second Edition
Hernan Murdock

CyRM℠: Mastering the Management of Cybersecurity
David X Martin

Why CISOs Fail, Second Edition
Barak Engel

Riding the Wave: Applying Project Management Science in the Field of Emergency Management
Andrew Boyarsky

The Shortest Hour: An Applied Approach to Boardroom Governance of Cybersecurity
Lee Parrish

Global Audit Leadership: A Practical Approach to Leading a Global Internal Audit (GIA) Function in a Constantly Changing Internal and External Landscape
Audley L. Bell

For more information about this series, please visit: https://www.routledge.com/Internal-Audit-and-IT-Audit/book-series/CRCINTAUDITA

Global Audit Leadership

A Practical Approach to Leading a Global Internal Audit (GIA) Function in a Constantly Changing Internal and External Landscape

Audley L. Bell

CRC Press
Taylor & Francis Group
Boca Raton London New York

CRC Press is an imprint of the
Taylor & Francis Group, an **informa** business

Designed cover image: Shutterstock

First edition published 2025
by CRC Press
2385 NW Executive Center Drive, Suite 320, Boca Raton FL 33431

and by CRC Press
4 Park Square, Milton Park, Abingdon, Oxon, OX14 4RN

CRC Press is an imprint of Taylor & Francis Group, LLC

Library of Congress Cataloging-in-Publication Data
Names: Bell, Audley L., author.
Title: Global audit leadership : a practical approach to leading a global internal audit (GIA) function in a constantly changing internal and external landscape / Audley L. Bell.
Description: First edition. | Boca Raton : CRC Press, 2025. |
Series: Security, audit and leadership series | Includes bibliographical references and index.
Identifiers: LCCN 2024004770 (print) | LCCN 2024004771 (ebook) |
ISBN 9781032075358 (hardback) | ISBN 9781032075372 (paperback) |
ISBN 9781003207559 (ebook)
Subjects: LCSH: Leadership. | Management audit.
Classification: LCC HD57.7 .B449 2024 (print) | LCC HD57.7 (ebook) |
DDC 658.4/092--dc23/eng/20240326
LC record available at https://lccn.loc.gov/2024004770
LC ebook record available at https://lccn.loc.gov/2024004771

ISBN: 978-1-032-07535-8 (hbk)
ISBN: 978-1-032-07537-2 (pbk)
ISBN: 978-1-003-20755-9 (ebk)

DOI: 10.1201/9781003207559

Typeset in Times
by KnowledgeWorks Global Ltd.

Contents

Preface

The journey of writing this book began in the summer of 2020 after a conversation with a friend and colleague Ann Butera, the President and Chief Executive Officer of the Whole Person Project. I was inspired to share my experience and knowledge with others, including established and aspiring leaders, professionals, practitioners, and students. During my professional career, I advocated for information sharing, continuous learning, and improvement, and this book is an extension of that value that I hold. My initial goal was to complete the book by November 2021. In hindsight, this completion date was overly ambitious, especially as a new author. Additionally, I experienced a few health challenges as I wrote the book as well as my computer system crashing midway through my writing process. Needless to say, it was very frustrating stopping and restarting the writing process and resetting the timing of the delivery of the manuscript to the publisher. I am grateful to CRC Press for affording me the opportunity to finish the manuscript.

Every leader across the globe has a common challenge. It is how to effectively lead and navigate the rapid and constant change and disruptions in the operating environment. Revisiting and rethinking how organizations operate occur more frequently in such an operating environment. The challenges, risks, and opportunities that come along with change must be effectively managed to assist in ensuring the survival, relevance, and success of the organization. Leaders and stakeholders need the team, particularly assurance service providers, to assist them in effectively addressing the risks, of which some are unprecedented, and capitalize on the opportunities that come along with change.

The purpose of this book, *Global Audit Leadership*, is to share lessons learned from leading internal audit functions during my 27 years as a chief audit executive (CAE) or head of internal audit. The sharing includes providing advice and guidance to leaders, particularly leaders of internal audit and other assurance service professionals and practitioners. Reading this book will assist leaders in improving and enhancing their ability to survive, be successful, and valuable to their organization in a dynamic operating environment. Sharing lessons learned is also one of the values ascribed to internal auditors and other assurance professionals and practitioners.

Topics covered in the book include guidance in preparing for a global CAE role and activities, measures, and tools to enhance the agility, effectiveness, and efficiency of a global internal audit (GIA) function. The book also shares challenges often encountered in a leadership role and advice and guidance on how to address them. Interpersonal skills, business acumen, relationship building, servant leadership, proactiveness, agility, and my engaging and collaborative nature played a vital role in my success as a CAE and are shared throughout this book.

My professional career spans over 40 years, including 35 in internal audit and 4 in public accounting. Additionally, I spent four years teaching accounting at the undergraduate level at the University of the West Indies, Jamaica. During my 27-year tenure leading internal audit functions, I served as the leader of internal audit for seven organizations, including two global organizations for 13 years. I also developed five internal audit functions and two in-house investigations units within GIA. Additionally, I served as a member of the ethics, compliance, and enterprise risk management leadership team at one organization, and oversaw the development of the plan for the implementation of an ERM program at another. My work experience covers several sectors and industries, including publicly traded companies, financial institutions, quasi-governmental entities, colleges and universities, construction, manufacturing, distribution, telecommunications, transportation, non-governmental organizations, micro-finance, and a credit union. The role included working closely with audit committees, senior management, and other internal and external stakeholders.

There is a message in this book for everyone whether you are a student, an entry-level staff, management trainee, an aspiring manager, a senior leader, executive, or a board member. It also applies to those in the internal and external audit, internal controls, governance, risk management, compliance, and fraud investigation professions. It is a good refresher for some stakeholders and a resource of actionable practices and ideas for others. This book will also assist stakeholders to effectively address the risks and capitalize on the opportunities of a dynamic operating environment. The following are examples of the value-added benefits that are afforded the reader of this book:

- Understanding why internal controls should be management's and the board of director's best friend
- Building and maintaining quality relationship with stakeholders
- Aligning GIA's plan with the organization's strategy, objectives, and risks
- Providing guidance in preparing for a global CAE role
- Driving engagement and collaboration with the Clean Sheet of Paper (CSOP) audit approach
- Using a combined assurance approach to get the most from an organization's assurance functions
- Utilizing a single source for risk assessment
- Understanding why in-sourcing of investigations under the umbrella of internal audit could be a double-edged sword
- Understanding and managing a multicultural team
- Understanding the pros and cons of a centralized, decentralized, and hybrid GIA organizational structure
- Transitioning to a risk-based internal audit operating environment
- Establishing an enterprise risk management program
- Managing transformational change, including the automation of the internal audit function
- Recognizing failure as an opportunity instead of being fearful of failing
- Providing guidance on how GIA can enhance its effectiveness and efficiency

I hope that my experience as a leader in the internal audit profession for 27 years with over 13 operating in a global environment will assist readers to effectively navigate the rapid change and disruption in the operating environment.

Author

Audley L. Bell, CPA, CIA, CISA, CFE, DHL, has a professional career that spans over 40 years, including 35 in internal audit and 4 in public accounting. Additionally, he spent four years teaching accounting at the undergraduate level at the University of the West Indies in Jamaica. During his 27-year tenure leading internal audit functions, he served as the leader of internal audit for seven organizations, including two global organizations for 13 years. He also developed five internal audit functions and two in-house investigations units within the internal audit function. Additionally, he served as a member of the ethics, compliance, and enterprise risk management leadership team at one organization, and he oversaw the development of the plan for the implementation of an ERM program at another. His work experience covers several sectors and industries, including publicly traded companies, financial institutions, quasi-governmental entities, colleges and universities, construction, manufacturing, distribution, telecommunications, transportation, non-governmental organizations, micro-finance, and a credit union. The role included working closely with senior management and audit committees and other internal and external stakeholders.

Prior to realizing his passion for internal audit, his first career was on the tennis court. He won several singles tennis tournaments at the junior and adult levels in Jamaica and represented Jamaica as a junior player and in Davis Cup competitions. He was the runner-up for the 1971 men's singles National Junior College Tennis Championships (NJCTC) while he attended Wingate Junior College, now Wingate University, on a tennis scholarship. The team, coached by Ronnie Smarr, won back-to-back national tennis championships in 1970 and 1971. Unbeknownst to him, Mr. Bell was the first Black tennis player in the Atlantic Coast Conference. He continued his college tennis journey at Wake Forest University on a full tennis scholarship, where he played in the number-one singles position in his senior year. After defeating the number-one tennis player from the University of North Carolina, Wake Forest's main rival, he decided to drop out of Wake Forest in the spring of his senior year in 1973 to pursue tennis professionally. In the summer of 1973, he lost in the third round of the National Collegiate Athletic Association Tennis Championships and in the final set of the final qualifying round of the US Open Tennis Championships. He also played Ilie Nastase, the number-one tennis player in the world at the time, in the Jamaica Invitational in November 1973 and lost to him 6-2, 7-5. After assessing his options, he did not believe he had a sustainable future in tennis as he was unable to financially support himself on the tennis tour.

Mr. Bell graduated cum laude with a BS in management studies and a concentration in accounting from Boston College. He is a Certified Public Accountant, a Certified Internal Auditor, a Certified Information System Auditor, and a Certified Fraud Examiner. He received an honorary Doctor of Humane Letters from Wingate University, where he is a member of the board of trustees and the chair of the audit committee. He is a former chair of Xcel's Federal Credit Union Supervisory Committee. He also served the Institute of Internal Auditors at the global and chapter levels in various roles in the past. This includes his being a member of the Board of Trustees of the Research Foundation, District Representative for the Caribbean, and Chair of the Government Relations Committee of the New York Metropolitan Chapter.

Acknowledgments

I could not have written this manuscript without the support of my family, colleagues, and friends who have contributed and encouraged me along my writing journey. Among my family, I want to recognize Dr. Ivylyn D. Davis-Bell, my wife, for her editing contributions. She is the epitome of a partner who supports and encourages one to achieve dreams, and I am so thankful we have spent 43 years together and counting! My children, Adrian and Andrea, also encouraged me along this journey. I want to thank my daughter Andrea for her role in editing the book. Finally Ms. Doret Chambers, my cousin, for her support, encouragement, and value-added contributions in editing the book.

Among my friends and colleagues, I want to thank the following people:

Brian Aryia – Chief Executive Officer, ICON

Laurence Brown, PhD, Inactive CPA, CIA, CGMA – Assistant Professor of Accounting, Clasin University, South Carolina, and Virginia Union University, Virginia, United States

Ann Butera – President and CEO, The Whole Person Project

Deloris Gordon, FCCA, CIA, M – Head of Internal Audit – Cayman Island Monetary Authority

Aaron Kantepa BACC, FCCA, MSc – Manager Risk Management, Malawi

Grace Lwanga II, MBA, BCOM, CIA, CRISC – Information Technology Professional

Jose Mendez, CIA, CFE, CRM – Internal Audit, Risk Management, and Compliance Professional

Coach Ronnie Smarr – Retired Tennis Coach, Rice University

Rebecca Smarr – Retired Home Health Regulatory Consultant

Dan Swanson – President at Dan Swanson and Associates

Maribel Walsh, CFE – Senior Investigation, World Vision International

Abbreviations

ACFE	Association of Certified Fraud Examiners
AI	Artificial intelligence
BOT	Robot
CAE	Chief audit executive
CDO	Chief diversity officer
CEO	Chief executive officer
CFE	Certified Fraud Examiner
CHRO	Chief human resources officer
CIA	Certified Internal Auditor
CISA	Certified Information System Auditor
CISO	Chief information security officer
CCO	Chief compliance officer
COSO	Committee of Sponsoring Organization
CPA	Certified Public Accountant
CPE	Continuing professional education
CPO	Chief people officer
CRO	Chief risk officer
CSOPA	Clean sheet of paper internal audit
CTO	Chief technology officer
ERM	Enterprise risk management
EU	European Union
GDPR	General Data Privacy Regulation
GIA	Global internal audit
HR	Human resources
IIA	Institute of Internal Auditors
IoT	Internet of Things
RPA	Robotics process automation
RBIA	Risk-based internal audit
SAAS	Software-as-a-service

1 Transformation to an Agile Leadership and Operating Environment

INTRODUCTION

The traditional approach of leading global internal audit (GIA) is a risk to its existence in a dynamic operating environment. The chief audit executive (CAE) and leaders of GIA must evolve, transform, and adopt the agile methodology for leading. This is required to effectively navigate the rapid and constant changes in the operating environment and remain relevant, successful, and valuable to the organization. The adoption of the agile methodology is the best option for the CAE and leaders of GIA to effectively manage the complexity, challenges, and demands of an ever-changing operating environment.

The transformation to an agile leadership and operating environment is a strategic undertaking. It must be effectively managed for it to be successful and sustainable. Agile leadership is also collaborative, stakeholder-focused, and solution-driven approach to leading.

The purpose of this chapter is to provide advice and guidance on why it is important for the leaders of GIA to evolve, transform, and adopt the agile methodology. Topics covered include the following:

- Overview of agile methodology
- Characteristics of agile leadership
- The need for the transformation to agile
- Managing the transformation to agile
- Change management
- Building a sustainable agile leadership and operating environment
- Agile organization structure
- Leadership development
- Investing in team members' development and well-being
- Readiness, resilience, and relevance
- Empowering team members
- Learn quick, share, and grow from failures
- Making the transformation to agile stick
- The value to GIA of adopting the agile methodology

DOI: 10.1201/9781003207559-1

Key learnings include the following:

- Understanding the characteristics of agile methodology and leadership
- Importance of the transformation to agile
- Key elements of effectively managing the transformation and building a sustainable agile leadership and operating environment
- Effectively managing expectations and resistance to the transformation
- Value in investing in the training, development, and well-being of team members
- Value in empowering team members
- Importance of learning quick, sharing, and growing from failures
- Making the transformation to agile stick
- Value to GIA and the organization of adopting an agile methodology

OVERVIEW OF AGILE METHODOLOGY

The agile methodology became popular with the creation and release of the Agile Manifesto in 2001.[1] It is a collection of software development methodologies based on a set of common values and principles for rapidly developing and delivering quality software to customers. It includes extreme programming, adaptive software development, scrum, dynamic system development method, crystal, feature-driven development, and pragmatic programming.[2] Agile methodology is a principle-based approach to software development, which allows for more flexibility and creativity. It also makes it easier to quickly pivot and adapt to change. It is unlike the traditional waterfall linear approach, which is structured, program-driven, and rigid.[3] A summary of the differences between the traditional waterfall and agile methodology project delivery is shown below in Figure 1.1.

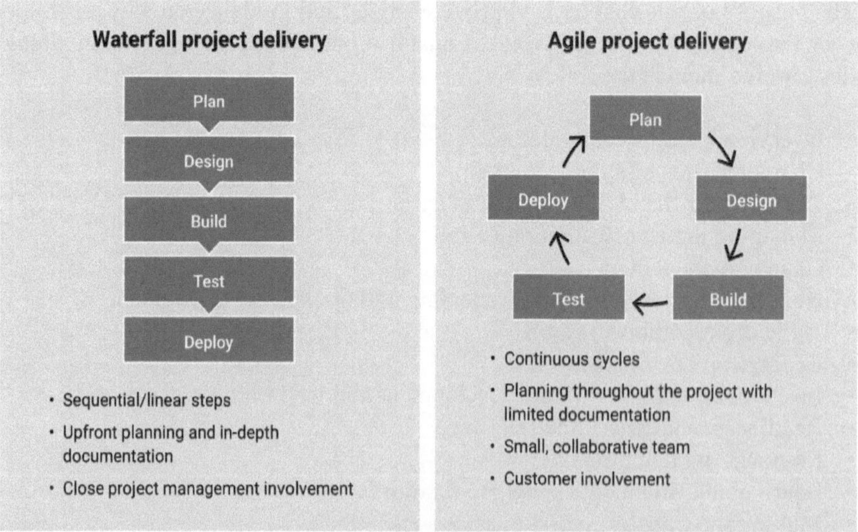

FIGURE 1.1 Waterfall and agile project delivery differences.[4] (Permission granted by ISACA)

TABLE 1.1
Agile Manifesto Four Key Values

Individuals and interactions	Over processes and tools
Working software	Over comprehensive documentation
Customer collaboration	Over contract negotiation
Responding to change	Over following a plan

The Agile Manifesto lays the foundation and provides guidance on how to become agile. The foundation and guidance are based on four key values and supported by 12 principles. The principles must be observed to effectively apply the agile methodology. The four values are shown above in Table 1.1.[5]

The 12 principles of the agile methodology are as follows[6]:

1. Our highest priority is to satisfy the customer through early and continuous delivery of valuable software
2. Welcome changing requirements, even late in development. Agile processes harness change for the customer's competitive advantage
3. Deliver working software frequently, from a couple of weeks to a couple of months, with a preference to the shorter timescale
4. Business people and developers must work together daily throughout the project
5. Build projects around motivated individuals. Give them the environment and support they need and trust them to get the job done
6. The most efficient and effective method of conveying information to and within a development team is face-to-face conversation
7. Working software is the primary measure of progress
8. Agile processes promote sustainable development. The sponsors, developers, and users should be able to maintain a constant pace indefinitely
9. Continuous attention to technical excellence and good design enhances agility
10. Simplicity – the art of maximizing the amount of work not done – is essential
11. The best architectures, requirements, and designs emerge from self-organizing teams
12. At regular intervals, the team reflects on how to become more effective, then tunes and adjust its behaving accordingly

Scrum is the most widely used methodology for the management and delivery of quality software development services and products as well as project management.[7] It is "a lightweight framework that helps people, teams and organizations generate value through adaptive solutions for complex problems."[8] The scrum approach breaks down complex projects into small units referred to as sprints.[9] The sprints are assigned to small teams working collaboratively toward a common goal with each sprint typically lasting 1–4 weeks.[10] Complex projects become easier to manage, and using an agile methodology enhances the likelihood of the timely completion of the overall project. Stand-up sprint updates are a key element of the scrum approach[11] as it helps to keep the team focused, minimizes surprises, and promotes a collaborative approach to completing tasks.

The information technology (IT) industry took the risk decades ago to transform and adopt the agile methodology for developing software. It has helped the IT industry to overcome the challenges frequently encountered with the traditional waterfall approach of software development. The challenges included missed deadlines, cost overruns, and lack of interaction with impacted stakeholders. Also, too much time was spent planning, designing, and documenting the software development process. Agile methodology is about working effectively and efficiently by simplifying and breaking projects into smaller and more manageable units. The process is a type of plan as you go and trial-and-error exercise. It includes engaging, collaborating, and exploring several iterations of the software with stakeholders to produce quality and workable software. Learning quickly from failures is vital to improving and delivering quality software to stakeholders.

Today, organizations from all industries are embracing and quickly adopting the agile methodology to survive and improve their effectiveness, efficiency, and sustainability. These improvements have allowed organizations to remain resilient, competitive, and successful in the ever-changing operating environment. The early adoption of the agile methodology has enabled the IT industry to be the primary driver of change, while other industries and organizations are struggling to survive, remain relevant, and competitive.

CHARACTERISTICS OF AGILE LEADERSHIP

The key characteristics of effective leadership do not change in an agile GIA leadership or operating environment. Key characteristics include the following:

- Effective tone at the top: Agile leaders lead by example and set the tone at the top to shape the ethical values and culture of the organization.
- Collaborative: Agile leaders listen, empathize, and share information closely with stakeholders on tasks or issue resolution.
- Inclusive: Agile leaders welcome the participation and ideas of key stakeholders in the decision-making process.
- Attentive: Agile leaders listen and seek input and advice from inside as well as outside of the team and are not afraid to admit to what they do not know.
- Creative and innovative: Agile leaders encourage and support creativity and innovation.
- Responsive and respectful: Agile leaders are respectful, responsive, and demonstrate that everyone in the organization has a role to play, which builds trust and confidence in leadership.
- Flexible and adaptable: Agile leaders are open to change and finding common ground.

- Accountable: Agile leaders take responsibility, do not blame others for failures, quickly take corrective action, and share lessons learned with others in the organization who can benefit from it.
- Problem-solving: Agile leaders focus on finding timely actionable solutions and not on finding faults or blaming others for problems.
- Servant leadership: Agile leaders know that their primary role is assisting and supporting others achieve their objectives.
- Transparency: Agile leaders readily share information regardless of the repercussions, including telling stakeholders the truth and not what they want to hear or what is convenient.
- Empowerment: Agile leaders empower team members to be proactive and build their business acumen through assignments that allow them to learn and expand their knowledge.

The following are 13 examples of what it takes to become a more agile leader according to the Forbes Coaches Council[12]:

- Embrace your team
- Know where you are going
- Think globally and embrace talent
- Go outside of your usual circle for insight
- Exercise your body and mind
- Step outside of your comfort zone
- Listen, Listen, Listen
- Think and move quickly
- Develop confidence with uncertainty
- Act like a scientist
- Know and develop yourself
- Act despite fear
- Be willing to fail

THE NEED FOR THE TRANSFORMATION TO AGILE

The traditional waterfall approach of leading GIA is a risk to its existence in an ever-changing operating environment. The approach is usually bureaucratic, slow, rigid, and reactive. The focus is on the past, historical data, and accomplishing the annual audit plan rather than on the present, the future, and what is most important to the organization and its stakeholders. The past should not be forgotten, but there should not be a fixation on the past when everything is constantly changing in the operating environment at a rapid speed. An agile GIA leadership is forward-looking and thinking. The focus is more on the present, the future, and what is most important to the organization and its stakeholders. The leaders of traditional GIA leadership and operations must evolve and transform to an agile GIA leadership and operating environment. This will enable them to be resilient, relevant, and more valuable to the organization and its stakeholders.

There are many reasons why a traditional leadership-driven GIA operation is a risk to the survival, sustainability, and success of GIA in an ever-changing operating environment. The reasons include the following:

- Autocratic and bureaucratic organizational structure
- Centralized operations
- Inability to quickly pivot and adjust to change
- Rigid and inflexible
- Reactive instead of proactive
- Backward thinking and looking
- Not inclusive or transparent
- Not conducive to continuous learning and improvement
- Risk-averse and fear of failing

The transformation to an agile GIA leadership and operating environment is a strategic undertaking. Transformation is a complex and challenging type of change. It is a journey due to the time it takes for the changes to become sustainable. The transformation to an agile GIA leadership and operating environment is strategic due to the following:

- Impact on the governance of the organization as the audit committee relies on the assurance and advice GIA provides to assist them in performing their governance oversight responsibilities.
- Usually requires the following:
  - Revisiting and reshaping of the mission, vision, organizational structure, strategy, and objectives of the organization.
  - Change in culture, including values, customs, and norms of the organization.
  - Support and approval from senior management and the board.
- Usually impacts team members and stakeholders across the organization.

A change in the culture of an organization takes years to stabilize and normalize. This is because a transformational change usually requires a change in the mindset and attitude of team members. This includes the way team members think, engage, communicate, and work with others.

The transformation to an agile GIA leadership and operating environment is a change to an engaging, collaborative, and solution-oriented operating environment. This is because agility requires ongoing interaction with stakeholders. The transformation is an opportunity for team members to enhance their knowledge and understanding of the organization including the following:

- The mission, vision, values, strategy, objectives, and risks to the organization.
- What is most important to stakeholders?
- What is working well and what needs to change?
- What keeps key stakeholders awake at night?
- What stakeholders expect from GIA?

TABLE 1.2
Comparative Summary of Traditional and Agile Leadership Operating Environment

Subject	Traditional GIA Leadership	Agile GIA Leadership
Organization	Hierarchical and formal structure	Flat and less formal structure
Focus	Compliance and task oriented	Stakeholders needs
Management style	Closed, rigid, authoritative, and exclusive	Open, collaborative, democratic, and inclusive
Decision-making process	Centralized, bureaucratic, and slow	Decentralized, distributed, delegated, and quick
Operating environment	Static	Dynamic
Communications	Top down	Ongoing and across the organization
Flow of information	Top down	Top down and bottom up
Risk appetite	Risk averse	Allows risk within the tolerance of the organization's risk appetite
Failure	Feared	Allowed
Collaboration and sharing of information	Low	High
Creative and innovative	Low	High
Response to change	Slow	Quick

The transformation also provides an opportunity for GIA leaders and team members to share their expertise, and knowledge of the business, as needed. It is also an opportunity to provide insight and foresight to stakeholders to assist them in making more informed decisions.

A comparison of traditional and agile GIA leadership and operating environments shows why agile is more effective and efficient as illustrated above in Table 1.2.

MANAGING THE TRANSFORMATION TO AGILE

The transformation to an agile GIA leadership and operating environment is a journey and requires effective management of the areas and activities that are most important to the transformation. It includes prioritizing, monitoring, and periodically updating stakeholders on the status of the transformation. Areas and activities that are most important and require effective management include the following:

- The plan
- Communication
- Execution
- Risk
- Change management
- Monitoring and reporting
- Post-implementation review

The Plan

The plan is the roadmap for effectively managing the transformation process. It paves the way and minimizes risks to the successful implementation of the transformation to agile. The leaders of GIA must have a plan and be intentional about keeping team members informed and engaged in the process. Effective planning supports participation and inclusion of input from those impacted by the transformation. This is particularly important for team members working at regional and local offices or remotely from their home. Effective planning also includes the following:

- Developing the strategy and objectives
- Identifying and assessing risk
- Determining the following:
    - Organization's structure, policies, processes, and procedures
    - Required resources to implement the transformation
    - Required coordination and collaboration to keep stakeholders informed
    - Required monitoring and periodic reporting on the status of the transformation
    - Communication strategy
    - Deliverables and timeline
    - Key performance indicators
- Assigning roles, responsibilities, authority, and accountability

Communication

The success of the transformation to agile depends in part on how well it is communicated to team members and stakeholders. Effectively communicated messages are delivered in the clearest and simplest way due to the diversity of cultures and languages in a global organization. It is important that messages are understood by team members and stakeholders to ensure everyone understands the message. The risk of miscommunication and misunderstandings is high in a global organization with diverse cultures and languages.

The communication of major organizational change initiatives usually comes from the chief executive officer (CEO), sponsor, and/or owner of the initiative. It may also include the chairperson of the board or a board sub-committee. Support from the chairperson of the board or sub-committee enhances the importance of the transformation to the organization. The communication exemplifies their support for the transformation and the importance of the change. It also contributes to the support and cooperation of management and staff across the organization for the transformation. The announcement should include the following:

- Justification
- Objective
- Risks and rewards
- Roles, responsibility, and accountability

- What will change, remain the same, or be eliminated
- Deliverables and timelines
- Help desk or contact person(s) for questions

Effective communication of messages requires confirming and reconfirming messages. This is to ensure that messages are clearly understood and interpreted the same way by everyone across the organization. Messages can easily be misunderstood or misinterpreted in a global organization due to the following:

- Ambiguous messages
- Misinterpretation of messages
- Distorted or lost messages
- Diverse culture and language barriers

Confirming and periodically reconfirming the understanding of messages is particularly important with team members and stakeholders in the field at the regional and local office levels. This is to ensure that the original or official messages, including updates, remain intact. Confirming and periodically reconfirming mission's critical messages help to keep the transformation on tract. This also helps to keep the messages at the forefront of team members' thinking and activities.

Miscommunicating and misunderstanding of the objectives of the transformation to agile can be costly. They can lead to missed opportunities in a dynamic operating environment. They can also derail the transformation and, although not intentional, can be as serious as someone sabotaging the transformation. The leaders of GIA must ensure that communication is clear, concise, and easy to understand for everyone across the organization.

Ongoing communication is critical in keeping team members and stakeholders engaged, informed, and connected. This is important in an ever-changing and disruptive operating environment. It minimizes the risks of miscommunication and misunderstandings. Ongoing communication helps to keep the objectives of the transformation at the forefront of the thinking and activities of the leaders of GIA, team members, and stakeholders. Communication must be up, down, and across the organization. This is particularly important for team members and stakeholders in the field that are impacted by the transformation. Ongoing communication includes the following:

- Confirming receipt of messages
- Reconfirming mission critical messages periodically
- Listening to input especially from team members and impacted stakeholders
- Providing timely, transparent, and honest responses to questions and feedback
- Timely sharing of adjustments and modifications to the plan with key stakeholders
- Timely sharing of failures, including mistakes, delays, and cost overruns with key stakeholders

Execution

Effective management of the transformation to agile requires effective execution. Effective execution is converting the plan into action or setting the plan into motion. The key objective of the execution phase is the successful implementation of the transformation to agile. A competent and experienced manager is required to lead and oversee the execution process. This includes directing, supporting, and motivating GIA's team, while monitoring and periodically reporting on the status of the activities and progress of the transformation.

The manager of the transformation must engage and invite stakeholders to participate in the decision-making process. The manager must also incorporate to the extent possible team members' and stakeholders' input into the transformation plan. This is particularly important to team members and stakeholders in the field. They are usually closest to the actions and activities of a major organizational change or transformation. This includes team members and stakeholders responsible for implementing, maintaining, monitoring, reporting, and complying with the objectives and/or activities of the transformation. They are usually more knowledgeable about the local context and operating environment and know what works best.

The participation of team members and stakeholders in the field can easily get lost or eroded if their input is ignored. Their participation and support strengthen and enhance the likelihood that the changes will be long lasting, thus enabling a successful transformation. It also gives team members and stakeholders a sense of part ownership of the transformation to agile.

Risk

Risks are known and unknown activities and events that must be effectively managed to mitigate threats to the achievement of the objectives of the transformation to agile. Effective risk management provides reasonable assurance of achieving the objectives of the transformation. It requires timely identifying, assessing, mitigating, monitoring, and periodically reporting on the risks to the transformation. Assessing risks includes evaluating and prioritizing the risks.

Identifying and assessing risks is one of the first tasks that leaders and managers must perform before undertaking a project or initiative. This must be an ongoing activity as risks are also constantly changing in the operating environment. Team members and stakeholders must be aware of the risks to effectively manage and mitigate them. Risks may include the following:

- Lack of buy-in and support from key stakeholders
- Lack of understanding of the transformation
- Misalignment
- Sabotage by team members who do not embrace change
- Staff taking a wait and see attitude by holding out or sitting on the fence to see if the change works
- Managers downplaying, deprioritizing, and delaying the completion of the initiative

- Resource constraints such as inadequately skilled staff and lack of access to technology
- Reluctance of team members to learn, improve, and grow from failure

Change Management

There is always going to be some resistance to a major organizational change or transformation. This is because a major change or transformation is usually a disruptive undertaking that needs to be effectively managed. The undertaking often requires a change in the mindset and attitude of team members and stakeholders. This includes the way team members think, engage, communicate, and work with each other. Emotions tend to run high in these situations. The emotions often give rise to uncertainties, stress, and anxiety of team members as it relates to:

- Losing power or control
- Becoming redundant and losing one's job
- Being transferred to another department
- Learning new ways of doing things
- Stepping out of one's comfort zone
- Finding a new job

Team members and stakeholders resisting the change may at times engage in activities to undermine and/or derail the transformation. The activities may include one or more of the following:

- Sabotaging the transformation initiative
- Ignoring the change
- Making excuses continuously for why work is not completed
- Resisting to learn, improve, and grow from failures
- Blaming others for failures, including missed deadlines, setbacks, mistakes, delays, and cost overruns

The leaders of GIA must collaborate closely with team members and stakeholders who are resisting the change. This is because the resistance can easily derail the transformation if not effectively managed. There will be early as well as late adopters of the change. The leaders must ensure there is a plan in place to maintain and strengthen the support for the transformation to agile. The plan will help to reduce skepticism and risks to the transformation. The plan should include ongoing communication of the status of the transformation to agile as well as the following:

- Timely, transparent, and consistent messaging
- Periodic reconfirmation of the objectives and value of the transformation to the organization
- Timely response to feedback, questions, and complaints
- Periodic project status update meetings and reports

- Encourage quick ownership of failures and learn, share, and grow from the experience
- Recognizing and rewarding staff and stakeholders for achieving their objectives

The leaders of GIA must set the expectation of the possibility of failure during the transformation to an agile GIA leadership and operating environment. They must manage expectations by sharing upfront with team members and stakeholders the possibility of failure and plans to mitigate that risk. There are going to be failures in any major change initiative. It is not a matter of whether there will be failures. It is a matter of when. Sharing that expectation upfront will reduce the fear, surprise factor, and negativity from the skeptics of the project should a failure occur. The leaders must learn and act quickly to address failures before they become disasters.

Monitoring and Reporting

Monitoring is to ensure the transformation to an agile leadership, and operating environment is progressing as planned. This includes operating effectively, efficiently, and in compliance with required laws, regulations, standards, policies, and procedures. Periodic reports are required to keep stakeholders informed of the status of the transformation initiative. Periodic reports assist the CAE and leaders of GIA in making more informed decisions regarding the implementation of the transformation initiative.

Post-Implementation Review

A post-implementation review is necessary to ensure that the transformation to an agile leadership and operating environment is occurring as planned. The review provides an opportunity for the CAE and leaders of GIA to address gaps in the planning and implementation process. This is to minimize subsequent risk or noncompliance with required laws, regulations, standards, policies, and procedures.

BUILDING A SUSTAINABLE AGILE LEADERSHIP AND OPERATING ENVIRONMENT

The key elements of building and maintaining a sustainable agile GIA leadership and operating environment include the following:

- Agile organization structure
- Leadership development
- Investing in team members' development and well-being
- Readiness, resilience, and relevance
- Empowering team members
- Learning quickly, sharing, and growing from failures

Each of the preceding are covered separately below.

Agile Organization Structure

An agile GIA organization structure must be nimble, adaptable, and flexible. This enhances the ability of the leaders and team members to quickly think, respond and work differently. The organizational structure enables stakeholders to meet existing challenges and new demands in a timely manner, which includes compromising, and modifying existing plans.

Nimbleness enables stakeholders to quickly respond and adapt to change or a new situation or condition. The reaction to change must be swift to remain relevant and effective in an ever-changing operating environment. It requires a lean team as well as effective structures, systems, policies, processes, and procedures. The decision or response is less likely to be as swift in a bureaucratic organization where the structure is usually hierarchical. Nimbleness is most effective in a flat organization structure.

Adaptability enables stakeholders to cope with and quickly adjust to changes such as technological innovations and industry trends. This includes adjusting to unexpected disturbances and disruption in the operating environment, which is often caused by external forces such as technological innovations, government regulations, and natural disasters.

An agile GIA organizational structure provides the highest level of interaction and collaboration with stakeholders, including GIA's team members. The flatter the organization structure, the greater the level of interaction and collaboration. The choice of a GIA's organizational structure is usually between centralized, decentralized, or hybrid. A centralized structure is one where the leaders of GIA at headquarters make all GIA's administrative and operating decisions. A decentralized structure is where most of GIA's administrative and operating decisions are made by leaders at the regional and/or local office level. A hybrid structure is a mix of a centralized and decentralized organization structure.

A flat organizational structure enables and enhances the agility and ability of the leaders of GIA to make quick decisions. The flat organization structure minimizes the back and forth of the bureaucracy that is often found in centralized organizational structures. In a decentralized structure, the leaders and team members in the field usually have a better understanding of the local context and operating environment. They are better able to respond and act quickly.

There is usually a GIA leadership presence at headquarters providing oversight and guidance regardless of the organization structure. Oversight at headquarters is usually provided by the CAE and a nimble support team. The support team is usually an executive assistant and may include leaders of GIA's operations, IT, data analytics, and fraud investigation. It is usually more cost-effective for the support team to operate from headquarters instead of each office having their own support team.

An agile GIA organizational structure is one that supports teamwork. Organizing, forming, and working in teams are key elements of an agile GIA leadership and operating environment. This enables the leaders and team members to engage and work collaboratively. It is an environment where leaders are willing to roll up their sleeves and get their hands dirty. The focus is on supporting and assisting stakeholders achieve their business, operating, reporting, and compliance objectives. Agile leaders rolling up their sleeves and getting their hands dirty will assist in motivating the team. It also enhances stakeholders' understanding, knowledge, and appreciation of the work being done by GIA's team.

Leadership Development

Leadership development is a key element of an agile leadership and operating environment. This is because it enables leaders to respond and act quickly with confidence when there is a leadership gap or disruption in the operating environment. Leadership development programs contribute to greater collaboration of current and future leaders and keep them informed of changes in the operating environment.

There are pros and cons associated with the inclusion of candidates external to the organization in GIA's succession plan. External candidates often bring innovative ideas, perspectives, and energy to an existing organization. They are also better able to move a static and ineffective operation forward because they are usually not beholden to one way of working within the organization. However, external candidates can be very disruptive when they do not spend the time to understand the organization's culture, business, and operations. Additionally, the learning curve and the time it takes for an external candidate to adjust to the new role can be lengthy compared to an internal candidate. An internal candidate is usually better able to adjust due to institutional knowledge.

The organization's leadership development program is integral to its succession plan. This is because there is no time in an ever-changing operating environment to engage in lengthy recruiting and training programs to fill leadership gaps. There are usually identified future leaders of the organization who must be ready to assume leadership roles in short notice. Organizations must be ready to act quickly to unexpected leadership changes and gaps. This includes a sudden resignation, life-threatening illness, or death of a leader. An organization's succession plan plays a key role in minimizing leadership gaps. Leadership gap exposes an organization to significant risks, including the following:

- Demise of the organization
- Breakdown in internal controls
- Fraud
- Abuse of authority and resources
- Noncompliance with laws and regulations
- Disruption of operations
- Delay in achieving objectives
- Missed opportunities
- Missed deliverables

Leadership development plays a key role in the sustainability and success of an organization through the following:

- Contributing to the maintenance of an agile leadership and operating environment

- Strengthening the readiness, resilience, and relevance of the organization and its leadership
- Minimizing the risk of disruption and lost opportunities for the organization
- Enabling relationship building and collaboration among current and future leaders of the organization
- Enhancing recruiting and retention of high-performing team members
- Enhancing team members' morale
- Driving and supporting continuous learning, improvement, and development

Leadership development programs vary from organization to organization. This includes homegrown, co-sourced, and outsourced. Homegrown leadership development programs are often conducted by senior leaders, managers, and subject matter experts within the organization. Homegrown leadership development programs are strengthened when the program includes external experts and executive development programs. These include specialized and condensed executive development and MBA programs offered by many universities. A co-sourced program is where the homegrown program is supplemented by partnering with subject matter experts outside of the organization. An outsourced leadership development program is where the program is contracted to a service provider such as a university, consultant, or specialty firm.

Investment in leadership development training and continuing education programs must be tailored to all levels of leaders in the organization. The investment will ensure that all leaders have basic leadership training. This includes being well-grounded in the mission, vision, values, and strategy of the organization, as well as the business, operating, reporting, and compliance objectives. There must also be a clear understanding of how their work contributes to the objectives of the organization.

Agile leaders must invest in self-learning to remain effective. Self-learning is a key contributor of knowledge, experience, and skills learned and developed over time. Self-learning must become a key element of a leaders' continuing education and professional development in a constantly changing operating environment. Leaders and team members cannot depend solely on the organization to satisfy all their career and professional developmental needs. They must invest time in self-learning to thrive and remain relevant.

Investing in Team Members' Development and Well-Being

Investing in team members' development and well-being contributes to a positive and effective agile GIA leadership and operating environment. The leaders of GIA must build and maintain a welcoming and supporting operating environment for agile to thrive. It is an environment where team members enjoy working, developing, and advancing their professional career within GIA or the organization. This requires investing in the hiring, developing, and retaining a high-performing, diverse, multicultural, and sustainable GIA team. This includes providing funding for ongoing continuing professional education and technological tools to meet leadership development goals.

Investing in GIA's team members' development and well-being also contributes to high-quality performance and retention of team members. Factors driving high-quality performance and retention of team members include:

- Diverse, equitable, and inclusive work environment
- Competitive health insurance coverage
- Vacation and sick time
- Employee assistance program, including counseling for addiction and mental health issues
- Maternal, paternal, and family leaves
- Compensatory time off for working overtime hours not eligible for payment

The investment in the development and well-being of GIA's team members has its risks. In countries where the organization operates the competition can be intense for high-quality staff, particularly in developing countries. Expect some high-performing team members to leave the organization after investing in their training and professional development. Organizations often offer lucrative compensation packages to regional and local staff to get them to join the organization. These packages often make it almost impossible for local employers, including the local government, to compete. As a result, there are countries that enact local laws to allow local employers to compete. Examples of such laws include taxation of benefits such as pension, housing, car, and child tuition allowance. The preceding is a reality that global organizations must effectively manage.

GIA's team members are its most important assets and must be effectively managed. It includes investing in their career, professional development, and well-being. This enhances attracting, hiring, and retaining a sustainable high-performing, diverse, and multicultural team. The key elements of effectively managing GIA's most important asset include:

- Competitive compensation package: The compensation package should be one that is commensurate with the candidate's experience, expertise, and qualifications. The package usually includes a base salary as well as one or more of the following: sign on and/or annual bonus; stock options; cash savings account; health and life insurance plans.
- Leadership succession plan: A leadership succession plan will minimize the risk of a leadership gap and disruption of GIA's operations. An effective leadership succession plan should include potential candidates outside of GIA and the organization. This is particularly effective where there are no internal candidates ready to fill a role should there be a sudden gap in leadership or a key vacancy.
- Leadership development plan: The leaders of GIA must have a leadership development plan for potential managers and leaders. An effective leadership development plan may include:
  - Leadership development training
  - Executive leadership development program
  - Executive MBA program

    - Secondments to other areas of the organization
    - Rotation of GIA's team members
- Mentoring program: Team members are provided with mentors who they can confide in, share thoughts, and use as a sounding board.
- Equity, growth, development, and promotional opportunities: This is at times skewed toward team members at headquarters. Regional and local team members often inquire about perceived and/or real inequities in salary and benefits, and little or no opportunities for growth, development, and promotion. GIA may be unable to address the perceived and/or real inequities in salary because of the difference in cost of living in developed and developing countries. However, the gaps and inequities in salaries are often offset by the offering of pension, housing, car, and tuition allowances to regional and local team members.
- Team member's career development plan: The plan outlines the short- and long-term goals and the required support to accomplish the goals. The team member's career development plan makes it easier for GIA to support team members with their career development needs and goals.
- Rotation: This is usually part of a team member's career development plan. It entails rotating to other areas of GIA to expand their understanding and knowledge of GIA's operations.
- Secondment: This is a tool that is used at times to either fill a vacancy or support team members with their career development plan. It is where a team member is requested to join another department or function to bridge a gap in staffing, management, or leadership for a specified period.

Continuous learning and improvement are key elements of the development of team members in an agile GIA leadership and operating environment. This is because continuous learning and improvement are critical to the survival, sustainability, and success of GIA in an ever-changing operating environment. An agile GIA leadership and operating environment must invest in the training, continuing professional education, and development of team members. Continuous learning and improvement enable the leaders and team members to be ready, resilient, and relevant. The training also keeps them connected, current, and informed of changes in the operating environment. This makes it easier for the leaders and team members to be proactive in quickly responding and adapting to change. The professional development also enables them to anticipate and be proactive in providing advice, including insight and foresight, to stakeholders on new and emerging risks and opportunities.

Readiness, Resilience, and Relevance

The readiness of the leaders of GIA depends on their ability to quickly think, respond, and adapt to rapid change. This includes focusing on what is most important to the organization and its stakeholders. The change can be either a new situation, condition, or simply working differently. Resilience is the ability to quickly pivot and recover from a failure, which requires quickly recognizing and acknowledging failure. Failure is a part of the journey to success. There is no time to fixate on failure in a fast-paced and disruptive operating environment. The experience must be used as an opportunity to learn, improve, grow, and become more effective and efficient. Timely sharing of lessons learned from the experience with stakeholders, who can benefit from it, enhances the collective knowledge on how to respond to any future similar issues within the organization.

Relevance is focusing on delivering what the organization and its stakeholders need most to be successful. The leaders and team members of GIA must keep at its forefront that GIA is a support function. The primary focus should be on assisting stakeholders succeed in achieving their objectives. The organization and stakeholders' success are also GIA's success. A relevant GIA is one that is constantly and consistently adding value to the organization. Relevance is maintained by:

- Quickly recognizing, embracing, and adapting to change in the operating environment
- Timely aligning GIA's work with the changing needs of the organization and its stakeholders
- Ongoing engagement, communication, collaboration, and sharing of information with team members and stakeholders
- Keeping abreast of technological innovations, regulatory developments in the industry and profession, and geopolitical developments
- Networking with peers and colleagues

Empowering Team Members

An agile GIA leadership is one that empowers team members and gives them the freedom to make decisions on behalf of GIA. It is a form of distributed leadership that should occur at all levels of an organization. Empowering team members gives them the freedom and flexibility to be more creative and innovative. It enhances their ability to determine the most effective way to achieve GIA's objectives. Empowered team members create and add value based on the local context and operating environment of the organization. They are accountable for their actions and decisions and are responsible for the following:

- Organizing and building teams
- Setting objectives
- Making major decisions on behalf of GIA
- Managing risks, including identifying, assessing, mitigating, monitoring, and reporting
- Providing periodic updates and status reports to headquarters

The complexity of the operating environment has strengthened the case for empowering team members to make decisions on behalf of GIA. The complexity is often caused by the constant and rapid pace of change and disruption in the operating environment. Empowerment is particularly important for team members in the field, at the regional and local office levels. This enables them to make decisions without the delays of the bureaucracy often found in a centralized operating environment.

Empowering team members in the field to make decisions on behalf of GIA tends to be more effective and efficient because of the following:

- Able to respond quickly and make decisions
- Closest to the actions and activities of the operating environment
- Have a better understanding of the local context and operating environment

It is important that empowered team members keep headquarters and other stakeholders impacted informed of major decisions made at the regional and local levels. This is particularly important regarding interdepartmental decisions that are critical to GIA's objectives.

Empowered team members' actions and activities must be in alignment with the strategy and the business, operating, reporting, and compliance objectives of GIA and the organization. Team members must become well-grounded and knowledgeable of the mission, vision, values, strategy, objectives, and risks to GIA and the organization as part of the empowerment process. Alignment is critical in achieving the overall objectives of GIA. Key factors contributing to the alignment include the following:

- Competent and experienced team
- Clarity of role, responsibilities, and authority
- Knowledge and understanding of GIA and the organization's strategic, business, and operational objectives, and risks
- Knowledge and understanding of key policies, processes, and procedures of GIA and the organization
- Knowledge and understanding of how their role contributes to the mission, vision, and values of GIA and the organization

Empowering team members to make effective decisions on behalf of GIA without the required resources and accountability is a recipe for failure and disaster. Empowering team members requires giving them the responsibility, authority, training, coaching, mentoring, and the resources required to take risks and make informed decisions. Empowered team members must be required to report periodically or as needed to the leaders of GIA on major decisions and actions taken on behalf of GIA. This is to avoid surprises and keep stakeholders informed. They must also be held accountable for their decisions and actions.

Learn Quick, Share, and Grow from Failures

An agile GIA leadership and operating environment is one that is ready and willing to deal with successes and failures, including the expected and unexpected. The leaders and team members must become comfortable dealing with sudden and rapid change and uncertainties in the operating environment. They must also quickly learn and share with stakeholders who can benefit from the experience. This includes the timely sharing of new and emerging trends, issues, risks, and improvement opportunities.

The outcome of actions taken by the leaders of GIA or team members may not meet expectations or may fail at times. Failure must be viewed as an opportunity to learn, improve, and grow. It is important that empowered team members quickly recognize and acknowledge failure and do the following:

- Be transparent and honest about failure
- Avoid surprises
- Quickly learn and take corrective action
- Timely share the lessons learned with stakeholders who can benefit from it

The implementation of the lessons learned will enhance future success and minimize the risk of the recurrence of the issue or problem.

Fear of failure is a major risk to an agile GIA leadership and operating environment. This is because fear of failure limits creativity, innovation, and growth. It encourages a status quo mindset and inhibits the development of working differently. As Thomas Edison once said when asked by a reporter, "How did it feel to fail 1,000 times?" Edison replied, "I did not fail 1,000 times. The light bulb is an invention with 1,000 steps."[13]

An agile operating environment is one where the leadership understands that there will be failures. This may include mistakes, setbacks, delays, missed deadlines, and budget overruns. Failure is an opportunity to learn and become more effective while adding value to the organization. Failure is part of the journey of successfully achieving the objectives of the organization. Agile leaders understand that failure is part of the learning process.

Sharing lessons learned from failures and acting quickly to resolve them are key elements of an agile GIA leadership and operating environment. This allows stakeholders to respond and act quickly to existing and emerging issues and risks to the achievement of objectives of the organization. The likelihood of the situation occurring in other locations where the organization operates is high. This is because employees tend to share information and follow similar practices to accomplish work. Withholding lessons learned from stakeholders due to fear of repercussions from the failure can be detrimental to the organization. The fear of failure may include:

- Embarrassment
- Poor performance evaluation
- Loss of or reduced bonus
- Loss of promotion opportunity
- Disciplinary action, including suspension or termination

Failures must be examined and analyzed to identify the root cause. Understanding the root cause will result in more sustainable solutions. This will also mitigate the risk of the recurrence and resources spent revisiting and addressing the issue. The recurrence is usually because of applying a quick fix to the issue without identifying the root cause.

MAKING THE TRANSFORMATION TO AGILE STICK

Stabilizing and normalizing the transformation to an agile GIA leadership and operating environment take time. A transformation to an agile leadership and operating environment is a journey due to the time it takes for the changes to be fully implemented throughout the organization. This is because a transformation often results in a change in culture, including values, customs, and norms of the organization. Additionally, it usually requires a change in the mindset and attitude of team members. The changes impact the way team members think, engage, communicate, and work with others within and external to GIA. Patience, commitment, and perseverance are required from those leading the changes as it usually takes years to adopt.

The transformation to an agile leadership and operating environment must remain at the forefront of how team members and stakeholders operate to make the change stick. It is easy for team members to continue or return to business as usual if the rollout of the change is not effectively managed. The rollout must be well planned, communicated, and implementers and users trained, and supported throughout the rollout process. There should also be periodic status meetings and reports to update team members and stakeholders on the progress of the initiative. This includes updates on what is working well and what needs to be changed. A post-implementation review is also required to ensure that the implementation of the change is operating as planned as well as effectively and efficiently.

The transformation to agile must be communicated in a manner that is easy to understand, memorize, and embrace. Simplifying and breaking down the key elements of the change into memorable communication make it easier and more likely to resonate with employees. How the impact of the transformation is communicated and rolled out across the organization is critical to a successful implementation. Elements of a successful rollout include transparent communication, clarity and understanding of the objectives, risks, and rewards of the transformation.

The leaders of GIA must keep team members and stakeholders informed and engaged to make the change sustainable. Information sharing is particularly important for team members working at regional and local offices or virtually. Transparent communication assists in maintaining:

- Buy-in and support for the transformation
- Alignment with GIA's mission, vision, values, strategy, and objectives
- Compliance with GIA's policies, processes, and procedures

There are certain steps that the leaders of GIA can take to make the changes stick. The steps include the following:

- Appointment of change management champions to support departments, functions, and offices
- Create and share a one-page memorizable flyer of the key elements of the change
- Post and display key elements of the change on the organization's website and communal areas

- Create a hotline where team members and stakeholders can call in with questions
- Provide refresher training on new ways of working due to the transformation
- Make the change initiative status update a standing agenda item at team meetings
- Make the change a key performance indicator for all team members
- Recognize and reward team members for outstanding performance
- Hold leaders accountable for the implementation of the change
- Create global dashboard of the status of the transformation and make it accessible to stakeholders
- Publish monthly global newsletter on the status of the transformation
- Send global alerts or blasts of the achievement of major milestones of the change

VALUE TO GIA OF ADOPTING THE AGILE METHODOLOGY

The adoption of the agile methodology best prepares the next generation of CAEs to effectively operate in an ever-changing environment. This is because its values and principles provide the framework for the leaders and team members of GIA to survive and remain valuable to the organization. The agile methodology enhances their readiness and resilience to change and relevance to the organization. The leaders and team members of GIA are also better prepared to meet the demands of GIA's stakeholders.

There are certain skills and expertise that are essential to an agile GIA leadership and operating environment. No one team member is expected to be an expert in all the skills. However, GIA should have at least one subject matter expert in each critical skill area. The leaders of GIA may also partner with a subject matter expert either in another department or hire a consultant to assist in areas where critical skills are lacking. The essential skills include the following:

- Strategic thinking
- Problem-solving
- Collaboration
- Communication
- Business acumen
- Change and project management
- IT
- Data analytics

Adopting the agile methodology will enable the leaders of GIA to effectively manage the complexity of GIA's operation in an ever-changing operating environment. Using this methodology will include building and strengthening relationships, breaking down barriers, eliminating silos and redundancies, and streamlining tasks and activities. This is due to the inclusive, engaging, collaborative, and stakeholder-focused nature of agile. Agility enables stakeholders to break down complex projects and tasks into smaller and more manageable units and usually expedites the completion and delivery of tasks and projects. The simplification and streamlining of activities include work plans, flows, policies, processes, and procedures. The simplification and streamlining make it easier for team members and stakeholders across the organization to understand and follow.

CHAPTER SUMMARY

The leaders of GIA must evolve and adopt the agile methodology to lead as the traditional approach of leading GIA is a risk to its existence. This is required for the survival, sustainability, and success of GIA. Adopting the agile methodology will enable the leaders of GIA to effectively manage the complexity, challenges, and demands of a rapid, constantly changing, and disruptive operating environment.

An agile GIA organizational structure and operating environment is an engaging, collaborative, stakeholder-focused, and solution-oriented environment. Adopting the agile methodology enables the leaders of GIA to build and strengthen relationships, break down barriers, simplify, and streamline GIA's operations and activities.

The transformation to an agile GIA leadership and operating environment is a strategic undertaking. It is a journey and a change in the culture and mindset of the leaders and team members of GIA. The transformation to an agile GIA leadership and operating environment requires the board and senior management's approval and support. The transformation must be effectively managed to be successful and sustainable. Effectively managing the transformation to agile includes effectively planning, communicating, executing, assessing, and mitigating risks. It also includes setting expectations and effectively managing the disruptions that the transformation to agile may cause.

Investing in the professional development and well-being of GIA's team members plays a key role in the sustainability, effectiveness and success of an agile leadership and operating environment. It is integral to the organization's succession plan. The investment contributes to continuous learning and improvement, and high-quality performance and the retention of team members. Agile leaders must also invest in self-learning to remain effective.

Investing in the development and well-being of GIA's team members, GIA's most important asset has its risks. They could begin to search for new opportunities outside their current organization, based on their new skills, if promotion opportunities are not available within the organization. Accordingly, an agile GIA leadership must effectively manage its most important asset.

An agile GIA leadership is one that empowers team members and gives them the freedom to make decisions on their own. The fast-paced, constantly changing, and disruptive operating environment has strengthened the case for empowering team members to make decisions on their own. Empowering team members in the field, who are closest to the actions and activities of the operating environment to make decisions on behalf of GIA, tends to be more effective and efficient. Empowered team members' actions and activities must be in alignment with the business and the operating, reporting, and compliance objectives of the organization.

The outcome of actions taken by the leaders and team members of GIA may not always meet expectations or may fail at times. Fear of failure is a major risk to an agile GIA leadership and operating environment. An agile operating environment is one where the leaders understand that there will be failures. The leaders must manage expectations by sharing upfront with team members and stakeholders the possibility of failure and plans to mitigate that risk. Failures must be examined and analyzed for lessons learned and opportunities. The lessons learned and opportunities must be utilized to improve and enhance GIA's value to the organization. Timely sharing of lessons learned with stakeholders who can benefit from it is valuable to an organization. The leaders of GIA must learn and act quickly to address failures before the failure damages the reputation of the organization or impacts the success of the overall business.

There is always going to be some resistance to a major organizational change or transformation. Team members and stakeholders resisting the change may at times engage in activities to undermine and derail the transformation. The leaders of GIA must collaborate closely with team members and stakeholders resisting the change. This is to understand and effectively address and minimize resistance to the transformation to agile.

The success of the transformation to agile depends on how well it is communicated to team members and stakeholders. Effective communication of messages requires confirming and periodically reconfirming the understanding of messages. Miscommunicating and misunderstanding of the objectives of the transformation, and the required coordination and cooperation can be costly at times.

The transformation to an agile GIA leadership and operating environment must remain at the forefront of how the leaders of GIA, team members, and stakeholders operate to make the changes stick. Implementing the transformation to an agile GIA leadership and operating environment takes time.

NOTES

1 Agile Manifesto, Alliance.Org/Jim Highsmith, History of Agile Methodology, Agile Alliance, Manifesto for Agile Software Development (agilemanifesto.org).
2 Ibid.
3 Mary Carmichael, Lead Developer, Incorporating Risk Management in Agile Projects, 2023 ISACA.
4 Ibid.
5 Agile Manifesto, Alliance.Org/Jim Highsmith, History of Agile Methodology, Agile Alliance, Manifesto for Agile Software Development (agilemanifesto.org).
6 Ibid.
7 What Is Scrum: A Guide to the Most Popular Agile Framework (scrumalliance.org).
8 Ibid.
9 Ibid.
10 Ibid.
11 Ibid.
12 Forbes Coaches Council, 13 Ways to Become an Agile Leader in Today's Fast Paced World, https://www.forbes.com/sites/forbescoachescouncil/2017/06/23/13-ways-to-become-an-agile-leader-in-todays-fast-paced-world/
13 The earliest known appearance of this quote is in a 1983 book called *The Forbes Book of Business Quotations* by Ted Goodman.

2 Role and Responsibilities of the Chief Audit Executive

INTRODUCTION

The chief audit executive (CAE) is viewed as the role model of global internal audit (GIA) and, at times, the organization. The CAE must set the tone at the top to shape the ethical values of GIA. The CAE is also expected to lead by example as the reputation of GIA lives and dies on the integrity, credibility, independence, and objectivity of the CAE. The success of the CAE largely depends on an understanding of the business and operations of the organization. There is no value to add or gain if there is no understanding of the organization's internal and external operating environment.

An essential requirement of the CAE's role is to assist and support stakeholders in achieving the objectives of the organization, which requires a servant leadership mindset. One of the most important responsibilities of a CAE is to provide assurance and advice, including insight and foresight, to stakeholders on the organization's governance programs. A key element of that responsibility is to ensure that GIA's plan and activities are aligned with the strategy, objectives, and risk mitigation plans of the organization. GIA's value basket must be adaptive to meet the constantly changing needs of stakeholders in an ever-changing operating environment. The CAE must also build and maintain effective relationships with stakeholders to build trust, stay connected, current, and informed.

The CAE needs to ensure that effective steps are taken to attract, hire, develop, and retain a high-performing diverse team. This includes an effective career development and leadership succession plan as this contributes to and enhances the readiness, resilience, and relevance of the team. As the organization and the operating environment evolve, so must the CAE and team members. A stagnant or complacent CAE and team members are of little value to an organization.

The purpose of this chapter is to share information on the key responsibilities of the CAE's role. It also provides guidance on how to prepare and be successful in an ever-changing operating environment. Topics covered include the following:

- Preparedness for the CAE's role
- Role and responsibilities
- Readiness, resilience, and relevance
- Servant leadership

DOI: 10.1201/9781003207559-2

- Tone at the top
- Seat at the c-suite table
- Value of GIA to the organization
- Building and maintaining relationships
- Alignment with the organization's strategy, objectives, and risk mitigation plans
- Educating and advising stakeholders
- Talent management
- Compliance with the Institute of Internal Auditors (IIA) Global Internal Audit Standards
- Training ground for the organization's managers and leaders

Key learnings from the chapter include the following:

- Key factors in preparing for the CAE's role
- Key responsibilities of the CAE's role
- Importance of remaining ready, resilient, and relevant
- Value of servant leadership to stakeholders
- Importance of setting the tone at the top
- Importance of having a seat at the c-suite table
- Importance of promoting GIA's value to the organization
- Benefits of building and maintaining effective relationships with stakeholders
- Importance of aligning GIA's plans and activities with the organization's strategy and objectives
- Value in enlightening, educating, and advising stakeholders
- Value in positioning GIA as a training ground for managers and leaders

PREPAREDNESS FOR THE CAE'S ROLE

A vital factor to the preparedness for the role of the CAE is obtaining an understanding of the organization, which should be done prior to accepting the role. As mentioned earlier, there is no value to add if there is no understanding of the organization's internal and external operating environment. Accordingly, there are important questions that a potential CAE must ask and obtain satisfactory answers for before undertaking the CAE's role. Knowledge of business and operations will minimize future surprises and disappointments. The questions include the following:

- What are the mission, vision, strategy, objectives, and risks of the organization?
- What are the size, nature, scope, and complexity of the operations?
- What are the governance structure and leadership of the organization?
- Is there an independent board of directors?
- Are there board sub-committees such as audit, risk, governance, finance, and nomination?
- Is the board involved in managing the daily operations of the organization?

- Is the board controlled by its chairperson or by the chief executive officer (CEO)?
- How are the financial stability and sustainability of the organization?
- Are there any unique regulatory requirements?
- Is there a risk management program?
- Who is the organization's external auditor?
- When was the most recent external audit performed and what were the results?
- Are there existing policies, processes, and procedures?
- Is there a contract administration function and procurement committee?
- Are there spending authorization limits?
- Is there proper segregation of duties in key areas of the organization?
- Who performs internal investigations of allegations of wrongdoings?
- Have there been any violation of laws and regulations in the past five years?
- Are there any pending litigations?
- Is there an internal audit charter?
- What is GIA's reporting relationship in the organization, including functional and administrative?
- Is GIA centralized or decentralized?
- What is the scope of internal audits?
- What is GIA's audit approach?
- Is GIA's operating environment manual, hybrid, or automated?

ROLE AND RESPONSIBILITIES OF THE CAE

The role and responsibilities of the CAE have evolved over the years. The CAE cannot remain stagnant or complacent in a dynamic operating environment. Accordingly, the role and responsibilities have become more holistic ensuring that all aspects of the organization are considered in the assessment of risk. Roles and responsibilities must be revisited periodically as needed to ensure alignment with the strategy and objectives of the organization.

The role of the CAE is kind of a balancing act as the CAE and GIA are often referred to as the eyes and ears of the board, audit committee, and senior management. The CAE must work collaboratively with the board and senior management so that it does not appear that GIA is spying on management. This should not be a concern if the board, senior management, and the CAE are aligned with the imperatives of the organization. This includes the mission, vision, values, strategy, objectives, and risks to the organization.

Agreement and alignment by stakeholders on what is most important to the organization must be the driver of GIA's plan and activities. Alignment means one team, common objectives, differing responsibilities but the same overall desired outcome. The overall desired outcome is the achievement of the objectives of the organization. Assisting stakeholders achieve their objectives, whether at the macro or micro level, needs to be at the forefront of the CAE and team members thinking and activities. Everyone needs to be in alignment in order for the organization to achieve its objectives.

The primary responsibilities of the CAE and GIA are standard from one organization to another. However, the nature of the work depends on the size and complexity of the organization. The key roles and responsibilities include the following:

- Attracting, hiring, developing, and retaining a high-performing multicultural GIA team
- Aligning GIA's plan and activities with the organization's strategy and objectives
- Overseeing the performance of independent and objective audits of the organization
- Overseeing and/or performing advisory reviews
- Providing stakeholders with periodic reports on the effectiveness of governance programs
- Keeping stakeholders informed of new and emerging risks, trends, and improvement opportunities
- Networking with key stakeholders, peers, and colleagues inside and outside of the organization
- Keeping current of changes in the internal and external operating environment
- Promoting GIA's value to the organization
- Building and maintaining effective relationships
- Enlightening, educating, and advising stakeholders
- Complying with the IIA's Global Internal Audit Standards

One of the primary responsibilities of a CAE is to provide assurance and advice, including insight and foresight, to stakeholders. This is to assist stakeholders in effectively performing their responsibilities and making informed decisions. Information that the CAE provides must be timely, actionable, and useful to stakeholders. This is important for the CAE to remain relevant and successful in the organization. Stakeholders expect the CAE to keep them up to date on the control environment, including new and emerging trends, issues, risks, and improvement opportunities. The CAE must engage in the following activities to assist in meeting stakeholders' expectations:

- Assessing the internal control environment, anticipating, and advising on improving controls
- Interpreting and connecting the dots from the results of data mining and analytics
- Networking with key stakeholders, peers, and colleagues inside and outside of the organization
- Keeping current with changes in the internal and external operating environment

The CAE's periodic reporting and meetings with the audit committee and senior management vary from organization to organization. CAEs typically meet with the audit committee in connection with the periodic meetings of the board of the organization. Board meetings are usually held on a quarterly basis. The CAE also has the option of meeting with the audit committee if needed in the case of a significant issue. Additionally, the CAE may have informal meetings with the chairperson of the audit committee if needed.

CAE's periodic report and meeting with the senior management team are usually more frequent than with the audit committee. The periodic report and meetings with the senior management team may take place either weekly, bi-weekly, or monthly. This may be done in connection with the periodic senior management meetings. However, it depends on whether the CAE is a member of the c-suite. It is also customary and best practice for the CAE to meet and brief the CEO periodically on significant, new, and emerging trends, issues, risks, and improvement opportunities. This includes the effectiveness of governance, risk, and compliance programs, and the organization's system of internal control.

READINESS, RESILIENCE, AND RELEVANCE

An essential responsibility of the CAE is to maintain a ready, resilient, and relevant GIA team. This is a basic requirement to survive and remain valuable to the organization in a dynamic operating environment. Change is no longer sporadic where organizations have time to research, test, and implement change. Taking a wait and see attitude or ignoring change until a major disaster occurs sometimes results in the demise of the organizations. Adapting to change must be timely if an organization is to survive and remain relevant.

The CAE must obtain a thorough understanding of the organization to be ready, resilient, and relevant. This includes spending time obtaining an understanding of the mission, vision, strategy, objectives, and risks to the organization. Understanding enables the CAE to effectively plan and align GIA's activities with what is most important to the organization and its stakeholders.

Readiness is being prepared to respond in a moment's notice to a situation. It is the ability to quickly recognize, acknowledge, and address change. The CAE and team members of GIA must be in a readiness mode to quickly think, pivot, and adapt to change. This requires staying connected, current, and informed of activities and changes in the operating environment. It also requires ongoing engagement and collaboration with team members and stakeholders internal and external to the organization.

Resilience is the ability to quickly acknowledge, pivot, and recover from a failure. There will be failures. It is not a matter of if but when. This may include setbacks, errors, missed deadlines, and deliverables. There is no time to fixate on failure in a fast-paced operating environment. The experience must be used as an opportunity to learn, improve, grow, and become more effective. The ability to quickly pivot and recover from a failure is an asset to an organization. It provides reasonable assurance of survival, sustainability, and success. Change is constant and quickly adapting to change is the most crucial element for survival. A CAE will not survive or succeed if failures are not quickly acknowledged and addressed.

Relevance is the ability to focus on what is most important to an organization and its stakeholders. A CAE must stay connected and informed of the activities in the internal and external operating environment. This enables the CAE to remain relevant and able to timely address what is most important to the organization and its stakeholders. The CAE must be included in all major organizational decisions to remain relevant to the organization in an ever-changing operating environment.

SERVANT LEADERSHIP

GIA is a support function whose primary focus is to assist stakeholders achieve the objectives of the organization. This requires a servant leadership mindset. It is a selfless approach that puts the needs of the organization and its stakeholders ahead of GIAs. The objectives and success of the organization must be at the forefront of the thinking and activities of the CAE, leaders, and team members. The CAE and GIA benefit from the success of the organization and its stakeholders. Similarly, their reputation is at risk should there be a major failure of the organization and its stakeholders.

There are servant leaders who believe that they are born to serve. They are reliable, ready, and willing to assist and serve stakeholders at a moment's notice. However, servant leaders need to be aware and that being always willing and ready to serve at a moment's notice could also be counterproductive. They need to serve smartly for self-preservation and to avoid burnout.

TONE AT THE TOP

The CAE is viewed as the role model of GIA and, at times, the organization. It is important that the CAE is the right fit for the organization. The reputation, including the integrity, credibility, independence, and objectivity of GIA, is at risk if the CAE is not the right fit for the organization. Team members will quickly emulate good as well as bad behaviors. Behaviors usually emulated by staff include the following:

- Respect for others
- Empathy and compassion
- Inclusion
- Transparency and honesty
- Open to other points of view

The CAE is expected to lead by example since the actions and behaviors of a leader are usually emulated by team members. The actions and behaviors of the CAE must be in alignment with the values of the organization and the Ethics and Professional Domain of the Global Internal Audit Standards. The guidance provided by the Standards helps the CAE to navigate through ethical issues.

Setting the tone at the top is a means of communicating GIA's values to the team and entire organization. The values of GIA are usually covered in the organization's Code of Ethics and Conduct. It is important that GIA's values are in alignment with the Standards including the following:

- Integrity: A behavior characterized by adherence to moral and ethical principles, including demonstrating honesty and the courage to act based on relevant facts, even when facing pressure to do otherwise, or when doing so might create potential adverse personal or organizational consequences.[1]

- Objectivity: An unbiased mental attitude that allows internal auditors to make professional judgments, fulfill their responsibilities, and achieve the Purpose of Internal Auditing without compromise.[2]
- Confidentiality: Internal auditors must follow the relevant policies, procedures, laws, and regulations when using information.[3]
- Competency: Requires developing and applying the knowledge, skills, and abilities to provide internal audit services.[4]

The reputation of GIA lives and dies on the integrity, credibility, independence, and objectivity of the CAE. The CAE must employ and display the highest level of professionalism, integrity, and credibility in the performance of the role and responsibility of the position. CAE is expected to have high ethical standards as well as being:

- Trustworthy
- Transparent and honest
- Independent and objective
- Factual and fair
- Reliable

The preceding are key drivers in building a positive GIA reputation. It is also important in setting the tone at the top as well as leading by example. As mentioned above, team members usually emulate the leader of an organization. A positive reputation is critical to the sustainability and relevance of GIA. A negative reputation can destroy in seconds what took years to build.

SEAT AT THE C-SUITE TABLE

The CEO and the chairperson of the audit committee must ensure that the CAE has a seat at the c-suite table. Securing a seat at the c-suite table enables the CAE to obtain firsthand knowledge of any major activity that the organization intends to undertake. The CAE obtaining firsthand knowledge mitigates the risk of miscommunication or misunderstanding that may occur from secondhand knowledge. A CAE manager or supervisor may, for example, forget to share important information or miscommunicate the information. A seat at the c-suite table allows the CAE to share relevant information GIA has regarding a topic of discussion or a major undertaking that will lead to a more informed decision.

A seat at the c-suite table is usually based on the knowledge and experience that the CAE can bring to the table. The CAE must demonstrate and market the value that GIA adds to the organization. This ensures that stakeholders are aware of the scope and value of GIA's work. It includes providing assurance and advice on new and emerging risks and improvement opportunities. Additionally, it assists stakeholders in making more informed decisions.

Securing a seat at the c-suite table enables the CAE to stay connected, ready, and relevant. It contributes to forward-thinking instead of backward-looking. A seat at the c-suite table also contributes to the following:

- Enhancing the CAE's agility
- Minimizing confusion and surprises
- Building trust and reducing friction
- Minimizing disagreements regarding audit findings and recommendations
- Keeping the CAE current and informed
- Minimizing miscommunication and misunderstanding

A seat at the c-suite table is an opportunity for the CAE to educate and enlighten and share information that can lead to more informed decisions by stakeholders. An engaged CAE is one of the most knowledgeable members of the senior management team of an organization.

VALUE OF GIA TO THE ORGANIZATION

An important responsibility of the CAE is to promote GIA's value to the organization. This includes making stakeholders aware of the services and scope of GIA's work. It also includes sharing how GIA supports and assists stakeholders and contributes to the effectiveness and efficiency of the organization. GIA's values to the organization include the following:

- Focusing on what is most important to the organization and its stakeholders
- Evaluating internal controls to assist in mitigating risks to the organization
- Providing assurance and advice on the effectiveness of governance programs
- Providing advice to improve the effectiveness and efficiency of the organization and mitigate risk
- Connecting the dots of data analytics to assist stakeholders in making more informed decisions
- Providing consulting and advisory services
- Conducting internal investigations
- Educating and enlightening stakeholders
- Offering GIA as a training ground for management trainees and leadership development

The CAE must quickly address any misperception of the scope of GIA's work and value. There are stakeholders in some organizations whose mindset of the scope of GIA work is financial compliance. They often refer to internal auditors as bean counters and internal policeman. The reference to policeman can be attributed in part to the fact that GIA is often asked to perform internal investigations. The scope of GIA's work goes beyond financial compliance and investigations. It includes the following:

- Governance
- Risk
- Regulatory compliance
- Cybersecurity
- Strategy
- Finance and administration
- Operations
- Information system
- Environmental, social, governance (ESG)
- Supply chain
- Third party reviews
- Advisory reviews

GIA's value basket needs to be adaptive in addressing the needs of stakeholders. This is necessary to be relevant and valuable to the organization. It also ensures that the CAE and team members of GIA keep current and align with the needs and what is most important to the organization and its stakeholders. This requires staying connected, current, and informed of activities in the internal and external operating environment. It also requires engaging in continuous learning and improvement activities, collaborating, and networking with stakeholders, peers, and colleagues within and outside of the organization. This is to ensure that the CAE and team members are informed early of new and emerging trends, risks, and opportunities to quickly advise stakeholders.

A CAE plays a vital role in supporting stakeholders in the performance of their responsibilities due to the breadth, depth, and scope of GIA's work. Connecting the dots requires engaging, collaborating, listening, sharing, and exchanging information and data with stakeholders. It includes coordinating, collecting, and incorporating information and data from various areas of the organization for analysis. Connecting the dots assists in identifying emerging trends, issues, anomalies, and unusual transactions and activities. This enables the CAE to be proactive, anticipate, and provide insight and foresight to stakeholders to assist in making more informed decisions. Sharing the results of connecting the dots with stakeholders enhances the agility of the organization and enables stakeholders to be proactive, anticipate, and quickly adapt to change.

The CAE and GIA's team play a key role in supporting and providing stakeholders reasonable assurance that internal controls are effective and working as expected to mitigate significant risks to the organization. The assurance is obtained from the performance of independent and objective assessment of risks and review of internal controls, including those that have been delegated to managers. The CAE and GIA's team also play a key role educating and enlightening stakeholders on the status of those risks and internal controls that they do not have the time to effectively monitor. This is particularly important in an operating environment where the risks are constantly changing.

BUILD AND MAINTAIN RELATIONSHIPS

CAE must build and maintain effective relationships with stakeholders. It requires staying connected, current, and informed. Factors that contribute to the CAE staying connected, current, and informed include the following:

- Obtaining a seat at the c-suite table
- Ongoing engagement and collaboration with stakeholders
- Becoming a trusted advisor
- Networking with peers and colleagues within and outside the organization
- Investing in training and continuing professional education
- Attending workshops, webinars, seminars, and professional conferences

Building and maintaining effective relationships with stakeholders are the foundation for building trust. Trust plays a key role in staying connected, current, and informed. This is because trust leads to more open, transparent, honest, and free sharing of information. Building and maintaining effective relationships with stakeholders pave the way for developing a trusted advisor relationship. A trusted advisor is one who is not afraid to share the truth and pros and cons with stakeholders seeking advice. A trusted advisor is also one who is patient, listens, and is empathic.

Networking plays a vital role in the CAE staying connected, current, and informed. This includes networking with stakeholders, peers, and colleagues internal and external to the organization. Networking enables the CAE and team members of GIA to be aware of any major activities and changes within the internal and external environment. This helps to keep the CAE and team members focused on what is most important to the organization and its stakeholders. It also enhances the CAE's and team members' ability to be proactive and quickly think, and respond to changes in the internal and external operating environment. Staying connected is a key factor to the relevance and effectiveness of the CAE and GIA.

ALIGNMENT WITH OBJECTIVES AND RISK MITIGATION PLAN

Aligning GIA's plans and activities with the strategy, objectives, and mitigation plans of the organization is one of the greatest values that a CAE can provide an organization. This include the business, operating, reporting, and compliance objectives of the organization. The alignment is also critical to the sustainability, relevance, and value of the CAE and GIA to the organization. This requires an understanding of the organization's internal and external operating environment. A key element of CAE's responsibility is to ensure that GIA's plans and activities are aligned with what is most important to the organization and its stakeholders. The achievement of the mission, vision, business, operating, reporting, and compliance objectives of the organization are usually what is most important to stakeholders. This includes the effective execution of the strategy and mitigation of significant risks to the achievement of the objectives of the organization. The alignment makes it easier for stakeholders to connect the dots.

The CAE and GIA's team members must engage and collaborate closely upfront with stakeholders on linking GIA's plans and activities to what is most important to them. Stakeholders' attention and interest in the results of an audit are enhanced when they are invited to participate in the planning and progress of the audit. Stakeholders are also more likely to listen to and act on GIA's recommendations when the focus is on what is most important to them. This includes assisting them in their efforts to mitigate risks to the achievement of their objectives. It also enhances the appreciation of the work of GIA.

EDUCATING AND ADVISING STAKEHOLDERS

The CAE is in a unique position to educate and enlighten stakeholders due to the broad scope of GIA's work and unique knowledge of the organization. Stakeholders include managers, senior management, and members of the audit committee. Topics covered may include fraud, new or emerging risks, trends, and recurring issues. The focus is on high-risk areas and areas where managers do not have the time and resources to effectively monitor. This includes areas where the risk may be low or acceptable according to the risk tolerance and appetite of the organization. Low-risk areas may quickly become significant and pervasive or irrelevant and disappear in a dynamic operating environment. The knowledge gained and lessons learned from reviewing those areas must be timely shared to educate and enlighten stakeholders. It will enable them to be proactive in allocating resources to the areas where risks have grown and eliminate resources to areas where the risks are no longer relevant.

The CAE plays a vital role advising stakeholders on new and emerging matters. This includes interpreting and connecting the dots from the results of data mining and analytics. It also includes identifying new and recurring trends, anomalies, unusual transactions and activities, risks, and improvement opportunities. Technological tools are now available for the CAE and team members to mine and analyze data in seconds that would normally take hours, days, and even weeks to do. Technological tools such as data analytics and artificial intelligence enable the CAE to quickly interpret, connect the dots, and share the results with stakeholders. This is a key value to the organization, especially in a fast-paced, constantly changing operating environment. It enables stakeholders to be proactive in taking required corrective action before the situation spreads to other areas of the organization.

The CAE and team members of GIA are in a unique position of keeping stakeholders informed of changes in the operating environment. This is because of their expertise, unique knowledge of the organization, and networking activities with peers and colleagues within and outside of the organization. Keeping stakeholders informed of changes in the operating environment enhances the organization's effectiveness over governance, risk, compliance, and internal controls. Topics covered may include new or emerging fraud risk, prevention, changes in regulations, recurring issues, gaps in internal controls, and recommended solutions. Informing stakeholders can be in the form of briefings and presentations during periodic meetings with senior management and/or the board. Briefings and presentations can also take place during stakeholders' team meetings and learning sessions. Stakeholders may also request GIA to conduct in-person or virtual training sessions for staff responsible for new or emerging issues and risks. This is to provide more detailed information on the matter, including the risks, root cause, and recommended mitigation controls.

TALENT MANAGEMENT

The acquisition and retention of a high-performing multicultural GIA team is one of the most challenging aspects of a CAE's responsibility. It is particularly challenging in a competitive and demand-driven job market. The CAE must ensure that policies, processes, and procedures are in place to attract and hire qualified, creative, innovative, and diverse candidates to meet the needs of GIA and the organization. The CAE must also ensure that plans are in place to develop and retain a high-quality-performing, diverse, and multicultural GIA team. This requires an effective career development and leadership succession plan that will enhance the readiness, resilience, and relevance of GIA. As the organization and operating environment evolve, so must the CAE and team members. A stagnant or complacent CAE and team members are of no value to an organization.

The CAE must ensure that GIA has an effective career development and leadership succession plan. This ensures that a successor is ready to quickly assume the CAE role should there be an unexpected separation of the CAE, such as immediate termination, sudden illness, or death. The usual tenure of a CAE in the role is between five and seven years. The objective of a progressive or forward-thinking CAE is to identify and develop internal replacement leaders. There are going to be times when it may be necessary to identify potential successors outside of GIA and/or the organization. They should also be included in the succession plan. The CAE must also ensure that there is a career development plan for each team member. The career development plan will assist in the retention of team members. Key elements of the plan include the following:

- Career objectives of team members
- Timing of the objectives
- Alignment with the objectives of the organization
- Required training and continuing professional education
- Key performance indicators
- Agreement and support

The CAE must ensure that effective steps are taken to retain a high-performing, diverse, and multicultural GIA team. This requires providing a positive and welcoming operating environment where team members can strive and succeed. It is an operating environment where team members enjoy coming to and working each day. It is also an environment where team members are motivated to work, learn, grow, and advance their career. The key elements of a positive and welcoming operating environment include the following:

- Embraces diversity, equity, and inclusion
- Offers competitive and equitable compensation package

- Provides the following:
  - Safe and secure working environment for team members
  - Reasonable work life balance
  - Quality resources, including specialized skills, expertise, and technological tools
  - Ongoing training and support for continuing professional education events
  - Career development and promotional opportunities, including secondment and rotation development opportunities for team members
  - Mentoring opportunities for team members
- Shares improvement opportunities with team members in a timely manner
- Empowers team members to act on behalf of the organization within their competence level

TRAINING GROUND FOR THE ORGANIZATION'S MANAGERS AND LEADERS

An often-underutilized value of a matured GIA function is to serve as a training ground for the organization's management and leadership development program. GIA can be an excellent training ground for developing future managers and leaders of the organization. This is because GIA is the only function within an organization where a staff can learn, gain knowledge, and experience about most, if not all, aspects of the organization. This is more than what most other staff will learn in a lifetime as a member of the organization. Rotating future managers and leaders through GIA as part of their career development program is a win-win option for the candidates, GIA, and the organization.

Secondment is a tool that is used at times by management to either fill a vacancy or support team members with their career development plan. It is where the team member is requested to join another department or function to bridge a gap in staffing, management, or leadership for a specific period. Team members may also request to join another function or department as part of their career development plan to obtain a deeper understanding of another area. A CAE may also request staff from another area of the organization to assist GIA in areas where it lacks the specialized skills or expertise to undertake an engagement.

The benefits to the organization and its staff for utilizing GIA as a training ground for future managers and leaders of the organization are unique to GIA. The learning and experience will remain valuable to staff for the rest of their career. This includes the following:

- Exposure to many areas of the organization
- Enhanced alignment with the organization's mission, vision, values, strategy, and objectives
- Enhanced understanding of risk management, including identification, assessment, and mitigation
- Enhanced understanding and appreciation of how different departments and functions operate

- Enhanced understanding of the value, importance, and appreciation of internal controls
- Enhanced ability of staff to connect the dots
- Enhanced appreciation and understanding of the value of GIA's work

There are certain things that must exist for GIA to be recognized as a valuable training ground for the organization's future managers and leaders. There must be a competent and experienced CAE, leadership team, and a mature GIA organization with the majority of the following in place:

- Internal audit charter
- Internal audit manual containing GIA's policies and procedures covering the functional (technical) and administrative activities of the function
- Competent and experienced managers and supervisors to oversee and support the team
- Team approach
- A forward-thinking and -looking team
- Risk-based audit approach
- Dynamic audit plans
- Stakeholder focus
- Welcome creative and innovative thinking
- Embraces and values diversity, equity, and inclusion
- Respects and open to different perspectives and points of views
- Mentorship program

One benefit to GIA for serving as a training ground for the organization's future managers and leaders is the opportunity to receive fresh and constructive feedback on its operation. It is also an opportunity to build relationships and trust with other departments and stakeholders, and expands GIA's knowledge and expertise including the following:

- Inflow of fresh ideas that drive and stimulate creativity and innovation
- Builds and strengthens relationships and trust
- Enhanced appreciation of GIA's work
- A fresh look at GIA's operations
- Learning from experts
- Open the door for secondment and guest auditor opportunities

COMPLYING WITH THE INSTITUTE OF INTERNAL AUDITORS GLOBAL INTERNAL AUDIT STANDARDS

The Institute of Internal Auditors (IIA) is the recognized standards setting body of the profession. Compliance with the IIA's Global Internal Audit Standards is a sign of maturity of a GIA operation. While it is not easy to quantify the return on investment (ROI) of complying with the Standards, it is an intangible asset to the organization and GIA to receive a "Fully Comply" rating from an independently conducted Quality Assurance Review (QAR). It is a badge of honor for complying with the Standards. It also enables and empowers the CAE to state in GIA's reports that the audit was conducted in accordance with the IIA's Global Internal Audit Standards. Key stakeholders such as investors, donors, bankers, and insurance brokers view compliance with the standards favorably in assessing governance, risk, and the internal controls environment of an organization.

Compliance with the IIA's Global Internal Audit Standards includes the implementation of a Quality Assurance Improvement Program (QAIP). A QAIP is a program established by the chief audit executive to evaluate and ensure the internal audit function conforms with the Global Internal Audit Standards, achieves performance objectives, and pursues continuous improvement. The program includes internal and external assessments.[5] A QAIP provides reasonable assurance of GIA's compliance with the Standards. The program also enhances the likelihood of receiving a "Fully Comply" opinion from the required or mandatory five-year QAR by an independent service provider. As mentioned above, a "Fully Comply" opinion affords GIA the opportunity to state in its internal audit report that the audit was conducted in accordance with the IIA's Global Internal Audit Standards. While the CAE should strive for a 100% QAR compliance rating, it is not required to receive an overall "Fully Comply" rating. The CAE must ensure that the QAIP and QAR reviews are not a checking-the-box exercise. The value of the QAIP and QAR is in engaging and collaborating with stakeholders on what is working well, needs to be changed, and improvement opportunities. This is necessary for GIA to remain ready, resilient, relevant, and valuable to the organization.

Compliance with the Standards enhances GIA's reputation, credibility, and integrity as well as the following:

- Indicates GIA's maturity
- Paves the way for a successful, "Fully Comply," independent QAR opinion of GIA's operation
- Enables and empowers the CAE to state in GIA's internal audit report that "The audit was conducted in accordance with the IIA's Global Internal Audit Standards"
- Drives and fosters consistency, standardization, and clarity of how the work is performed across the organization
- Serves as a guide to GIA staff in performing their professional responsibilities and duties
- Attractive to prospective candidates
- Increase in the marketability of GIA team members

The rapid change taking place in the technological space and pandemics have required CAE's and GIA leaders, in some cases, to abandon and refresh their audit approach. This is necessary for GIA to remain effective, ready, relevant, resilient, and valuable to the organization. It requires an agile CAE and GIA's team to successfully navigate and lead GIA in this fast-paced, constantly changing operating environment. The CAE must be able to quickly respond and adapt to change. It requires spending more time partnering and collaborating with stakeholders and less time complying with the traditional detail planning and documenting of workflow and control processes. However, the objectives, scope, audit approach, audit trail of the work performed, and results must be documented in accordance with the IIA's Global Internal Audit Standards. This is to ensure that a third party can easily reperform the work and arrive at a similar conclusion as GIA.

Partnering and collaborating with stakeholders may at times appear to be an independence gray area. However, this is in alignment with the primary objective of GIA of assisting stakeholders achieve the objectives of the organization. Accordingly, CAEs must become more flexible and take more risk after assessing and weighing the risks and rewards of the decision rather than sticking to the norms of the past.

CHAPTER SUMMARY

A CAE is viewed as the role model of GIA and, at times, the organization. The CAE is expected to lead by example and must set the tone at the top. Setting the tone at the top is a means of communicating GIA's values to the team and the entire organization. The reputation of GIA lives and dies on the integrity, credibility, independence, and objectivity of the CAE. The primary focus of the role of the CAE is to assist and support stakeholders in achieving the objectives of the organization. It requires a servant leadership type of mindset. This is where the success of the organization and its stakeholders is at the forefront of the CAE and team members' thinking and activities.

The key to the preparedness and success in the role of the CAE is obtaining an understanding of the business and operations of the organization. This must be done before accepting the CAE role as it is critical in becoming a valuable member of the organization. There is no value to add or gain if there is no understanding of the organization's internal and external operating environment.

The CEO and chairperson of the audit committee must ensure that the CAE has a seat at the c-suite table. A seat at the c-suite table is usually based on the knowledge and experience that the CAE can bring to the table. It enables the CAE to stay connected, ready, and relevant. It is also an opportunity for the CAE to educate and enlighten and share information that can lead to more informed decisions by stakeholders, particular senior management, and the audit committee. A seat at the c-suite table is also an opportunity for the CAE to build and maintain effective relationships with senior management, and to stay connected, current, and informed. It is the foundation for building trust and a trusted advisor relationship. Networking also plays a key role in building and maintaining effective relationships, staying connected, current, and informed.

The CAE must promote GIA's value to the organization and quickly address misperception of the scope of GIA's work and value basket. GIA's value basket must be dynamic in addressing the needs of stakeholders in an ever-changing operating environment. The CAE also plays a valuable role supporting stakeholders in the performance of their responsibilities. It is particularly important to senior management and the audit committee in performing their governance responsibilities. Connecting the dots and timely sharing the results of GIA's work with stakeholders are key elements of GIA's value to the organization.

The role and responsibilities of the CAE have evolved over the years. The key responsibilities are fairly standard from one organization to another. However, the CAE's periodic meeting and reporting to the audit committee and senior management vary from organization to organization. One of the most important responsibilities of a CAE is to provide assurance and advice, including insight and foresight, to stakeholders. A key element of that responsibility is to ensure that GIA's plans and activities are aligned with what is most important to the organization and its stakeholders. It is one of the greatest values that a CAE and GIA can provide an organization. The CAE must understand the internal and external operating environment to effectively align with the objectives of the organization. This is required for the CAE to provide stakeholders with meaningful value-added assurance and advice. The CAE is also in the unique position to educate and enlighten stakeholders on new, emerging, and recurring trends, issues, risks, and improvement opportunities.

Talent management is a key responsibility of the CAE as team members of GIA are an invaluable asset. Therefore, the CAE must ensure that effective steps are taken to attract, hire, develop, and retain a high-performing multicultural team. This includes an effective career development and leadership succession plan as it contributes to and enhances the readiness, resilience, and relevance of GIA's team. As the organization and the operating environment evolve, so must the CAE and team members of GIA. A stagnant or complacent CAE and team members are of no value to an organization.

NOTES

1 Global Internal Audit Standards.
2 Ibid.
3 Ibid.
4 Ibid.
5 Ibid.

3 Laying the Foundation for the Success of the Chief Audit Executive

INTRODUCTION

A chief audit executive (CAE) can be one of the most valuable team members of an organization. This requires the right candidate and the support of key stakeholders. The right candidate is one that is competent, knowledgeable, and has the required experience and qualifications for the role. A CAE needs the support of senior management, particularly the chief executive officer (CEO), and the audit committee to be successful in the role. The CAE's authority is diminished without senior management and the audit committee support.

A CAE must have a mentor or a confidant to share and seek advice and guidance as the role can be a lonely one at times. The CAE's manager, CEO, and the board and audit committee chairpersons are the usual individuals that the CAE confides in for advice and guidance. The CAE must exercise good judgment in sharing sensitive information.

The purpose of this chapter is to provide advice and guidance on laying the foundation for the success of a CAE in an organization. Topics covered include the following:

- Support of key stakeholders
- Reporting line in the hierarchy of the organization
- Seat at the c-suite table
- The internal audit charter
- Empowering the CAE
- Mentoring
- Quality resources
- Continuing professional education

Key learnings from the chapter include the following:

- Vital role that the support of key stakeholders plays in the success of the CAE
- Importance of the CAE's reporting line in the hierarchy of the organization
- Value of the CAE at the c-suite table
- Important role the internal audit charter plays empowering the CAE

DOI: 10.1201/9781003207559-3

- Value mentoring plays ensuring the success of the CAE
- Importance of providing the CAE quality resources
- Importance of ongoing training and professional education

SUPPORT OF KEY STAKEHOLDERS

The success of the CAE depends on the level of support that is provided by key stakeholders. Key stakeholders in this case are the CAE's manager, senior management, particularly the CEO, and the audit committee. It is impossible for a CAE to be successful in an organization without their support. Their support sets the tone at the top of the organization's commitment to the role. It is also a key indicator and message to all employees of the organization of the importance of the role and value of the CAE and global internal audit (GIA) to the organization.

The support of senior management and the audit committee plays a key role in laying the foundation for effectiveness and efficiency of the CAE and GIA. It includes the following:

- Enhancing the agility of the CAE and GIA in quickly responding and adapting to change
- Enhancing the ability and influence of the CAE in effecting value-added changes
- Making it easier for the CAE and team members to access staff and the assets of the organization
- Providing support for the approval of the required resources that the CAE needs to be successful

A CAE's authority is diminished without the support of key stakeholders. Their support sets the tone for the role and value of the CAE and GIA to the organization. If it appears that the CAE is not respected or not seen as adding value to the organization, the sentiment will spread across the organization and make it difficult for the CAE to be effective and successful. This is a risk to the CAE and GIA especially in countries or organizations where an internal audit function is mandatory or required by law.

There are actions that the CEO and the audit committee can take to show their support and commitment for the success of the CAE. The actions include the following:

- Positioning the CAE to report to the highest practical level in the organization
- Giving the CAE a seat at the c-suite table
- Supporting the internal audit charter
- Empowering the CAE
- Providing the necessary resources

The risk to the success of the CAE is high if there is a lack of support from key stakeholders. The risks include the following:

- Damage to the reputation of GIA
- Damage to the credibility of GIA

- Loss of respect for GIA and the CAE
- Lack of interest in GIA's work
- Denial or restriction of access to key stakeholders, information, and data
- Lack of the required resources to be successful

REPORTING LINE IN THE HIERARCHY OF THE ORGANIZATION

The reporting line of the CAE in the hierarchy of the organization matters. The value of the role of the CAE to the organization is likely to be underutilized and underappreciated if the function reports several levels deep in the hierarchy of the organization. The higher the reporting line and visibility of the CAE in the organization, the higher the likelihood of a creative, innovative, agile, effective, and successful CAE. A reporting line to the highest and most visible position in the hierarchy of the organization is a recognition of the importance of the role and value of GIA to the organization. It is also a key factor in the assessment of the governance and the control environment of the organization.

The lower the reporting line of the CAE in the organization the likelihood that the function will be less agile, creative, and innovative. The function is likely to be slower in responding, acting, and adapting to change. This is because of the bureaucracy and the levels of reviews and approvals that may be required before an issue is shared with or reported to senior management, the CEO, and the audit committee. The bureaucracy usually delays or extends the review and approval process that is required to get major decisions approved. Bureaucracy is also a risk to creativity, innovation, agility, and the effectiveness of the CAE and GIA in an ever-changing operating environment. A low-level reporting line of the CAE may also lead to a negative perception and undermining of the role of the CAE and GIA as well as the following:

- Reduces the visibility and presence of GIA, which is an inherent benefit to the organization
- Reduces the relevance and influence of the CAE
- Lessens the collaboration and timely sharing of information
- Lessens the agility, creativity, and innovation of the CAE and GIA

It is generally accepted that the CAE should report functionally to the audit committee of the board of directors and administratively to a member of the senior management team. It is a dual reporting line in the hierarchy of an organization. There is debate at times over who the CAE should report to administratively. The suggestion that the CAE should report functionally and administratively to the chairperson of the audit committee does surface at times. However, it is a major undertaking for the chairperson of an audit committee to be responsible for the functional and administrative responsibilities of the CAE. The chairperson and members of the audit committee usually have other obligations and responsibilities. Moreover, this school of thought of the CAE reporting administratively to the chairperson of the audit committee has the potential of isolating the CAE from the management of the organization. It is also likely to dampen the collaboration, relationship, and trust with senior management. The oversight of the functional responsibility of the CAE's role by the audit committee includes the following:

- Approval of the hiring and termination of the CAE
- Participation in the annual evaluation and review of the compensation of the CAE
- Adequacy of GIA's budget
- Approval of GIA's audit plan
- Review of internal audit report findings and recommendations
- Follow-up on the implementation of audit recommendations

Reporting administratively to the CEO is the preferred option for CAEs. However, the question is whether it is the best use of the CEO's time. A possible solution is for the CEO to delegate that responsibility to his or her chief of staff. The chief of staff will be required to alert the CEO of unresolved issues. The CEO can then discuss unresolved issues with the CAE during their periodic status update meetings. A lower-level administrative reporting line for a CAE from time to time raises the issue of bias and questions regarding the independence and objectivity of the CAE and GIA.

The CAE reporting administratively to another member of the senior management team such as the chief financial officer (CFO) may make other leaders feel that GIA's audits and reports are biased. Other members of the senior management team may at times view GIA's audits and reports as more punitive and less favorable of their areas of responsibility than it is for the CFO. The reasons why reporting administratively to the CEO is the preferred option for CAEs include the following:

- Contributes to the independence and objectivity of the CAE
- Enables the CEO to receive information firsthand directly from the CAE
- Eliminates bureaucracy and enables the organization to respond and act quickly to significant issues and change
- Enhances the agility of the CAE and GIA
- Contributes to good governance and accountability
- Mitigates the perception and accusation of bias and favoritism

The administrative responsibility for the CAE's role covers the day-to-day activities of GIA's operations. This includes the following:

- Approval of GIA's annual spending budget
- Approval and monitoring of GIA's expense budget
- Review and approval of the:
    - CAE's timesheets, expense reports, vacation, sick time, training events, and conferences
    - Requests for salary increase, promotion, bonus, and sabbatical for team members
- Collaborate with the CEO and the chairperson of the audit committee on the annual evaluation of the performance of the CAE

There are leaders who do not care for the CAE's administrative reporting responsibility. This is because the CAE is not always the bearer of the good news. These leaders are mostly interested in hearing and sharing good news and what stakeholders want to hear. They have little interest in the bad news. The reasons include the following:

- To claim ignorance or no knowledge of a major issue
- Fear of losing existing investors, donors, customers, and suppliers
- Negative impact on attracting potential investors, donors, and customers
- Negative impact on performance evaluation, including salary increase, promotion, and/or bonus

The CAE must collaborate with key stakeholders and senior management on resolving issues before escalating them to the audit committee. This of course does not apply if there is a major unresolved disagreement with management, especially if the issue involves a member of the senior management team. This usually includes escalating the issue up the hierarchy of the organization, which may be up to the level of the CEO and the board. The CAE is required to report unresolved disagreements with management to the audit committee. The process for escalating disagreements in an organization is more effective when supported with a policy and procedures.

SEAT AT THE C-SUITE TABLE

A CAE can be one of the most valuable team members of an organization. This requires the right candidate and the support of key stakeholders. The right candidate is one that is competent, knowledgeable, and has the required experience and qualifications for the role. A CAE needs the support of senior management, particularly the CEO, and the audit committee to be successful in the role.

A seat at the c-suite table is a recognition of the importance of the role of the CAE and GIA to the organization by senior management. The c-suite table usually includes the CEO, chief financial and chief operating officers. The number of chiefs at the c-suite table varies from organization to organization and may include other chiefs such as the chief human resources or people, legal, risk, compliance, and information security officers, and the CAE. A seat at the c-suite table enables the CAE to be more proactive and enhances the effectiveness, success, and value of GIA to the organization. It also opens the door for enhanced engagement, collaboration, understanding, and clarity of what matters most to senior management. Additionally, it paves the way for enhanced contribution to the value creation, preservation, and protection initiatives of the organization as well as the following:

- Timely inform senior management of new risks and improvement opportunities
- Timely sharing of relevant information regarding major undertakings for more informed decisions
- Enables the CAE to have knowledge of major activity the organization plans to undertake
- Minimizes time stakeholders need to spend from their core activities to brief team members of GIA

- Enables the CAE to build lasting relationships and trust with senior management
- Enhances access to senior management and information
- Enhances the readiness, agility, effectiveness, and relevance of the CAE and GIA
- Minimizes surprises and enhances transparency and trust between GIA and senior management
- Minimizes the risk of miscommunication, misunderstanding, and suppression of information
- Paves the way for the CAE to become a trusted advisor
- Sharpens the focus of GIA's activities on what matters most to the organization
- Contributes to forward-thinking and proactive internal audits
- Provides an opportunity for the CAE to educate and enlighten stakeholders

There are many organizations where the CAE is not a member of the c-suite although the "C" requirement is met. It is a waste of a valuable resource if you have the right fit as the CAE. This is because an engaged CAE is one of the most knowledgeable members of the senior management team of an organization.

INTERNAL AUDIT CHARTER

The internal audit charter plays a key role in laying the foundation for the success of the CAE. It is one of the first documents that a CAE must ensure exists or develops as soon as possible to get off to a good start. The internal audit charter sets the tone for the performance of internal audit across the organization. It provides guidance regarding the CAE's reporting relationship with the audit committee, senior management, and the external auditor of the organization. It also governs the performance of internal audit of the organization's operations and activities.

The CAE is usually responsible for developing the internal audit charter for review and approval by the CEO and the audit committee. The approval plays a key role in gaining managers and staff support for the role of the CAE and GIA across the organization. The internal audit charter is usually updated periodically, for example, every two or three years, or as needed and submitted to senior management and the audit committee for approval. A good practice is to include the internal audit charter in the new employee orientation program and handbook as well as reshare it when it is updated.

The internal audit charter empowers and enables CAEs to effectively perform their responsibilities. It provides the framework and guidance on how a CAE should operate. It also provides guidance on the reporting relationships, responsibilities, authority, accountability, scope of internal audit work, hire, termination, performance, and evaluation of the CAE as follows:

- Reporting relationship: It covers who the CAE reports to functionally and administratively. It is standard practice that the CAE reports functionally to the audit committee and administratively to a senior leader such as the CEO. It also covers the frequency of meetings with the audit committee.

- Relationship with the external auditor: It supports collaborating periodically with the external auditor on the coordination and sharing of audit plans, results, new and emerging trends, issues, and risks.
- Responsibilities: It covers the key areas, including overseeing and directing independent and objective internal audits of the organization's administration and operations.
- Authority: It gives the CAE unrestricted access to employees, functions, operations, and assets of the organization, including documents, reports, data, and emails.
- Scope of audit work: The scope of the role may include compliance, financial, operational, information technology (IT), third-party reviews, investigations, and advisory services.
- Independence: Defined as the freedom from conditions that impair the internal audit function's ability to carry out its responsibilities in an unbiased manner.[1] The CAE should avoid taking on management or operational responsibilities outside of GIA. Controls should be implemented to avoid conflict of interest should it become necessary for the CAE or team members to engage in such activities to assist the organization in achieving its objectives.
- Objectivity: An unbiased mental attitude that allows internal auditors to make professional judgments, fulfill their responsibilities, and achieve the Purpose of Internal Auditing without.[2] The CAE must have the freedom and ability to make his or her own decisions based on facts and free of influence, and bias.
- Hire and termination of the CAE: The audit committee, usually the chairperson of the audit committee, must concur with the hiring or termination of the CAE. Management should not be allowed to unilaterally terminate the CAE.
- Performance and evaluation of the CAE: Annual performance evaluation of the CAE is usually a collaborative or joint exercise between the CEO or the administrative manager of the CAE and the chairperson of the audit committee.

The internal audit charter is a requirement of the IIA's Global Internal Audit Standards. The internal audit charter is and needs to be in alignment with the Standards. This is because it is one of the areas that is reviewed and rated in a Quality Assurance Review (QAR) of GIA once every five years. It is an important element of the QAR process for receiving a "Fully Comply" QAR report.

The role and responsibilities of the CAE are often misunderstood. The internal audit charter provides clarity of the role and responsibilities of the CAE. It addresses the question that CAEs are often asked. What does GIA do? There are stakeholders who perceived the role of the CAE and GIA to be financial compliance and fraud investigations. Of course, the role and responsibilities go beyond financial compliance and fraud investigations. The scope of the role may include compliance, financial, operational, IT, third-party reviews, investigations, and advisory services.

EMPOWERING THE CAE

Empowering the CAE enhances the creativity, innovativeness, and agility of GIA. It provides the CAE with the freedom, authority, and flexibility to be creative and innovative. It also enhances the effectiveness of the CAE's in assessing and taking risks in quickly responding and adapting to change. The freedom and authority to act without prior approval, in most cases, are critical in a fast-paced, constantly changing, and disruptive operating environment. It is also critical in a tall GIA organizational structure where the approval of requests is often delayed. Requests usually must flow up the chain of command through the bureaucracy before they are reviewed and approved. This at times leads to missed opportunities to timely mitigate significant risks to the objectives of the organization and remain relevant.

The freedom and authority to make decisions on behalf of GIA enables the CAE to exercise professional judgment and quickly make important decisions. The decisions can have a positive or negative impact on the organization. Therefore, a process must be in place to oversee and hold the CAE accountable for his/her actions. This is to mitigate risks of abuse of empowerment.

There are certain factors that must be considered in empowering the CAE. The factors to consider include the following:

- Agreement: There must be clarity, understanding, and agreement on objectives and deliverables.
- Competence: Team members must be qualified and equipped with the required education, training, knowledge, experience, skills, and technical expertise to do the job.
- Objective: This requires decisions to be based on facts and the exercise of good judgment.
- Accountable: CAEs must be willing to accept responsibility and be held accountable for their actions.
- Servant leadership mindset: This requires putting the interest of stakeholders ahead of the interest of the CAE and GIA.

Empowerment without the required resources, accountability, and a competent team is a recipe for failure. This includes damage to the reputation of the organization. Senior management and the audit committee must ensure that they hire and empower the right person to be the CAE. Empowerment needs to be based on the qualifications of the candidate, including knowledge, experience, expertise, and skills. Organizations do at times assign key roles to staff who are not ready to undertake the role. This is often based on one or more of the following:

- Required to quickly fill a leadership gap
- Required or mandated by law
- High performance and leadership potential of the staff
- Leadership development opportunity for the staff
- Nepotism, loyalty, favoritism, and affiliations

It is a risk to the organization to empower a member of staff who is not qualified for the role. It could be a major reputational damage to the organization and a career-ending event for the staff.

MENTORING

The CAE role is a lonely one at times. A CAE must have a mentor and/or a confidant as a sounding board to share ideas and concerns. It must be someone that the CAE can trust and confide in for advice and guidance. There is highly sensitive information that CAEs receive at times that needs to be shared for advice and guidance. The CAE's manager, CEO, and the chairpersons of the board and the audit committee are usually the individuals that the CAE confides in for advice and guidance. The CAE must exercise good judgment in sharing sensitive information.

There are organizations that have mentorship programs for their staff. This is a valuable tool for onboarding staff. Assigning new staff to a mentor makes it easier for them to learn and adjust to the organization's culture and how it operates. It helps to minimize the anxiety and frustration that often come along with adjusting to a new job. Additionally, it contributes to the career development and retention of staff and team members. The onus is on staff to find a mentor if the organization does not have a mentorship program.

Care should be taken to ensure that the mentor knows and understands the value of being a mentor. A mentor can be a professional internal or external to the organization who the mentee can trust and confide in. A mentor should also be a professional who can provide advice to improve and enhance a mentee's development, career, and dealing with challenging situations.

Mentors must be willing to spend time periodically or as needed to listen, share experiences, lessons learned, insight, and provide guidance to mentees. A mentor should be candid with the mentee. The mentee should be candid with the mentor, listen, and follow through on actions agreed on to pursue and keep the mentor informed of progress. This is important as the engagement and the time commitment must be meaningful to the mentor and the mentee. It is rewarding for a mentor to see a mentee quickly overcome challenges and thrive in their development and career.

The benefits of mentoring include the following:

- Makes onboarding and adjusting to an organization's culture easier
- Provides different perspective of thinking and viewing an issue or problem
- Assists in effectively addressing professional challenges
- Assists in the professional development and success of leaders and team members
- Assists in retaining team members

QUALITY RESOURCES

CAE must have quality resources to be successful in a fast-paced, constantly changing, and disruptive operating environment. The success of the CAE is dependent on the quality of the resources that are provided by the organization. CAE is not able to effectively add value and assist the organization in achieving its objectives without the required or necessary resources. This includes investment in competent staff, technological tools, continuous training and education, and a reasonable spending budget. The quality of GIA's resources determines the quality of its work product. If the quality of GIA's team is mediocre so will the quality of the work. It is more effective to spend GIA's staffing budget on a nimble or small high-quality-performing team armed with technological tools rather than a large average-quality-performing team. The provision of quality resources enables the CAE to do the following:

- Attract and retain talented and diverse team members
- Acquire the required expertise and tools that GIA needs to be effective, ready, resilient, and relevant
- Provide valuable advice to assist stakeholders in making more informed decisions
- Provide ongoing training opportunities to keep the team fresh on activities in the environment

Organizations cannot expect the CAE to be successful keeping up with the pace of an ever-changing environment doing things with a business-as-usual mindset. The organization or senior management must provide funding for the acquisition of the required expertise and technological tools. They must also invest in continuous training and professional education of team members of GIA. This enables the CAE and team members to keep current and informed of changes in the operating environment. This also enables them to quickly think, respond, and adapt to change. The acquisition of required expertise includes expertise in IT, Cybersecurity, Data Analytics, Data Protection and Privacy, Environmental, Social, Governance (ESG).

The primary driver of quality in an ever-changing operating environment is technological innovations. This includes the following:

- Artificial intelligence
- Automation
- Data analytics
- Digitalization
- Drones
- Global positioning system
- Internet of things
- Robotic process automation
- Robotics

The above technological tools are playing a key role in enhancing the effectiveness and efficiency of organizations. This is by speeding up processes and improving the quality of services and products across organizations. For example, the COVID-19 vaccine was developed for use in warp speed, within a year, compared to the past where it took years or even decades to develop a vaccine for use. Digitalization played a key role in developing and fast tracking the vaccine to market and the population. The acquisition of technological tools will replace most, if not all, of GIA's manual and mundane work. It includes manual and sample testing of transactions, controls, compliance, and physical count of inventories. This can now be done utilizing technological tools, including continuous auditing and monitoring. These tools play a key role in freeing up the CAE and team members' time to focus on what really matters most to the organization and its stakeholders. This includes the strategy, objectives, risk mitigation, and the core business of the organization.

The return on investment (ROI) in GIA is hard to quantify and defend at times. However, the intrinsic and intangible value of the presence of a capable and well-equipped GIA is a deterrent to one who is thinking or considering unacceptable or fraudulent activities. As the saying goes, an ounce of prevention is better than a pound of cure. GIA is that ounce of prevention.

INVESTMENT IN CONTINUING PROFESSIONAL EDUCATION

An organization must invest in the continuing professional education of the CAE and team members of GIA. This is to ensure the continued success of the CAE and the team. The investment enables them to stay connected, current, and informed of the activities in the internal and external operating environment. It includes technological innovations, new laws, and regulations as well as technical and professional updates. The investment in continuing training and professional education will enable the CAE and team members to be proactive in responding and adapting to rapid change in the operating environment. This is necessary for the CAE and team members to be successful in staying ahead of the curve and remain ready, resilient, relevant, and valuable to the organization. It also plays a key role in the advice, including insight and foresight, the CAE provides stakeholders to assist them in making more informed and timely decisions.

The risk of the CAE and team members of GIA becoming isolated, complacent, irrelevant, and obsolete is high in an ever-changing operating environment. Change is continuous and so too should be learning. Continuous learning is required for the CAE and team to be successful. They must be aware of current and emerging trends, risks, and opportunities in the operating environment. There is no guarantee that what worked well yesterday will work well today or what worked well today will work well tomorrow.

The benefits to the organization, the CAE, and team members from investing in continuing training and professional education events are priceless. They include the following:

- Keep team members fresh on emerging issues, trends, risks, opportunities, laws, and regulations
- Enhance the organization's image to external stakeholders such as regulators
- Provide opportunities for networking and benchmarking
- Stimulate creativity, innovation, and forward-thinking
- Reduce the risk of the CAE and team members becoming obsolete
- Supports the CAE and team members in maintaining their professional certifications and license

There are various methods for the delivery of continuous training and professional education. This includes in-person or virtual conferences, webinars, workshops, and professional meetings as well as self-study and learning. The training and education can be offered onsite at the organization's office or offsite by a professional organization. In-person offerings are one of the most effective forms of training and education. This is because it allows for more effective networking, collaboration, building of professional relationships, and benchmarking opportunities.

CHAPTER SUMMARY

The success of the CAE depends on the level of support that is provided by key stakeholders. The support of senior management and the audit committee enhances the effectiveness of the CAE. A CAE's authority is diminished without the support of key stakeholders. There are actions that the CEO and the audit committee can take to show their support and commitment for the success of the CAE. The risk to the success of the CAE is high if there is a lack of support from key stakeholders.

The reporting line of the CAE in the hierarchy of the organization matters. The lower the level of the CAE reporting line in the organization the likelihood that the function will be less agile, creative, and innovative. It is generally accepted that the CAE should report functionally to the audit committee of the board of directors and administratively to a member of the senior management team. Reporting administratively to the CEO is the preferred option for CAEs. The functional responsibility for the CAE's role covers the technical aspects of GIA's operations, while the administrative responsibility covers the day-to-day activities.

A seat at the c-suite table is a recognition and acknowledgment of the importance of the CAE and GIA to the organization by senior management. It opens the door for enhanced engagement, collaboration, understanding, and clarity of what matters most to the organization. Additionally, it is an opportunity for the CAE to educate, enlighten, and share information that can lead to more informed decisions by stakeholders.

The internal audit charter plays a key role in laying the foundation for the success of the CAE. The existence or timely development and approval of the internal audit charter sets the tone for the role and responsibilities of the CAE. It is a requirement of the IIA's Global Internal Audit Standards for the Professional Practice of Internal Auditing. It also empowers and enables the CAE to effectively perform the roles and responsibilities of the position. Empowering the CAE enhances the creativity, innovativeness, agility, and effectiveness of the role. An empowered CAE is given the freedom and authority to make decisions on behalf of the organization without prior approval. However, empowerment without accountability is a recipe for abuse, failure, and damage to the reputation of GIA and the organization.

The CAE role is a lonely one at times. A CAE must have a mentor and/or a confidant from whom to seek advice and guidance. The CAE's manager, CEO, and the board and the audit committee chairpersons are the usual confidants of the CAE in organizations. There is highly sensitive information that CAEs receive at times that needs to be shared for advice and guidance. The CAE must exercise good judgment in sharing sensitive information.

A CAE must have quality resources to be successful in a fast-paced, constantly changing, and disruptive operating environment. Organizations cannot expect a CAE to be successful keeping up with changes in the operating environment with a business-as-usual mindset. An organization must invest in the continuing professional education of the CAE and team members of GIA. The risk of the CAE becoming isolated, complacent, obsolete, and irrelevant is high in a dynamic operating environment. The ROI in GIA is hard to quantify and defend at times. However, the intrinsic value to the organization and its stakeholders is priceless.

NOTES

1 Global Internal Audit Standards.
2 Ibid.

4 Building and Maintaining Relationships with Stakeholders

INTRODUCTION

The chief audit executive (CAE) must build and maintain effective relationships with stakeholders to stay connected, current, and informed of activities in the operating environment. It enhances GIA's agility and enables the team to remain ready, resilient, and relevant. It also contributes to GIA's effectiveness, efficiency, and value to the organization. There is no need to spend time reinventing the wheel, especially in a fast-paced, constantly changing, and disruptive operating environment.

A CAE cannot keep up with the fast pace of change without proactively building and maintaining effective relationships with stakeholders and others with mutual interest. This includes team members of GIA, the chairperson of the audit committee, senior management, the leaders of assurance functions, external auditors, regulators, peers, colleagues, and professional organizations. There are mutual benefits to stakeholders in building and maintaining effective relationships. There is no other time that building and maintaining effective relationships with stakeholders are as important as in an ever-changing operating environment.

The purpose of this chapter is to provide advice and guidance on the importance of building and maintaining effective relationships with internal and external stakeholders. Topics covered center around the CAE building and maintaining effective relationship with the following:

- Team members of GIA
- Audit committee
- Senior management
- Leaders of assurance functions
- External auditor
- Regulators
- Peers and colleagues
- Professional organizations

Key learnings from the chapter include the following:

- Value in building and maintaining effective relationships with team members and stakeholders

DOI: 10.1201/9781003207559-4

- Guidance on building and maintaining effective relationships
- Role building and maintaining effective relationships play in:
    - Performance of assurance services
    - Compliance with laws and regulations

RELATIONSHIP WITHIN GIA

The CAE must build and maintain effective relationships with team members of GIA. The team members are an invaluable asset to GIA and the organization. They are the ones who perform the detailed work and provide information to support the CAE in performing GIA's governance-related responsibilities. Their work and reports are the source for the CAE's reports and presentations to stakeholders. The information enables the CAE to provide reasonable assurance and advice, including insight and foresight, into the effectiveness and efficiency of the organization's system of internal control to stakeholders. Senior management, the chief executive officer (CEO), and the audit committee rely on this information to assist in performing their management and governance oversight responsibilities, respectively.

GIA's team must be effectively managed to ensure that the organization and the members of the team get the most from the relationship. This of course is dependent on the resources that are available to GIA. There are steps that a CAE can take to maintain effective relationships with team members of GIA, including the following:

- Meeting and spending time periodically with the team to listen, share, and reconfirm priorities
- Providing periodic update on GIA's activities, challenges, and opportunities
- Keeping team members informed and current on key activities
- Embracing diversity, equity, and inclusion
- Providing a positive and nurturing environment for the team to work, grow, and become successful
- Providing the necessary resources that team members need to be successful
- Encouraging and supporting creativity and innovation
- Obtaining and including input from team members in GIA's decision-making process
- Providing mentoring opportunities for team members
- Showing compassion and empathy for the well-being of team members and families
- Making team members feel welcomed and appreciated
- Recognizing and rewarding outstanding performance, and value-added contributions
- Providing opportunities for continuous learning and professional development
- Providing timely feedback on performance

There should be clarity and understanding of what is most important to team members, the CAE and GIA. The needs of the team are usually different at the various levels of the GIA organization. Additionally, team members are usually closer to the action. They are the ones, for the most part, engaging with stakeholders and doing the detail work. They usually have a good understanding of the local context and the operating environment. They are also familiar with the challenges and have ideas, advice, and insight on the root cause and potential solutions to regional and local issues. Therefore, it is important for the CAE to listen and understand what is most important to team members. This will enable the CAE to be proactive in responding to their needs and minimize turnover. Similarly, there must be clarity and understanding by team members of the strategic and operating objectives and what is most important to the CAE and GIA. Listening and sharing will help to find common ground on what will work best for team members and the organization. It is a team effort.

The sustainability and success of GIA depend on the relationship between the CAE and team members. The benefits of effective relationships between the CAE and team members include the following:

- Enhancing clarity and understanding of roles and responsibilities
- Enhancing alignment with GIA's strategy and objectives
- Enhancing openness, transparency, and ease in sharing of information
- Building trust and confidence
- Keeping team members informed and engaged
- Minimizing turnover of team members

Effective relationship with the CAE and team members of GIA is likely to improve their retention. However, there is always going to be turnover of team members. The return on the investment in training and developing team members is not always realized. High-performing team members leave at times for better opportunities because the opportunities for internal promotion within GIA are usually limited. The risk of turnover of team members can be minimized by the existence of the following:

- Effective relationship with the CAE and team members
- Positive and nurturing working environment
- Career development plan for each team member
- GIA's leadership succession plan

Building and maintaining effective relationships with team members of GIA enhance the effectiveness, efficiency, and quality of GIA's work. Collaborating with team members as the work progresses eliminates the revisiting and reworking of tasks. The CAE will be aware and able to provide timely feedback on key issues as they arise. This minimizes surprises and reduces the revisiting of the issue with stakeholders. It also speeds up the delivery of the findings and recommendations to stakeholders.

Building and maintaining effective relationships with team members of GIA make them feel appreciated, valued, and part of the team. This, along with adopting a positive and nurturing operating environment, is likely to minimize turnover. This also paves the way for building trust, a lasting relationship, and a sense of job security. A positive and nurturing operating environment is one that:

- Values all team members
- Cares for the safety and security of team members
- Supports openness, transparency, and honesty
- Encourages creativity and innovation
- Embraces change and technological innovations
- Embraces agility, flexibility, and adaptability
- Embraces proactive and forward-thinking
- Embraces diversity, equity, and inclusion
- Provides opportunities for continuing education, learning, career growth, and professional development

RELATIONSHIP WITH THE AUDIT COMMITTEE

The audit committee of the board of directors (herein after the board) plays a key role in certain governance oversight responsibilities of the board. It comprises independent, non-executive board members. Certain board governance oversight responsibilities are delegated to the audit committee. The delegated oversight responsibilities usually include the following:

- Financial reporting, including Sarbanes-Oxley (SOX)
- External Auditor
- Internal Audit
- Internal controls
- Risk Management
- Compliance

Risk management and compliance, in some organizations, are assigned to other board sub-committees.

The chairperson of the audit committee and the CAE must work collaboratively to build and maintain an effective working relationship. It provides an understanding and clarity of what is most important to the audit committee and the CAE. This is necessary for the CAE to be successful in achieving GIA's objectives. The chairperson of the audit committee plays a key role in ensuring that the relationship is developed, maintained, and supported. The relationship between the chairperson of the audit committee and the CAE is enhanced by:

- Staying connected and accessible to each other as needed
- Holding executive session with only the CAE and members of the audit committee after each audit committee meeting but no less than annually
- Having periodic or as needed catch-up calls and/or meetings

The audit committee needs the CAE and GIA's support in performing its governance oversight responsibilities. As mentioned earlier, the audit committee has governance oversight responsibilities for certain of the organization's governance programs. However, the members' time is limited since they may also have a full-time job as well as other board commitments. Additionally, the operating environment is constantly changing and introducing new risks to the board and the organization. Ignoring or refusing to quickly adapt to change to mitigate new and/or emerging risks can lead to the demise of an organization. It includes ignoring or refusing to embrace technological innovations, adopting new laws and regulations, or improving internal controls. This can damage the reputation of the board and expose board members and officers of the organization to legal liability. What took organizations years and decades to build can be destroyed in no time. The CAE can enhance GIA's value to the audit committee and the organization by doing whatever it can to make the audit committee governance oversight easier. This will enable the audit committee to spend more time on what matters most to the board and the organization.

The audit committee relies on the CAE to oversee and manage the performance of independent and objective audits of the organization's administration and operations, including its governance programs.

The performance of independent and objective audits provides assurance and advice, including insight and foresight, into the effectiveness and efficiency of the organization's governance, risk, and compliance (GRC) programs. A key focus of governance programs is to mitigate risks to the achievement of the mission, vision, strategy, and business, operating, reporting, and compliance objectives of the organization. The support and assistance the CAE and GIA provide the audit committee are usually in the form of periodic reports and presentations. The information is to assist the committee in the effective performance of its governance and oversight responsibilities. The following information is usually included in the CAE's report and presentation to the audit committee:

- Audit findings and recommendations, including:
  - Fraudulent activities
  - Effectiveness and efficiency of the organization's system of internal control, risk management, and compliance programs
  - Advice, including insight and foresight, on improving the effectiveness and efficiency of the organization's governance programs
  - Update on significant existing, new, and emerging issues, risks, and opportunities
- Actions taken by management beyond the organization's risk appetite and tolerance
- Status update on the implementation of outstanding audit recommendations
- Status update on the execution of the internal audit plan
- Competence, qualifications, and level of staffing to effectively perform the audit work

The CAE normally reports functionally to the audit committee and administratively to the highest level possible in an organization. This reporting relationship enhances the independence and objectivity of GIA's operations. Additionally, the

CAE needs the audit committee's support for GIA's strategic initiatives as well as the following:

- Setting the tone at the top of the organization to indicate their support and the importance of GIA to the organization
- Obtaining the required resources that the CAE and GIA need to be effective
- Providing advice and assist in resolving major disagreements with the CAE and senior management
- Serving as a confidant or sounding board for the CAE

RELATIONSHIP WITH SENIOR MANAGEMENT

The CAE, CEO, and members of the senior management team must work collaboratively to build and maintain effective working relationships. The CAE and the CEO need each other's support to effectively perform their governance-related responsibilities. The CEO is accountable to the board for the establishment and overall effectiveness and efficiency of the organization's governance programs. The CEO usually delegates the responsibility for developing, implementing, and maintaining governance programs to the senior management team. Organization's governance programs usually cover the myriad of risks and internal controls across the organization. The CEO does not have the time and capacity to directly manage the requirements of the programs. This includes the responsibility for financial reporting, risk management, compliance (including SOX), and internal controls. The CEO and senior management need the CAE's independent and objective assurance and advice, including insight and foresight, into the effectiveness and efficiency of the organization's governance programs. This is to assist them in performing their governance-related responsibilities and making more informed decisions. Working collaboratively requires ongoing engagement, communication, and coordination. It is particularly important in a fast-paced, constantly changing, and disruptive operating environment. It will ensure the following:

- Enhance alignment of GIA's plans and activities with the following:
  - Business, operating, reporting, and compliance objectives of the organization
  - What is most important to the CEO, senior management, and the CAE
- Allow for the timely receipt of unfiltered or firsthand information
- Pave the way for building trust and lasting relationships
- Enhance understanding and appreciation of GIA's value to the organization

The senior management of an organization is typically the CEO and his or her direct reports. This usually includes the following:

- Chief financial officer (CFO)
- Chief operating officer (COO)
- Chief legal officer (CLO) or General counsel (GC)

Other members of the senior management team who may not be a direct report of the CEO include the following:

- Chief audit executive (CAE)
- Chief compliance officer (CCO)
- Chief human resources officer (CHRO)
- Chief information security officer (CISO)
- Chief of diversity, equity, and inclusion (CODEI)
- Chief risk officer (CRO)
- Chief technology officer (CTO)
- Head of investigations

Building and maintaining effective working relationships with senior management requires ongoing engagement, communication, and timely sharing of information. This is for the CAE and senior management to stay connected, current, and informed. It is necessary to effectively address risks and opportunities in a fast-paced, constantly changing, and disruptive operating environment. Additionally, the benefits of the relationship to the CAE and senior management include the following:

- Securing a seat at the c-suite table for the CAE
- Keeping the CAE in the loop of any significant changes in the organization
- Ensuring there is clarity and understanding of what is most important to the CAE and senior management
- Making it easier for senior management to satisfy their responsibilities for the organization's governance programs

Senior management, particularly the CEO, needs GIA's assistance to effectively perform their governance-related responsibilities. As mentioned earlier, the CEO is accountable to the board for the establishment and overall effectiveness and efficiency of the organization's governance programs. Also, the CEO usually delegates the responsibility for developing, implementing, and maintaining governance programs to members of the senior management team. Senior management is responsible for developing, implementing, and maintaining effective governance programs for their area(s) of responsibility. It includes governance structures, policies, processes, and procedures. Senior management may, in turn, delegate the responsibility to managers in their reporting line. Senior management must periodically report to the CEO on the status of their governance programs. The information is required to be incorporated into the CEO's periodic report on the organization's governance programs to the board. This is where the CEO needs the independent and objective assurance and advice, including insight and foresight, from the CAE. It gives the CEO reasonable assurance that the information provided by senior management is reliable, valid, accurate, complete, and consistent.

GIA is the only assurance function that is usually mandated to operate independent of management and the day-to-day operations of an organization. This enables the CAE to provide independent and objective assurance and advice into the effectiveness and efficiency of the organization's governance programs. The benefits to senior management from the services that the CAE and GIA provide include the following:

- Providing independent and objective assurance and advice, including insight and foresight, into the effectiveness and efficiency of the organization's governance programs
- Sharing of early warning indicators of new and emerging trends, recurring issues, risks, and opportunities
- Providing status update on the implementation of agreed on audit recommendations
- Anticipating and sharing with senior management risks to the achievement of the business, operating, reporting, and compliance objectives of the organization
- Evaluating and providing impactful advice to improve internal controls, including governance structures, policies, processes, and procedures

The CAE and team members' comprehensive knowledge of the organization enables the CAE to assist senior management with their governance program responsibilities. This includes educating and timely sharing lessons learned with the CEO, members of the senior management team, and other stakeholders who can benefit from the experience. This enables them to be proactive in addressing new and emerging trends, issues, risks, and improvement opportunities. The educating and sharing of lessons learned can be in the form of workshops and lunch and learning sessions covering topics such as:

- Fraudulent activities
- Trends and emerging issues, risks, and recommended mitigation activities
- Findings and remediation activities
- Risk assessment
- Internal controls
- Compliance
- Policies, processes, and procedures
- Change management

The CAE needs senior management's support to effectively perform GIA's governance-related responsibilities. The CAE must engage and collaborate regularly with senior management. This includes ongoing communications, sharing, and coordination with senior management. Their support is critical in setting the tone at the top of the organization for GIA. The CAE's effectiveness and efficiency depend on the level of support GIA receives from the CEO and members of the senior management team. The benefits to the CAE and GIA from the engagement and collaboration include the following:

- Maintain effective working relationship with the CEO and members of the senior management team

- Set the tone at the top of the organization of the importance of the CAE's role and value of GIA to the organization
- Send the message to employees of the organization's commitment and support for GIA
- Keep the CAE current on what matters most to senior management
- Confirm and strengthen the alignment of GIA's plan and activities, including audit findings and recommendations, with the objectives and risk management plans and activities of the organization
- Ensure clarity and understanding of what matters most to the CAE and GIA
- Provide support for GIA's plans and objectives
- Enhance support for the required resources the CAE needs to effectively perform and add value to the organization
- Enhance the timely sharing of information to keep the CAE informed of major changes in the organization
- Provide and ensure easy access to staff and assets of the organization, including information and data
- Enhance and strengthen the CAE and GIA's readiness, relevance, and value to the organization
- Enhance transparency and minimize surprises
- Pave the way for building trusted advisor relationships

RELATIONSHIP WITH THE LEADERS OF ASSURANCE FUNCTIONS

The leaders of assurance functions and external assurance service providers play a key role in supporting and assisting stakeholders perform their governance responsibilities. They are responsible for providing reasonable assurance and advice on the effectiveness and efficiency of the organization's governance programs. Senior management and the board rely on the information presented by the leaders of assurance functions to assist them in performing their management and governance oversight responsibilities, respectively.

Leaders of assurance functions and assurance service providers include the following:

- CAE – Internal audit
- Head of investigation – Fraud investigation
- CRO – Risk management
- CCO – Compliance
- CISO – Information security
- External auditor – Financial statements audit

Leaders of assurance functions operating in silos hinders the organization and stakeholders from getting the most from the functions. They often do not communicate, coordinate, or share information on a regular basis or in a timely manner with each other. They prepare and present their periodic assurance report to senior management and the board. The lack of coordination and sharing of information and reports at times lead to gaps and duplication of work, and inconsistent information in presentations and reports to senior management and the board. This poses a risk to the effectiveness, efficiency, and quality of the assurance services and reports to stakeholders. The risks are higher in a fast-paced, constantly changing, and disruptive operating environment that is overwhelmed with data.

The lack of communication, coordination, and sharing of information with other leaders of assurance functions is a risk and disservice to the organization. It makes it more difficult for senior management and the board to effectively perform their management and governance oversight responsibilities, respectively. The risks include the following:

- Inconsistent reporting
- Conflicting findings and recommendations
- Hidden gaps in assurance work
- Duplication of work
- Waste of resources

The leaders of assurance functions must work collaboratively to improve the quality and value of their services to the organization. This includes improving and enhancing the effectiveness and efficiency of assurance services. Working collaboratively includes ongoing engagement, communication, listening, sharing, and coordinating assurance services activities. It requires the buy-in and support of the leaders of assurance functions, senior management, and the board. Working collaboratively will require a change in culture and mindset of the leaders of assurance and staff. The impact can be significant, including:

- Breaking down and eliminating silos
- Eliminating the performance of some activities to avoid duplication of work
- Standardizing and consolidating assurance functions processes, procedures, and reports
- Streamlining compliance testing
- Using a common platform and software such as GRC software
- Utilizing common technological tools such as data analytics, robotics, machine learning, and artificial intelligence
- Utilizing common terminology

RELATIONSHIP WITH THE ORGANIZATION'S EXTERNAL AUDITOR

Building and maintaining an effective relationship with the CAE and the organization's external auditor require regular communication and meetings where update and topics of mutual interest are shared. It is particularly important in an ever-changing operating environment. The sharing, updating, and coordinating are usually between the CAE and the audit partner assigned to the engagement. However, the leaders of GIA and the senior members of the external audit team are often in attendance.

The relationship with the external auditor is an opportunity for the CAE and the external audit partner to share information of mutual interest. This is a valuable resource for advice and information for the CAE, leaders and team members of GIA, and the organization. Matters of mutual interest include the following:

- Audit committee-related information, including pre-read materials, agenda, timing, and minutes
- Technical updates on accounting and auditing matters
- Trends and emerging issues in the profession and industry
- Internal audit reports, findings, and recommendations
- Status of the implementation of external audit recommendations
- Events that may be of interest to the CAE and team members such as technical briefings and training

There is value to GIA and the organization in building and maintaining an effective relationship with the external auditor. The organization's external auditor is an excellent source of information and advice for the CAE and leaders of GIA. This enables them to keep current and informed on activities that are most important to GIA and the organization. Benefits of the relationship with the external auditor to GIA and the organization include the following:

- Minimize increase in the annual external audit fees
- Minimize the risk of audit fatigue of internal stakeholders
- Provide insight into relevant emerging issues and trends in the industry
- Provide technical advice and updates on accounting and auditing matters
- Provide access to the external audit firm's events and publications, including training, research, and industry newsletters

There is value to the organization's external auditor in building and maintaining an effective relationship with the CAE. An effective relationship with the CAE can enhance the effectiveness and efficiency of the annual external audit of the organization. Value to the organization's external auditor of the relationship with the CAE includes the following:

- Access to GIA's internal audit plan, workpapers, and audit reports
- Minimize duplication of audit work by coordinating audit plans and schedules
- Streamline testing of internal controls by relying on GA's work
- Support from GIA staff in performing the annual external audit

RELATIONSHIP WITH REGULATORS

An organization should embrace rather than fear regulators as there are benefits available to both. There is nothing to fear if an organization is committed to and is doing the right things to comply with laws and regulations. Of course, there are at times gaps and instances of non-compliance with laws and regulations for various reasons. Reasons may include the following:

- Lack of resources, such as staffing, technological tools, and internal controls
- Misunderstandings
- Ambiguity of laws and regulations
- Cost benefit of compliance
- Rogue or defiant staff

Building and maintaining effective relationships with regulators keep the CAE and team members current and informed of changes in laws, regulations, and compliance requirements. This enables the CAE to be proactive in informing stakeholders of such changes, which, in turn, can be proactive and timely in addressing. The relationships assist in enhancing the effectiveness of the organization's compliance with laws and regulations. External stakeholders that have an interest in compliance include government agencies such as the Security and Exchange Commission, bankers, insurers, rating agencies, and watchdog organizations.

Regulators are usually interested in how quickly non-compliance with laws and regulations is identified, corrected, and, if applicable, reported to the regulatory body. A regulator may be more lenient if management is proactive in addressing non-compliance with laws and regulations and demonstrates commitment to comply. Management's commitment to complying with laws and regulations includes the implementation of effective internal controls as well as organizational structures, policies, processes, and procedures, to mitigate the risk of non-compliance.

A regulator's audit, review, or inquiry can at times be very disruptive to an organization. The disruption is usually driven by fear, stress, and additional demand on staffs' time by a regulator. The CAE's relationship with the regulator can help to reduce and ease the fear, stress, and demand on staffs' time. This is by sharing relevant information with the regulator in connection with their work. There are staff who at times would prefer not to share information with regulators unless they request it. The mindset of such staff is the belief that what the regulators do not know will not hurt the organization. That may work sometimes, but honesty and transparency work better. Regulators are not happy if they find out that the organization had been withholding issues from them. They may extend their time at the organization to determine if there are other issues that the organization is withholding.

Organizations and regulators usually want the audit, review, or inquiry to be done expeditiously. As mentioned earlier, a regulator's audit, review, or inquiry can at times be very disruptive. The fear, stress, and the additional demand on staff time are often a distraction to the core business of the organization. This can lead to productivity issues. Therefore, it is important for a regulator's audit, review, or inquiry to be done expeditiously. Regulator's staff usually want to get into the organization, perform their work, and leave as quickly as possible. They are usually under pressure to get their work done in accordance with the budget requirements for the assignment. Therefore, the opportunity for a regulator to rely on GIA's work will be seriously considered in developing the plan for their work. The CAE can assist regulators in effectively performing their work by sharing relevant information. The information shared will assist the regulator in determining the timing, scope, and nature of their work. This will also minimize the stress and time that staff must spend gathering information for regulators. Information often shared by GIA includes the following:

- Process flow documentation
- Internal controls test workpapers and results
- Relevant audit reports

The CAE and leaders of GIA can play a key role in reducing the stress and demand on staff time from a regulatory audit, review, or inquiry. It includes reducing the hostility that may arise at times from a regulator's findings and recommendations. This is because of the CAE and team members of GIA knowledge, experience, and expertise overseeing and conducting audits. However, a senior member of GIA needs to be the organization's liaison for regulatory audits, reviews, or inquiries to maximize this value.

Effective relationships with regulators contribute to the CAE and team members' agility, readiness, resilience, relevance, and value to the organization. These relationships enable the CAE and team members to stay connected, current, and informed of changes in existing, new, and emerging laws and regulations. The CAE will also have a contact person(s) at the regulators office to reach out to for assistance such as:

- Provide advice and guidance on new and emerging regulations
- Provide training on existing and new regulations
- Share emerging issues and risks in the industry and operating environment
- Share common areas of non-compliance and recurring issues

There is value to GIA and the organization in building and maintaining effective relationships with regulators. The benefits to GIA and the organization include the following:

- Enhancing timely compliance with new and existing laws and regulations
- Minimizing ambiguity of laws and regulations
- Minimizing fear, stress, and demand on staff time
- Minimizing hostility that may develop between management and regulators regarding disagreements over findings and recommendations

There is also value to regulators in building and maintaining an effective relationship with the CAE. The value to regulators from the relationship includes the following:

- Assist in streamlining the timing, scope, and nature of the regulator's work by relying on GIA's work
- Enhance the effectiveness and efficiency of the regulator's audit, review, or inquiry
- Reduce hostility that may develop between management and regulators regarding disagreements over findings and recommendations

A regulator usually performs a review of GIA and its work to determine whether the work can be relied on. The review includes the following:

- Verification of the integrity, independence, objectivity, and competence of team members of GIA
- Verification of compliance with the IIA's Global Internal Audit Standards
- Reperform tests of a sample of GIA's work to determine if it can be relied on

RELATIONSHIP WITH PEERS AND COLLEAGUES AT OTHER ORGANIZATIONS

Building and maintaining effective relationships with peers and colleagues at other organizations enhance the agility of the CAE and team members of GIA. This includes the readiness, resilience, relevance, and value of GIA to the organization. The benefits of building and maintaining effective relationships with peers and colleagues at other organizations are priceless. Benefits include the following:

- Share lessons learned to the extent possible on matters of mutual interest, including new, emerging, and recurring risks, opportunities, and avoid reinventing the wheel and making the same mistakes
- Access to early warning indicators of risks, which enables the CAE and leaders of GIA to anticipate and be proactive in providing advice, including insight and foresight, to stakeholders
- Serve as a sounding board for obtaining feedback on innovative ideas
- Enable the CAE to stay connected and keep current with technological innovations, new laws, regulations, and trends in the industry and profession
- Pave the way for benchmarking and joint training opportunities

The peers and/or colleagues should be professionals who the CAE can trust. The objective of the relationship is to discuss, share, exchange ideas, and information on areas of mutual interest. These are areas that do not expose confidential and proprietary information of either organization. The relationship should not be limited to peers and colleagues in the same industry. Building and maintaining effective relationships with peers and colleagues in other industries can lead to more learning and thinking outside of the box. There is value in listening to different perspectives on solving problems and sharing with stakeholders.

Building and maintaining effective relationships with peers and colleagues at other organizations require periodic touch base calls and/or informal meetings. This is to share and exchange ideas, experiences, lessons learned, and solutions to common issues and risks. It requires finding areas of mutual interest that, as mentioned earlier, do not expose either organization's confidential or proprietary information. Areas of mutual interest include the following:

- Cybersecurity
- Fraud
- Technological innovations

- Experience with software and tools
- Implementation of new laws and regulations
- Staffing matters
- Joint training opportunities

RELATIONSHIP WITH PROFESSIONAL ORGANIZATIONS

Building and maintaining effective relationships with professional organizations enable team members of GIA to stay connected, current, and informed of changes in the operating environment. This includes changes in laws and regulations, technological innovations, and trends in the profession, industry, and operating environment. There are benefits to the CAE and team members as well as the organization in building and maintaining effective relationships with professional organizations. The benefits include opportunities for career and professional development as well as the following:

- Learn early about changes in laws and regulations, technological innovations, and trends in the operating environment
- Access to the results of research, studies, surveys, professional journal, and newsletters
- Access to continuing professional education training courses and career development programs, including webinars, workshops, seminars, and conferences
- Discount to members for events sponsored by the professional organization

The relationship with professional organizations usually requires membership. Membership usually has some entry-level requirements such as education, knowledge, and experience as well as a sponsor in some cases. Membership categories include the following:

- Full membership includes the following:
  - Licensed members such as a Certified Public Accountant (CPA) and Chartered Accountant (CA)
  - Certified members such as the Certified Internal Auditor (CIA), Certified Information System Auditor (CISA), Certified Fraud Examiner (CFE), and Certified Management Accountant (CMA)
- Associate members such as qualifying candidates for membership into the professional organization

Most professional organizations offer professional certifications to their members. This includes the following:

- The CIA certification issued by the Institute of Internal Auditors (IIA)
- The CPA issued by the Institute of Certified Public Accountants (AICPA)
- CA issued by the Fellow of the Institute of Chartered Accountants (FCA)
- CISA issued by the Information Security and Control Association (ISACA)
- CFE issued by the Association of Certified Fraud Examiner (ACFE)
- CMA issued by the Institute of Management Accountant (IMA)

A member must engage in continuing professional education to maintain membership in a professional organization. Most professional organizations require a minimum of 20 hours of CPE annually and a total of at least 120 hours of CPE over a three-year period. For example, the preceding is required to maintain the CPA, CIA, CFE, and CISA designations. The CAE must encourage members to engage and participate in the activities of professional organizations. The professional activities include the following:

- Joining a professional organization
- Attending membership meetings regularly
- Sharing experience and expertise
- Volunteering to serve on a committee
- Advocating and promoting the value of the profession

The traditional and most common professional organizations that GIA members are affiliated with include the following:

- The IIA
- Information System Audit and Control Association
- ACFEs
- Professional accounting organizations, such as the American Institute of Certified Public Accountants, American Accounting Association, Institute of Management Accountants, Fellow of the Institute of Chartered Accountants
- Association of Chartered Accountants
- Financial Executive International

There are benefits to professional organizations in building and maintaining effective relationships with CAEs and team members of GIA. The benefits of the relationship to professional organizations include the following:

- Increase in membership
- Increase revenues from membership fees and professional training and development events
- Increase attendance at membership meetings and events such as conferences, webinars, and workshops
- Source of research
- Increase in the source of volunteers to serve on committees

CHAPTER SUMMARY

The CAE must build and maintain effective relationships with team members of GIA. The team members must be effectively managed to ensure that the organization and team members get the most from the relationship. There must be clarity and understanding of what is most important to the team, the CAE, and GIA. The CAE must engage, listen, and timely share information with the team. The sustainability and success of GIA depend on the relationship between the CAE and team members, GIA's most valuable asset. An effective relationship with team members is likely to improve their retention and enhance the effectiveness, efficiency, and quality of GIA's work. Building and maintaining effective relationships with team members make them feel appreciated and valued.

The audit committee of the board of directors plays a key role in certain governance and oversight responsibilities of the board. The chairperson of the audit committee and the CAE must work collaboratively to build and maintain an effective working relationship. The audit committee needs the CAE and GIA's support in performing its governance oversight responsibilities. The committee relies on the CAE to oversee and manage the performance of independent and objective internal audits of the organization's administration and operations, including its governance programs. The CAE normally reports functionally to the audit committee and administratively to the highest level possible in an organization.

The CAE and senior management must work collaboratively to build and maintain effective working relationships. Building and maintaining effective working relationships with senior management require ongoing engagement, collaboration, and timely sharing of information. Senior management needs GIA's assistance to effectively perform their governance-related responsibilities. GIA is the only assurance function that is usually mandated to operate independent of the management of the day-to-day operations of the organization. The CAE's and team members' comprehensive knowledge of the organization enables them to assist senior management with their governance-related responsibilities. This includes educating and timely sharing lessons learned with senior management and stakeholders. Similarly, the CAE needs senior management's support to effectively perform GIA's governance-related responsibilities.

The leaders of assurance functions and external assurance service providers are expected to play a key role in supporting and assisting stakeholders perform their governance-related responsibilities. The leaders of assurance functions must work collaboratively to improve and enhance the value of assurance services to the organization. Leaders of assurance functions operating in silos pose a risk to the assurance services they provide to their organization. Operating in silos prevents the organization and key stakeholders from getting the most from the organization's assurance functions. This is usually due to the lack of communication, coordination, and sharing of information with other leaders of assurance functions.

Building and maintaining an effective relationship with the organization's external auditor require periodic communications. This relationship is an opportunity for the CAE and the external audit partner responsible for the annual audit to share information on matters of mutual interest.

An organization should embrace rather than fear regulators. Building and maintaining effective relationships with regulators keep the CAE and team members of GIA current and informed. This relates to changes in laws, regulations, and compliance requirements. Regulators are usually interested in how quickly issues are identified, corrected, and, if applicable, reported to the regulatory body. A regulator's audit, review or inquiry can be disruptive to an organization at times. Organizations and regulators usually want the audit, review, or inquiry done expeditiously. The

CAE and leaders of GIA can play a key role in reducing the stress and demand on staff time. Building and maintaining effective relationships with regulators contributes to the CAE and team members' agility.

Building and maintaining effective relationships with peers and colleagues at other organizations enhance the agility of the CAE and team members of GIA. The peers and/or colleagues should be professionals who the CAE can trust. The relationship with peers and colleagues should not be limited to peers in the same industry. Building and maintaining effective relationships with peers and colleagues at other organizations require periodic touch base catch-up calls and/or meetings.

Building and maintaining effective relationships with professional organizations enable the CAE and team members to stay connected and informed. This relates to changes in the industry, profession, and the operating environment. The relationship with a professional organization usually requires membership. Most professional organizations offer professional certifications to their members. A member must engage in continuing professional education to maintain membership in a professional organization.

5 Managing a Multicultural Global Internal Audit Team

INTRODUCTION

There is no value added if there is no understanding of what is most important to the members of a multicultural global internal audit (GIA) team. A multicultural GIA team comprises team members from different countries and cultures where the organization operates. There are inherent risks associated with the culture in some countries where the organization operates due to the diverse values, customs, norms, and languages that exist on a multicultural team. Ongoing communication of important messages must be a planned activity for effectively managing the team. Keeping multicultural team members engaged and motivated is critical to the effectiveness and success of GIA.

Effectively managing a multicultural GIA team is a role for a competent and experienced audit manager who embraces diversity. It requires patience and understanding as one shoe does not fit all in the operating environment. Attracting and retaining talented multicultural team members require providing and maintaining a welcoming operating environment and resources that the team needs to be successful. Understanding the strengths and areas for improvement is critical in effectively managing multicultural teams to yield the highest quality work product, growth, and experience for team members.

Inclusion of multicultural team members at the decision-making table enhances the quality of the discussion and leads to more informed decisions. A GIA function that comprises team members only from the home country is shortchanging itself of the true value of a multicultural team. A multicultural GIA team is an asset to an organization that is often underutilized.

The purpose of this chapter is to provide advice and guidance on how to effectively manage a multicultural GIA team. Topics covered include the following:

- No understanding no value
- Managing a multicultural GIA team
- Barriers
- Communication, engagement, and collaboration
- Talent management
- Diversity, equity, inclusion, and a multicultural team

DOI: 10.1201/9781003207559-5

Key learnings from the chapter include the following:

- Benefits of understanding what is important to the members of a multicultural team
- Effectively managing a multicultural team
- Reasons why one shoe does not fit all
- Understanding cultural and language barriers
- Importance of ongoing communications, engagement, and collaboration
- Attracting and retaining talented multicultural team members
- Value and challenges of diversity, equity, and inclusion
- Contribution of multicultural teams to the organization

NO UNDERSTANDING NO VALUE

There is no value added if there is no understanding of what is most important to the members of a multicultural GIA team. The effectiveness and success of managing a multicultural GIA team lie in obtaining an understanding and focusing on what matters most to the members of the team. The manager must assist in addressing their needs to the extent possible. This includes career development, advancement opportunities, and the well-being of team members. Understanding, respecting, and giving grace to each other's culture help to pave the way for teamwork and a productive and positive GIA-operating environment.

The manager and multicultural team members must have a common understanding of GIA's strategy, objectives, and risks. This includes GIA's plans, policies, processes, and procedures. Understanding is necessary to set and manage expectations. It enhances the focus and engagement of the team and assists in ensuring that multicultural team members' activities are in alignment with GIA's plans and objectives. Alignment is critical in effectively managing a multicultural GIA team.

The manager and multicultural team members must have a mutual understanding of what is most important to the team. This includes obtaining an understanding of the team members' career plan and objectives, strengths, and opportunities for development. This is critical in effectively managing the team. The manager must also pay attention to the well-being, including the safety and security, of team members.

One shoe does not fit all in managing a multicultural team due to the diverse nature of the team. It is important that the manager obtains an understanding of the culture, including values, customs, and norms of the members of the team. The key is to understand the diverse background and characteristics of the members of the team and tailor interaction and engagement keeping the characteristics in mind.

MANAGING A MULTICULTURAL GIA TEAM

Effectively managing a multicultural GIA team is a role for a competent and experienced audit manager who embraces diversity. A multicultural GIA-operating environment is a diverse and complex operating environment consisting of diverse cultures and languages. The effectiveness and success in managing a multicultural GIA team to become a high-performing team depend on the quality of the team.

This includes having the right fit of the multicultural team members. The manager must be able to leverage the cultural diversity in the countries where the organization operates to enhance GIA's effectiveness and efficiency. It is advantageous for the manager to have experience managing a multicultural team.

Effectively managing a multicultural GIA team requires patience. Patience and understanding are required to effectively manage diverse cultures, including beliefs, values, customs, norms, and languages that are usually present in a multicultural team. The manager must genuinely care for the well-being and safety of multicultural team members, particularly those working offsite in their home country or remotely. They often encounter challenges that could disrupt their performance. The challenges include different time zones, lack of access to the internet, frequent power outages, and transportation issues. As a result, it is not realistic to expect multicultural team members working in their home country or remotely to consistently perform at the same level as team members at headquarters.

The effectiveness and success of managing a multicultural team require a manager who takes time to engage and collaborate with team members. The manager must understand what matters most to them. This includes the work, their career, well-being, and challenges that they are experiencing. This enables the manager to effectively address their needs to the extent possible and set mutual expectations. Effectively managing a multicultural GIA team includes the following:

- Setting the tone at the top
- Setting realistic goals and metrics
- Providing a welcoming and nurturing operating environment where team members can grow
- Providing the necessary resources that team members need to be successful
- Encouraging and supporting creativity and innovation
- Obtaining and including input from team members in GIA's decision-making process
- Ensuring alignment with the mission, values, strategy, and objectives of GIA and the organization
- Meeting periodically with the team to listen, understand, share, discuss, and reconfirm priorities
- Keeping team members informed and current on key activities of GIA and the organization
- Empowering team members to make decisions on behalf of GIA
- Embracing diversity, equity, and inclusion
- Providing mentoring opportunities for team members
- Showing compassion and empathy for the well-being of team members and families
- Making team members feel welcomed and appreciated
- Recognizing and rewarding outstanding performance and valuable contributions
- Providing opportunities for continuous learning, growth, career, and professional development
- Providing timely feedback on performance

BARRIERS

Language barriers are often challenging when managing a multicultural team where English is the official language of the organization. The level of the English language varies on a multicultural team. The manager of the team must ensure that the spoken words are in alignment with the written words as there are at times differences in the spoken and written words. It is best to focus on the substance rather than the form. This requires listening intently and ensuring that there is mutual understanding. There are organizations that have either an internal or external report writing service provider to assist in the writing of multicultural team reports.

There are inherent risks associated with the customs and norms in some countries where the organization operates. The risks include favoritism, nepotism, fraud, including bribery, kickbacks, and extortion. Staff are at times reluctant to report observed wrongdoings in such cultures as it is not the custom or norm to do so. This usually occurs when it relates to senior executives, managers, elders, and family members. The risks to staff include intimidation, retaliation, termination, and abandonment by family members. Bribery and kickbacks are prohibited by law in many countries; however, it occurs, and it goes without saying even in countries where it is prohibited.

There are steps that an organization can take to minimize inherent risks to its reputation. The steps include the following:

- Implement ethics policy
- Implement effective management policies, processes, and procedures
- Implement an anonymous confidential whistleblower hotline
- Monitor compliance with policies and procedures
- Conduct internal audits and/or proactive investigations of vulnerable areas based on risk

COMMUNICATION, ENGAGEMENT, AND COLLABORATION

Ongoing communication of key messages must be a planned activity in managing a multicultural team. This includes the confirmation and reconfirmation of important messages. Ongoing communications keep the focus on what matters most not only to the organization but also to the members of the team. Messages are at times lost, ambiguous, misinterpreted, misunderstood, distorted, or manipulated. These incidents can disrupt, delay, and/or cause cancelation of major initiatives. Confirmation and reconfirmation of messages minimize disruption as well as mission drift, and misalignment with mission, vision, strategy, and objectives.

Communication must be clear, concise, and easy to understand. This is particularly important in a GIA multicultural operating environment where there are inherent cultural and language barriers. Actions that can be taken to overcome some of the challenges communicating with multicultural teams include the following:

- Set clear and easy to understand objectives, policies, processes, and procedures
- Hold virtual town-hall-style meetings to communicate important messages
- Confirm and reconfirm important messages

- Standardize systems and applications
- Respect, appreciate, and celebrate cultural diversity
- Include multicultural team members in GIA's decision-making process

The message must be consistent across the organization and followed up to ensure that it was received, interpreted, and delivered as intended. Steps that can be taken to ensure that messages are received, interpreted, and delivered as intended include the following:

- Confirm receipt by the recipient
- Recap of messages by recipients
- Reconfirm important messages
- Reshare important messages periodically until the objective is achieved

Keeping a multicultural team engaged is critical to the success of GIA. Multicultural teams working at a regional, local office or remotely from home must feel that they are an important and valued member of the team. The manager must effectively manage the risk of the members of a multicultural team working in silo, becoming distracted, or feeling isolated. Their buy-in and support are critical to the success of any major GIA initiative. Multicultural team members are usually more familiar with the culture and the local operating environment. They are also closest to the action. Actions that a manager can take to enhance the engagement of a GIA multicultural team include the following:

- Empower members of multicultural teams working remotely to act on behalf of GIA
- Conduct periodic virtual team and town-hall-style meetings
- Provide timely response to multicultural team's questions and inquiries
- Attend multicultural team meetings
- Conduct periodic onsite visits with multicultural team members
- Understand and leverage multicultural team members' strengths and provide the support and training to improve areas that need improvement
- Offer mentoring opportunities
- Provide multicultural teams opportunity to participate and provide input to major GIA's decisions
- Provide annual training opportunities
- Provide opportunities for career development and advancement
- Support multicultural team training and certification programs
- Provide opportunities for multicultural teams to work remotely in their home country
- Ensure that information flows up, down, and across multicultural teams

TALENT MANAGEMENT

Attracting and retaining talented multicultural team members require providing and maintaining a welcoming operating environment and resources for team members to be successful. It must be an environment where multicultural team members enjoy working, growing, and advancing their careers. This includes attracting, hiring, training, developing, retaining, and providing opportunities for the advancement of the careers of multicultural team members. It is a major investment of an organization that must be effectively managed. Losing high-performing multicultural team members to other organizations is costly and draining on the organization and its resources. It often requires having to restart the recruiting process. Organizations can minimize this risk by taking an interest in the career goals and development plan of multicultural team members and supporting them on their journey toward their career goals. Steps that can be taken to support multicultural team members on their career journey include the following:

- Provide training and leadership development opportunities
- Advocate for the promotion of multicultural team members to other areas of the organization
- Provide mentoring opportunities
- Assist multicultural team members seeking secondment in other areas of the organization
- Provide rotational opportunities
- Support multicultural team members candidacy for management development programs
- Support continuing professional education programs
- Support professional certification programs

Understanding the strengths and areas for improvement is critical in effectively managing a multicultural team. This is important in the assignment, supervision, training, and development of multicultural team members. Understanding assists in yielding the highest quality work product, growth, and experience for team members. The sooner the areas of strength and improvement are identified, the more effective it is in leveraging team members' strength while providing support to address areas needing improvement. This enhances team members' confidence, skills, expertise, and their value to the organization.

The manager must pay attention to the well-being of multicultural team members. This includes the impact of localized challenges such as crime, climate change, and severe weather conditions that may require a remote or hybrid approach to work. The COVID-19 pandemic has brought to the forefront the importance of the well-being of team members to an organization. This is because their well-being is critical to the quality of work and success of the organization. Caring for the well-being of team members minimizes the risk of turnover, the work being delayed, not done, or done poorly. Factors that impact the well-being of team members include the following:

- Safety and security
- Stress
- Lack of time off or vacation
- Working while sick
- Constantly working long hours or more than one shift

DIVERSITY, EQUITY, INCLUSION, AND A MULTICULTURAL TEAM

A diverse and multicultural GIA team is an asset to an organization. It is a sign of a diverse workforce and goodwill in the countries where the organization operates. There is usually no lack of diversity in a GIA-operating environment. GIA's team usually includes team members from the countries where the organization operates. It reflects positively on GIA and the organization within those countries. However, care must be exercised to ensure that the organization addresses not only the diversity element but also the equity and inclusion elements. An organization can be diverse but lacks equity and inclusion. Adding equity and inclusion to the mix enables the organization to unleash and realize its full potential, including growth, value creation, preservation, and protection. This is from the creative and innovative energies that DEI provides an organization.

Equitable compensation packages for multicultural team members are an inherent challenge at times in countries where the organization operates as is usually the case in developing countries. The national and local pay scales are often below the pay scale of the home country of the organization. Pay scales are at times controlled by the government of the developing country. This allows national and local employers and governments to compete for high-performing staff in competitive job markets. To minimize the gap in salary, regional and local compensation packages often include housing and car allowance, tuition reimbursement for team members and their children. These benefits are often taxed by local and/or national governments.

Organizations at times tend to make decisions without engaging with the members of multicultural teams at the regional and local offices. This is a missed opportunity to obtain valuable advice, including insight and foresight, on initiatives and projects that the organization plans to undertake. Headquarters at times tend to impose their will on the staff and team members in the countries where they operate. It is usually based on the mindset that staff at headquarters know what is best for staff at the regional and local offices. However, staff at headquarters must engage and collaborate with multicultural teams in the field for their input on what is most important to them. This is necessary to obtain their buy-in and support for initiatives and projects that the organization plans to undertake. The success of the initiative is often in the hands of staff at the regional and local offices.

Inclusion of multicultural team members at the decision-making table leads to more informed decisions. Multicultural teams enhance the creative and innovative energies of GIA. It is an opportunity to obtain different perspectives from across the organization. This, no doubt, leads to more informed decisions, buy-in, and support from team members across the organization. They are the ones who will enhance the ability of the chief audit executive (CAE) and the leaders of GIA to anticipate and provide valuable advice, including insight and foresight, into the next big, new, or emerging risks and opportunities. Emerging risks and opportunities in a remote area or location in the organization could be the next big economic breakthrough or a global pandemic.

A GIA function that is based in and comprises team members only from the home country is shortchanging itself of the true value of a diverse and multicultural GIA team. The CAE and leaders of GIA must embrace and leverage their organization's diverse and multicultural operating environment to build and unleash the creative and innovative energies of an inclusive GIA team. Studies and research have shown that organizations that embrace diversity and inclusion are more creative and innovative.[1] The value of a diverse and multicultural team to the organization and GIA includes the following:

- Leads to a more creative and innovative operating environment
- Enhances the opportunity for growth, value creation, and preservation
- Leads to better understanding of the regional and local context and culture
- Improves transparency of activities at the regional and local offices
- Contributes to more timely identification and notification of early warning signs, red flags, trends, emerging risks, and opportunities in the field
- Results in more timely response to regional and local issues
- Improves the quality of advice, including insight and foresight, to assist stakeholders in making more informed decisions regarding issues in the field

Diversity, equity, and inclusion concerns are driving organizations to revisit and reshape their mission, vision, strategy, and objectives. This is to enhance and/or incorporate a DEI program into their operations. There is increased scrutiny of the social responsibility of organizations by investors, boards, governments, and watchdog organizations across the globe. DEI is one of the key elements of that scrutiny and social responsibility reporting of organizations. Organizations must periodically demonstrate progress and/or action taken in the DEI space.

CHAPTER SUMMARY

There is no value added if there is no understanding of what is most important to the members of a multicultural GIA team. A multicultural GIA team comprises team members from different countries and cultures where the organization operates. They may be located at headquarters, regional and/or local offices. This may also include team members working remotely from their home. The manager and multicultural team members must have a common understanding of GIA's strategy, objectives, and risks. There must also be a mutual understanding of what is most important to the team. This is because one shoe does not fit all in managing a multicultural team.

Effectively managing a multicultural team is a role for a competent and experienced audit manager who embraces diversity. The effectiveness and success of managing a multicultural team require patience and a manager who takes time to engage and collaborate with multicultural team members.

There are inherent risks associated with the customs and norms in some countries where the organization operates. There are also language barriers associated with managing a multicultural team. Ongoing communication of important messages must be a planned activity. Keeping multicultural team engaged and motivated is critical to the effectiveness and success of GIA. Communication must be clear, concise, and easy to understand. The message must be consistent across the organization. Follow-up is required to ensure that messages are received, interpreted, and delivered as intended.

Attracting and retaining talented multicultural team members require providing resources and a welcoming operating environment. It is an environment where team members enjoy working and advancing their careers. The manager must pay attention to the well-being of the team members. This is a major investment of an organization that must be effectively managed. Losing high-performing multicultural team members to other organizations is costly and draining on the organization and GIA's resources. Understanding the strengths and areas for improvement is critical in effectively managing multicultural teams. This is important for the assignment, supervision, training, and development of multicultural team members. It is also necessary to yield the highest quality work product, growth, and experience for team members.

A diverse and multicultural GIA team is an asset to an organization that is often underutilized. Diversity, equity, and inclusion concerns are driving organizations to revisit and reshape their mission, vision, strategy, and objectives. Equitable compensation packages for multicultural team members are an inherent challenge at times in countries where the organization operates. A GIA function that comprises team members only from the home country of the organization is shortchanging itself of the true value of a diverse and multicultural GIA team.

NOTE

1 The Importance of Diversity and Inclusion for Today's Companies (forbes.com).

6 Managing Change

INTRODUCTION

Change is not an option but a necessity for the survival, sustainability, and success of an organization in an ever-changing operating environment. Technological innovation is the primary driver of the changes in the operating environment. Senior management and the board of directors (hereinafter board) must quickly embrace and adapt to relevant changes. Ignoring or refusing to embrace and adapt to change is a recipe for disaster and the possible demise of the organization. Embracing change requires becoming comfortable with the uncomfortable.

The change management process is a journey that must be effectively managed. This requires prioritizing and effectively managing the areas that are most important in driving the successful implementation of the change initiative. The owner of the initiative must share and obtain the buy-in and support of stakeholders impacted by the change, particularly those at the regional and local office levels. The approval and success of the change initiative are unlikely if the owner of the initiative does not have the support of staff and stakeholders.

Making the changes stick is a journey due to the length of time it takes to stabilize and normalize the changes. A change management initiative must remain at the forefront of staff and stakeholders' thinking. Communicating the change in a manner that is easy to understand is crucial for stabilizing and normalizing a change initiative.

The purpose of this chapter is to provide advice and guidance on why change should be embraced and not feared. Topics covered include the following:

- Embrace change or become obsolete
- Characteristics of change
- Support for the change initiative
- The business case
- Managing the change initiative
- Making change sustainable
- Misuse of change

The key learnings from the chapter include the following:

- Importance of timely embracing and adapting to change
- Understanding the characteristics of change
- Importance of sharing and obtaining the buy-in and support of stakeholders
- Role of the business case
- Importance of effectively managing change, including expectations, failures, and resistance
- Quickly learning, sharing, and growing from failures

DOI: 10.1201/9781003207559-6

- Steps that can be taken to assist in making change stick
- Risk to the organization from the misuse of change

EMBRACE CHANGE OR BECOME OBSOLETE

Embracing change is not an option but a necessity for the survival, sustainability, and success of an organization in a fast-paced, constantly changing, and disruptive operating environment. Change is doing things differently rather than doing the same thing repeatedly and expecting a different result. This type of mindset is also a risk to an organization. Change enables an organization to remain competitive and prosper. Success in an ever-changing operating environment requires organizations and their stakeholders to be ready for the unexpected. There is no guarantee that what worked well yesterday will work well today and what worked well today will work well tomorrow.

Ignoring or refusing to embrace and adapt to change is a recipe for disaster and the possible demise of an organization. Organizations that ignore or refuse to embrace change often create their own demise. Fortune 500 companies that paid the ultimate price of ignoring or refusing to embrace change include the following[1]:

- Blockbuster Video: Filed for bankruptcy in 2010 because of refusing to change to digital.
- Polaroid: Failed to anticipate the impact that digitalization would have on the film business.
- Kodak: Failed to transition to digital.
- Borders: Failed to transition to digital online books or e-books.
- Tower Records: Failed to keep up with digital disruption in the music industry.

Senior management and the board must quickly embrace and adapt relevant changes in the operating environment or become obsolete. Embracing change requires becoming comfortable with the uncomfortable. Quickly embracing and adapting to relevant change better prepare an organization to timely address risks and capitalize on the opportunities that come along with change. Stakeholders must quickly embrace and adapt to change to survive, succeed, and remain valuable to the organization. It also enables senior management to quickly address what matters most to internal and external stakeholders.

CHARACTERISTICS OF CHANGE

Change is internally and/or externally driven. The primary internal drivers are usually for the survival and success of the organization as well as to:

- Create, protect, and preserve organizational values
- Adapt to technological innovations
- Improve effectiveness, efficiency, and competitiveness of the organization
- Improve and enhance structures, processes, and procedures
- Comply with laws and regulations

The key external drivers of change include the following:

- Technological innovations
- Regulations, including data security, privacy, environmental, social, and governance (ESG)
- Geopolitical issues, including war, terrorism, migration, tariffs, sanctions, and embargoes
- Natural disasters and global pandemic
- Technical and professional pronouncements, including new professional standards
- Health, safety, and security of staff

There must be clarity about the type of change that is being undertaken. Developmental, transitional, and transformational are the most common type of organizational change.[2] Developmental change is the most common type of organizational change. It is usually to revisit, rethink, and improve the efficiency and effectiveness of existing systems, policies, processes, and procedures. It is less dramatic and radical than transformational or transitional change.

An overview of the most common type of change is illustrated in Table 6.1.

TABLE 6.1
Overview of the Most Common Types of Organizational Change

Subject	Developmental	Transitional	Transformational
Definition	"This type of change involves the enhancement and correction of existing systems without aiming for any radical changes."[3] This is usually to revisit, rethink, and improve the efficiency and effectiveness of existing policies, processes, and procedures	"In a transitional change, companies replace an existing procedure with a new one for increased efficiency and performance."[4] This is usually to improve the effectiveness and efficiency by revising, rethinking, and replacing existing systems policies, processes, and procedures, and systems	"Changes that completely reshape business strategies and processes and redefine a business are called transformational changes."[5] This is a dramatic and radical change and usually requires reimagining the operations of the organization, which includes revisiting, rethinking, reshaping, or re-inventing the entire or some aspects of the organization. It may include a change in the mission, vision, structure, business model, and/or strategy of the organization. It impacts the culture mindset of staff and stakeholders, including the way they engage, communicate, and work with each other
Impact of change	Low	Medium	High
Level of disruption	Low	Medium	High
Frequency of change	High	Medium	Low
Expertise required	Low	Medium	High
Training needed	Low	Medium	High

SUPPORT FOR THE CHANGE INITIATIVE

The owner of the change initiative must informally test the appetite of trusted stakeholders to obtain their feedback and preliminary support for the change initiative. The approval of a strategic or major change initiative is often dependent on their support. Trusted stakeholders in this case include the manager of the owner or requestor of the change initiative, the owner's leadership team, the chief executive officer (CEO), and the chairperson of the board or sub-committee. Testing the appetite of trusted stakeholders must be done before time and resources are invested in developing the business case. The owner of the initiative must be able to articulate the driving force behind the change and be prepared to share the key elements of the change with stakeholders, including the following:

- Justification
- Objective
- Support for the initiative
- Leadership of the initiative
- Impact of the initiative, including what is expected to change or remain the same
- Potential risks and rewards
- Estimated cost and return on investment (ROI)
- Funding source
- Key performance indicators (KPI)
- Deliverables and timelines

In addition to, testing the appetite of trusted stakeholders, the requestor of the change initiative must also share and obtain preliminary support from key stakeholders. Key stakeholders in this case include senior management and stakeholders most impacted by the initiative. Senior management support is usually required to expedite the approval process of a strategic or major change initiative. This includes assistance in identifying and securing the required resources for the initiative. The preliminary support of key stakeholders is the green light for the owner of the change initiative to develop the business case. The success or failure of a strategic or major initiative is often dependent on the level of support it receives from trusted and key stakeholders.

The owner of the change initiative must also share and obtain the buy-in and support of stakeholders most impacted by the change. Staff and stakeholders at the regional and local office levels are usually the ones most impacted. They are usually closest to the activities and know what will work best in their operating environment. Additionally, they are usually the ones responsible for implementing, using, monitoring, maintaining, and reporting on the status of the initiative. Engaging, collaborating closely, and incorporating, to the extent possible, their input into the project plan and implementation process are critical to the successful implementation of the initiative. It also empowers and gives them a sense of part ownership of the initiative. Staff and stakeholders' support can easily be eroded if their input is ignored. Headquarters, corporate or home office staff should be careful not to take a know-it-all attitude of what is best for staff in the field. That attitude is a risk to maintaining their support. Losing their support could delay or derail the implementation of the initiative.

The owner of the change initiative must ensure that steps are taken to maintain the support of stakeholders. Maintaining their support, particularly those most impacted, requires keeping them engaged and motivated. Actions that can be taken to keep staff engaged and motivated include the following:

- Sharing and welcoming input from stakeholders on the change initiative
- Including key stakeholders in the change initiative's decision-making process
- Ongoing communication of the progress of the change initiative, including periodic status update
- Providing timely, honest, and consistent messaging as staff roles may change or be eliminated
- Creating a culture where staff are empowered to make decisions on their own
- Encouraging the timely sharing of failures and mitigation plans and activities
- Providing timely response to feedback, questions, concerns, and complaints
- Reconfirming the objectives and value of the initiative to the organization
- Assigning subject matter experts and contact persons at the global, regional, and local office levels
- Recognizing and rewarding staff and stakeholders for achieving their objectives

THE BUSINESS CASE

A business case is required for a strategic or major change management initiative whether initiated by senior management and/or the board. It is the mechanism for getting the change initiative officially approved. It can either be a one- or multipage document depending on the organization's approval process. A preliminary project plan, if available, may be attached to the business case, which usually includes the following:

- Initiative or project title
- Sponsor
- Owner or requestor
- Justification
- Strategy and objectives
- Project management team
- Current state, proposed changes, and expected future state
- Impact of the change initiative, including what is expected to change or remain the same
- Alternative solutions
- Risks and rewards
- Source of funding
- Cost/benefits of the initiative, including ROI
- KPI

- Timeline and deliverables
- Approvals

The manager of the requestor of the change initiative and certain members of the senior management team's approval may be required before the business case is submitted for final approval. Senior management's approval may include the following:

- Chief financial officer (CFO): To address the availability of funding for the initiative.
- Chief human resources officer (CHRO) or chief people officer (CPO): To address staffing concerns such as redundancies, budget cuts, redeployment, severance packages, among other things.
- Chief legal officer (CLO): To ensure compliance with local labor laws, assist with contractual agreements and negotiations with unions, if applicable.
- Chief operating officer (COO): To ensure alignment with operation strategy and objectives.
- Chief risk officer (CRO): To discuss support, sharing, and coordination of activities.
- Chief technology officer (CTO): To address information technology matters such as system security, connectivity, integration, reliability, availability, and accessibility.

Final approval of the business case is usually given by the CEO and the chairperson of the board or a sub-committee, if applicable.

MANAGING THE CHANGE INITIATIVE

As mentioned earlier, change is not an option but a necessity for the survival of an organization in a fast-paced, constantly changing, and disruptive operating environment. An organization and its stakeholders must embrace and quickly adapt to change to remain competitive, successful, and sustainable. This is particularly important in an ever-changing operating environment where risks and opportunities are constantly changing. It also enhances the resilience and relevance of the organization. Change must be effectively managed to ensure a smooth transition and achievement of the objectives of the change initiative.

Agility, nimbleness, adaptability, and flexibility are key elements of effective change management. These key elements are essential to the timely and effective implementation, and achievement of the objectives of the change initiative. Agility is a key driver of effective and efficient change management processes and procedures. It enables stakeholders to quickly engage, think, respond, and adapt to change or do things differently. More time is spent engaging and working collaboratively with stakeholders on what works best for them. Less time is spent on planning, designing, and documenting policies, processes, and procedures. Agility plays a key role in how quickly things get done. This is by breaking down or simplifying complex tasks into smaller units or parts and working collaboratively on a meaningful outcome and solution. It makes the change initiative more manageable, quicker, and easier to complete. An agile leadership environment is one that is receptive and open to change. Change drives creativity and innovation that usually results in new and more effective and efficient ways of getting things done.

Nimbleness refers to a lean or small staff and/or organizational structure, systems, policies, processes, and procedures. The reaction to change must be swift or quick and often rapid in an ever-changing operating environment. The decision or response is less likely to be as swift in a bureaucratic structure where the organization structure is usually tall. Nimbleness enables stakeholders to be agile and to quickly think, respond, and adapt to change or a new situation or condition.

Adaptability and flexibility enable stakeholders to adjust, find common ground, compromise, modify existing positions, and quickly adapt to change. It includes adjusting to unexpected disturbances and disruption in the operating environment such as those from technological innovations, government regulations, natural disasters, and global pandemics. This enables an organization to align with what matters most to internal and external stakeholders. Additionally, it enables the organization to timely meet the existing challenges and new demands of a fast-paced, constantly changing, and disruptive operating environment.

The key requirements of the change must be documented and shared with stakeholders. The requirements of a major change initiative usually include the following:

- Senior management and the board support and approval
- Buy-in and support of stakeholders
- Inclusion and participation of impacted stakeholders in the decision-making process
- Project plan
- Justification and objective for the change initiative
- Clarity of objectives, roles, responsibilities, and accountability
- Clarity regarding what is expected to change or remain the same
- Competent leadership and project management team
- Communication strategy
- Availability of required resources
- Cost benefit analysis and ROI
- Testing, training, rollout, and post-implementation plan
- KPI
- Deliverables and timelines

The change management process is a journey that must be effectively managed. It requires prioritizing and managing the areas and activities that are most important in driving the successful implementation of the change initiative. The areas and activities that are most important include the following:

- The plan
- Communication
- Execution
- Risk
- Change management

- Monitoring and reporting
- Post-implementation review

The Plan

The plan is the roadmap for effectively managing a transformational or major change initiative. It paves the way and minimizes risks to the successful implementation of the initiative. The plan should not be developed in isolation. Effective planning will ensure that the transformation process is collaborative and includes input from staff and stakeholders most impacted by the initiative. Effective planning includes the following:

- Developing objectives and strategy
- Identifying and assessing risk
- Determining the following:
  - Organization's structure, policies, processes, and procedures
  - Required resources to implement the transformation
  - Required coordination and collaboration to keep stakeholders informed
  - Required monitoring and periodic reporting on the status of the transformation
  - Strategy for communicating the transformation
  - Deliverables and timeline
  - KPI
- Assigning roles, responsibilities, authority, and accountability

Communication

Communication is how messages, whether oral or written, are conveyed and understood by the recipient or audience. The announcement of the change initiative to the organization is the official starting point of the communication process. The origin of the communication or the message of the change initiative depends on the nature of the change. The communication of a strategic change initiative usually comes from the CEO. The announcement may also include the chairperson of the board, and the senior leader or owner of the change initiative. This sets the tone at the top of the organization of the importance and support for the change. Additionally, it contributes to the support and cooperation of management and staff across the organization for the initiative. Staff and stakeholders are usually more receptive to the message when it comes from senior management and the board. The announcement should include the following:

- Justification
- Objective
- Risks and rewards
- Project leader
- Roles, responsibility, and accountability

- What will change, remain the same, or be eliminated
- Deliverables and timelines
- Help desk or contact person(s) for questions

The success of the change initiative depends on how effective it is communicated to staff and stakeholders from the beginning to the completion of the initiative. Well-communicated messages are usually those that are delivered in the simplest of forms. This is due to the diverse culture and language in a global organization. Additionally, it is important to have various mediums to communicate the message such as emails, virtual meetings, and visual aids. It is important to remember the diversity of ways people consume information and vary the way updates are provided to keep all staff and stakeholders engaged in the change journey.

Ongoing communication is one of, if not, the most important elements of an effective change management process. It plays a key role in keeping the project management team, staff, and stakeholders engaged, informed, and focused on the change initiative. It also minimizes surprises and risks of misunderstandings, misinterpretations, misinformation, and manipulation of information. This is particularly important for staff and stakeholders in the field and those most impacted by the initiative. Staff and stakeholders in the field include implementers, users, maintainers, and monitors of the change who can make or break the success of the initiative. Periodic status reports, meetings, and newsletters are effective actions that can be taken to keep staff and stakeholders engaged and informed.

Effective communication is a three-way and ongoing activity going up, down, and across the organization. It requires confirming and periodically reconfirming the understanding of messages. This is particularly important for staff and stakeholders in the field at the regional and local office levels. It minimizes the risk of excluding impacted staff and stakeholders from receiving messages. Additionally, it reduces the risks of mission drift and ensures that the original messages, including updates, remain intact and at the forefront of staff thinking and activities.

Communication needs to be timely, clear, and concise to be effective. Timely communication is critical for stakeholders to stay engaged, connected, current, and informed. Gone are the days of lengthy oral or written communications. Time and speed are valuable organizational assets in a fast-paced and disruptive operating environment. Stakeholders do not have the time to listen to long presentations, and read lengthy documents, and reports. Technological innovations have made communicating faster, easier, and cheaper to transmit information to staff and stakeholders. This includes the use of emails, virtual meetings, visual aids, and infographics to keep staff and stakeholders engaged and motivated.

Miscommunicating and misunderstanding of the initiative's objectives and required coordination and cooperation can be costly. They can derail the change initiative. Although not intentional, they can be as deadly as someone sabotaging the change initiative. The leader of the change initiative must ensure that communication is clear, concise, and easy to understand for everyone across the organization. Miscommunication and misunderstanding of messages can also lead to missed opportunities in a fast-paced, constantly changing, and disruptive operating environment. The reasons include the following:

- Ambiguous messages
- Misinterpretation of messages
- Distorted or lost messages
- Diverse culture and language barriers
- Use of multiple modes of communication mediums and devices

There are steps that can be taken to mitigate the risks of miscommunication, misunderstanding, and manipulation of information. These include the following:

- Recapping of message by recipients
- Confirming receipt of messages
- Reconfirming periodically mission's critical messages, including benefits of the transformation
- Listening to input particularly from stakeholders most impacted and closest to the activities
- Providing timely, transparent, and honest response to questions and feedback
- Timely sharing of failures, including delays, and cost overruns with key stakeholders
- Timely sharing of modifications to the transformation and project plan with key stakeholders

Communication is one of the key beneficiaries of technological innovations. The mobile phone and social media tools have made communication faster and easier. Communication mediums are available 24/7 to stakeholders anywhere in the world where the internet is available. These benefits include:

- Using mobile phones to conduct transactions remotely, including answering emails, reviewing, editing, and approving documents, taking and scanning pictures of documents and evidential matter
- Conducting virtual meetings with team members and stakeholders thousands of miles apart
- Dictating instead of typing or writing
- Reading aloud
- Using internet of things (IoT) such as doorbells, smart watches, and Fitbit to share information with other electronic devices such as smartphones, computers, and laptops without any human intervention

The wide range of communication mediums and devices can impact the effectiveness of communicating with staff and stakeholders. Timely response to messages is critical when working in a fast-paced and disruptive operating environment. The risk of delayed, missed, or unread messages is high when too many communication mediums and devices are used. Senior management must standardize the preferred mode of communication staff should use for business. This will mitigate the risk of delayed, missed, or unread messages.

Execution

Change management requires effective execution of the change initiative. Effective execution is converting the plan into action. The key objective of the execution phase is the successful implementation of the change. This includes obtaining the buy-in and support of staff and stakeholders who are using and benefiting from the outcome or results of the change. The outcome or results may include new or updated structures, systems, policies, processes, and procedures. Obtaining the buy-in and support of staff and stakeholders in the field at the regional and local office levels is particularly important in the execution phase. Staff and stakeholders in the field are usually closest to the action and activities of the change initiative. They are usually more knowledgeable of the local context and operating environment and know what works best. It also empowers and gives them a sense of part ownership of the initiative.

Staff and stakeholders buy-in and support, particularly those in the field, can easily get lost or eroded if their input is ignored. Collaborating closely with them includes engaging, sharing, listening, learning, and incorporating, to the extent possible, their input on the implementation process into the project plan. Their buy-in and support strengthen and enhance the likelihood that the changes will stick.

The execution of the change initiative requires an experienced and competent leader to oversee and lead the project team. The team should include any required subject matter expertise to effectively implement the change. Leading and overseeing a change initiative include directing, supporting, and motivating the team. It also includes monitoring and periodically reporting on the status of the activities and progress of the change. Effectively overseeing the change initiative includes the following:

- Ongoing communication to:
  - Keep staff and stakeholders engaged, informed, and motivated
  - Keep the change initiative at the forefront of the thinking and activities of staff and stakeholders
  - Provide periodic status updates on the implementation of the change
  - Provide transparency and avoid surprises
- Providing periodic reminders to staff and stakeholders of the justification and benefits of the change
- Testing of the changes to minimize risks of errors, faults, gaps, and bugs during the rollout
- Training staff and stakeholders to minimize stress, fears, and frustration regarding the change
- Supporting the rollout and implementation of the change
- Following up to ensure that the change was implemented as planned and is functioning effectively

There are required steps that must be taken to ensure the successful execution and implementation of the plan. The steps include the following:

- Obtain and document a detailed understanding of stakeholder' requirements of the change initiative
- Confirm and prioritize stakeholders' requirements
- Develop and document specifications for prioritized stakeholders' requirements
- Confirm specifications are in alignment with stakeholder' requirements
- Design the system
- Confirm system design is in accordance with the specifications
- Perform stress test of the system
- Develop migration plan and strategy
- Develop electronic user manual
- Test the functionality of the system
- Train and coach stakeholders
- Rollout and implement system, including structures, policies, processes, and procedures
- Perform post-implementation review

Risk

Risks are known and unknown activities or events that present a threat to the achievement of the objectives of the organization. Simply put, risks are anything that will prevent an organization from achieving its objectives. Change management risk is a growing concern for organizations due to the rapid speed of change and disruption in the operating environment. With change comes risks and opportunities that need to be effectively managed. Change management risks must be effectively managed if the organization wants to successfully implement the change initiative and capitalize on emerging opportunities.

Risks must be effectively managed to a reasonable level and within the risk tolerance and appetite of the organization. This requires timely identifying, assessing, mitigating, monitoring, and periodically reporting on the status of risks impacting the change initiative. Identifying risks includes brainstorming sessions with staff and key stakeholders, thinking out of the box, and the inclusion of "what if scenarios." Assessing risks includes evaluating and prioritizing risks to the initiative. Staff and stakeholders need to be aware of the risks to effectively manage and mitigate them. Risks include the following:

- Lack of buy-in and support by key stakeholders
- Lack of understanding of the change initiative
- Misalignment and mission drift
- Sabotage by team members who do not want to change
- Resource constraints such as inadequate skilled staff and technological tools

- Taking a wait-and-see attitude by holding out or sitting on the fence to see if the change works
- Suppressing information regarding the change initiative
- Spreading misinformation about the change initiative
- Downplaying or ignoring the change initiative
- Deprioritizing and delaying the competition of required tasks and deliverables
- Resisting to learn, improve, and grow from failures

Ongoing communication, monitoring, and reporting are required to effectively manage risks to the change initiative as risk is constantly changing in an ever-changing operating environment. Effectively managing risks includes clarity of authority, responsibility, and accountability as well as the following:

- Simplifying the transformation process since complexity is a driver of risk
- Including input from stakeholders most impacted by the initiative in the decision-making process
- Providing adequate resources, including competent management team and subject matter experts
- Providing timely status updates to stakeholders, including changes and risks to the initiative
- Providing timely, transparent, and honest response to stakeholders' questions and feedback
- Managing expectations, failures, and resistance to the change initiative
- Agreeing on realistic deliverables and timelines
- Providing adequate training

Change Management

There is always going to be some resistance to change, which needs to be effectively managed. Resistance can easily derail a change initiative if not effectively managed. There will be early adopters of the change as well as those who will take a wait-and-see attitude. There are also those within and external to the organization who will resist the change. The fear of doing things differently can be traumatic and uncomfortable for staff and stakeholders within or external to the organization. Those resisting the change may at times engage in activities to undermine and/or derail the initiative. Such activities may include one or more of the following:

- Sabotaging the change initiative
- Ignoring the change
- Making excuses continuously for why things are not getting done
- Resisting to learn, improve, and grow from failures
- Blaming others for failures, including missed deadlines, setbacks, mistakes, delays, and cost overruns

Staff and stakeholders' emotions can lead to resistance to the change, if not acknowledged and effectively managed. Emotions tend to run high during a strategic or major change initiative. These emotions are usually from fear of doing things differently. Doing things differently can be traumatic and uncomfortable for staff and stakeholders due to the uncertainty and insecurity that change attracts. Resistance is usually from staff and stakeholders who want to continue doing business as usual or maintain the status quo as well as fear of the following:

- Losing power and control
- Being assigned to a different role
- Increasing workload
- Going outside of one's comfort zone
- Uncovering of wrongdoings
- Becoming redundant and losing one's job
- Learning new ways of doing things

There is pushback at times regarding the timely sharing of failures with key stakeholders. Failures may result in missed deadlines, setbacks, mistakes, delays, and cost overruns. The pushback is often caused by the fear of the consequences from the delivery of bad news which may result in:

- Reduction or loss of funding for the project
- Cancelation or cutback on the scope of the initiative
- Reassignment or replacement of the project management team
- Impact on performance evaluation

Senior management must ensure that there is a plan in place to maintain and strengthen the support for the change initiative. This will help to reduce skepticism, and resistance to the change. The plan should include ongoing communications of the status of the change as well as the following:

- Provide timely, transparent, honest, and consistent messaging
- Reconfirm periodically the objectives and benefits of the initiative, including the following:
  - Senior management and the board ongoing support and commitment
  - Purpose, objectives, and value of the initiative to the organization
  - Justification for the change initiative
  - What is expected to change or remain the same
- Provide timely response to feedback, questions, and complaints
- Meet and share periodic project status updates and reports with key stakeholders
- Encourage quick ownership of failures and learn, share, and grow from the experience

Senior management and/or the project leader of the change initiative must engage with staff and stakeholders resisting the change. They need to engage and work collaboratively with the resistors on finding common ground where there are disagreements. Those resisting should be given an opportunity to share their feedback and concerns. The owner and project leader of the change initiative must be open to and listen to their feedback and concerns. This is particularly important for those staff and stakeholders most impacted and closest to the activities. Their feedback and concerns should be considered and incorporated where feasible in the project plan. Mutual separation is usually the most effective decision where there is failure to find common ground over disagreements. This is because ongoing resistance will be a constant risk to the success of the change initiative. The CAE must collaborate with human resources and legal to mitigate risks of claims of wrongful termination and monetary damages against the organization.

Senior management must set the expectation for the possibility of failure when undertaking a change initiative. There will be failures in any major change initiative. It is not a matter of whether there will be failures. It is a matter of when. Organizations should view failure as an opportunity for staff to learn, improve, grow, and build resilience from experience. There is no time to be fixated on failure in a fast-paced, constantly changing, and disruptive operating environment.

Effectively managing failures requires transparency, timely sharing of the event, learning, and improving from the experience. This minimizes surprises and mission drift as the truth will surface eventually. Delay in sharing failures can be costly to the organization and senior management. There could be damage to the integrity, credibility, and reputation of the organization, senior management, and the board.

The possibility of failure and mitigation plans must be shared with staff and stakeholders upfront. This will reduce the fear, surprise factor, the "I told you so," and the noise from the skeptics of the project should a failure occur. The project management team must learn and act quickly to address failures before they become a disaster. A failure could be the end of an initiative or project. Causes of failures may include changes in the operating environment due to technological innovations and changes in laws and regulations as well as the following:

- Inadequate resources, including inadequate funding, staffing, expertise, and tools
- Incompetence or mismanagement of the project, including lack of expertise and negligence
- Modification to the project plan, including change in user requirements, process, and tasks
- Defective project design, including not in alignment with the user requirements and specifications
- Outdated policies, processes, and procedures
- Fatigue and burnout of staff

Senior management must ensure that controllable activities are effectively managed, including the following:

- Selection of the project management team
- Acquisition of required resources
- Assessment of users' needs and requirements
- Design and documentation

- Testing
- Training
- Rollout and implementation

Additionally, there should be contingencies, redundancies, and flexibility built into the project plan to allow for quick adjustment to changes in the operating environment.

The senior leader or owner of a change initiative must learn and act quickly to address failures. Failure is a major risk to the successful implementation of an undertaking whether small or large. A failure could be the end of a project. The senior leader or owner of a change initiative must take the necessary steps to minimize the risk of failure. This includes quickly acknowledging, learning, and addressing failures before they become disasters. Failure can be costly and may include any of the following:

- Cancelation of the project
- Reduction in funding for the project
- Restart of the project
- Scale back of the project where only a fraction of the project is pursued
- Budget cuts in other areas to cover project cost overruns

Monitoring and Reporting

Monitoring and reporting are key elements of an organization's governance program. Monitoring is to ensure that the change is progressing as planned. This includes operating effectively, efficiently, and in compliance with required laws, regulations, standards, policies, and procedures. Periodic reports are required to keep stakeholders informed of the status of the change initiative. These reports assist the board and senior management in making more informed decisions in performing their governance oversight and management responsibilities, respectively.

Post-Implementation Review

A post-implementation review is necessary to ensure that the change initiative is operating as planned. This includes operating effectively, efficiently, and in compliance with laws, regulations, standards, policies, and procedures. It provides an opportunity for senior management to timely address gaps in the planning and implementation process to minimize subsequent risk.

MAKING CHANGE SUSTAINABLE

Stabilizing and normalizing a transformational or strategic change initiative is a journey because of the length of time it takes to make the change sustainable. This often results in a change in the culture, including the values, norms, and customs as well as the mindset of staff. It also usually impacts the way staff think, engage, communicate, and work with others in an organization. Patience is required as a change in culture of the organization takes years to adopt, stabilize, and normalize.

The change initiative must remain at the forefront of staff and stakeholders' thinking and activities to make the changes stick. It is easy for staff to continue or return to business as usual if the rollout of the change is not effectively managed. The rollout must be well planned and communicated. The implementers and users must be trained and supported throughout the rollout process. There should also be periodic status meetings and reports to update staff and stakeholders on the progress of the change initiative. This includes updates on what is working well and needs to be changed or stopped. A post-implementation review is also required to ensure that the change is operating as planned as well as effectively and efficiently.

Change must be communicated in a manner that is easy to understand, memorize, and embrace. Simplifying and breaking down the key elements of the change into memorable one liner make it easier and more likely to be long-lasting. A complex change initiative process is a risk to the successful implementation of the initiative. How the change is communicated and rolled out across the organization is critical to the successful implementation of the change. This includes transparency, clarity of responsibility, accountability, and understanding of the objectives, risks, and rewards of the change.

There are steps that managers can take to make the changes stick. These include the following:

- Appointment of change management champions to support departments, functions, and offices
- Create and share a one-page memoizable flyer of key elements of the change
- Post and display key elements of the change on the organization's website and communal areas
- Create a hotline where staff and stakeholders can call in with questions
- Provide periodic training to keep staff educated about the change initiative
- Make the change initiative status update a standing agenda item at staff meetings
- Make the change a KPI for all staff
- Recognize and reward staff for outstanding performance
- Hold leaders accountable for the implementation of the change initiative
- Create a global dashboard of the status of the change initiative and make it accessible to stakeholders
- Publish periodic global newsletters on the status of the change initiative
- Send global alerts or blast of the achievement of major milestones of the change initiative

MISUSE OF CHANGE

Using change as a tool to avoid accountability is a major risk to an organization, especially when used to avoid making tough decisions. This includes holding staff accountable for wrongdoings, especially fraudulent activities, hiding, suppressing, and/or blaming others for failures. In such situations, the issue remains unresolved, lessons not learned or shared, and the root cause of the issue is not examined and addressed. In the case of wrongdoings, the financial risk to the organization could be significant. Eventually, the truth will surface and often resulting in disruption of the operations and possible financial loss. It may also result in fines and penalties in case of non-compliance with laws and regulations.

Change must be justifiable and adds value to an organization. The change must be reviewed and validated to ensure that it is clearly defined, specific, measurable, achievable, realistic, and timely. The review process must include input from stakeholders, particularly those most impacted by the change. This will assist in ensuring that the change is justifiable and adds value to the organization. Frequent changes need to be examined carefully to assess the risks and determine their true intent.

Management sometimes avoids an issue or situation by restructuring, renaming, or repurposing roles within the organization. This is often in lieu of making the tough decisions of holding staff accountable and being transparent and honest about the issue or situation. It is often easier for management to make the case to change the narrative or deflect attention from the issue or situation. It is important that time is spent to understand the root cause of the issue for the change and identify sustainable solutions. Understanding the root cause includes investigating, assessing, and confirming the justification for the change. It is highly likely that the issue will resurface if the root cause is not identified and effectively addressed. Any other solution to the issue is likely to be short term or a band aid that could eventually become a significant risk. Change red flags include the following:

- Frequent reorganizing or repurposing roles instead of counseling or terminating poor performers
- Modifying the project plan, renaming the project, or broadening the scope of the change initiative
- Changing the project objectives, deliverables, timing, and expectations

The fear of failure is a key driver and motivator for misusing change. This is due to the fear of the potential consequences of delivering bad news, including the following:

- Reduction or loss of funding for the project
- Cancelation or cutback on the initiative
- Reassignment or replacement of the project management team
- Impact on performance evaluation

The fear of failure must be effectively managed. This includes the following:

- Setting the tone at the top for the initiative
- Setting realistic goals
- Sharing potential risks to the change initiative up front
- Taking ownership and quickly addressing failures

CHAPTER SUMMARY

Change is not an option but a necessity for the survival, sustainability, and success of an organization in a fast-paced, constantly changing, and disruptive operating environment. Technological innovation is the primary driver of most changes in the operating environment. Senior management and boards must quickly embrace and adapt relevant changes as delaying or ignoring change is a recipe for disaster and possible demise of the organization. Embracing change requires becoming comfortable with the uncomfortable.

Change is internally and/or externally driven. There must be clarity about the type of change that is being undertaken. This includes developmental, transitional, or transformational. The owner of the change initiative must informally test the appetite of trusted stakeholders on the concept of the change before sharing it with other stakeholders. Sharing the concept of the change with key stakeholders is the beginning of the journey of gathering support for the approval of the change initiative. The preliminary support of senior management is usually required to expedite the approval process of a strategic or major organizational change initiative. The approval and success of the initiative are unlikely if the owner of the initiative does not have the support of key stakeholders. The owner of the initiative must also share and obtain support from stakeholders most impacted by the change, particularly those at regional and local office levels. Staff and stakeholders at the regional and local office levels of an organization often know what will work best in their operating environment.

The change management process is a journey that must be effectively managed. Agility, nimbleness, adaptability, and flexibility are key elements of effective change management. It requires prioritizing and managing the areas that are most important in driving the success of the change initiative. Stabilizing and normalizing a change initiative and making the changes stick is a journey due to the length of time it takes for the changes to stabilize and normalize. A change management initiative must remain at the forefront of staff and stakeholders' thinking and activities in order for the changes to stick and achieve the objectives of the initiative. The change must be communicated in a manner that is easy to understand, memorize, and embrace.

Finally, change must be justifiable and add value to the organization. Using change as a tool to avoid accountability is a major risk to an organization. The possibility of this risk must be considered in any organizational change initiative as the fear of failure is a driver and motivator for misusing change.

NOTES

1 Ten companies That Failed to Innovate, Resulting in Business Failure by Francis Goh on Enterprise Innovation.
2 Three most common organizational change – Search (bing.com).
3 What is Organizational Change? (Benefits, Types And Reasons) | Indeed.com India.
4 Ibid.
5 Ibid.

7 Transformation to a Risk-Based Internal Audit Operating Environment

INTRODUCTION

The transformation of global internal audit (GIA) from a compliance to RBIA approach of performing internal audit is one of the most valuable contributions that a chief audit executive (CAE) can make to an organization. Organizations cannot rely on a compliance-driven GIA-operating environment to fulfill its internal audit needs. A holistic and dynamic internal audit approach is required particularly in an operating environment where risks are constantly changing. The transformation to RBIA is a journey due to the length of time it takes for the changes to stabilize and normalize. It is a strategic and transformational initiative that requires the support of key stakeholders.

The purpose of this chapter is to provide advice and guidance on the importance of transforming GIA from a compliance to an RBIA approach of performing internal audit. It is a transition to a risk-driven GIA-operating environment. Topics covered include the following:

- Overview of RBIA
- Comparison of RBIA and compliance audit approach
- Strategic and transformational nature of RBIA
- Support for the RBIA initiative
- The business case
- Managing the transformation to RBIA
- The RBIA implementation roadmap
- Making the change sustainable
- Value to the organization and GIA

Key learnings from the chapter include the following:

- Key differences between RBIA and a compliance audit approach
- Understanding the strategic and transformational nature of RBIA
- Importance of obtaining and maintaining support for the initiative
- Importance of the participation of stakeholders in the decision-making process
- Understanding the key elements of the business case
- Importance of effectively managing the transformation process
- Value of RBIA to the organization, stakeholders, and team members of GIA

DOI: 10.1201/9781003207559-7

OVERVIEW OF RISK-BASED INTERNAL AUDIT (RBIA)

The transformation to RBIA approach of performing internal audit is one of the most valuable contributions that a CAE can make to an organization. The value is derived from the fact that the focus is on risk, which is critical in an ever-changing operating environment. The CAE and leaders of GIA must revisit and adjust their approach of performing internal audit to address the challenges of a constantly changing risk landscape. What worked well yesterday is not necessarily going to work well today and what worked well today is not necessarily going to work well tomorrow.

The transformation to RBIA is an opportunity for the leaders and team members of GIA to learn and obtain an understanding of what is important to the organization and its stakeholders. This includes an understanding of the following:

- Mission, vision, strategy, objectives, and risk mitigation plan and activities
- What is most important to stakeholders
- What is working well and what needs to be changed, including improved or stopped
- What keeps key stakeholders awake at night
- What stakeholders expect from GIA
- Any known emerging issues and risks

The transformation to RBIA also provides an opportunity for the leaders and team members of GIA to listen, learn, improve, and enhance their soft skills and business acumen. Stakeholders are usually an excellent source of information about the organization's business and operations. They are often subject matter experts for their area(s) of responsibilities. This is also an opportunity for the leaders and team members to share their knowledge and expertise of the business.

COMPARISON OF RBIA AND COMPLIANCE AUDIT APPROACH

Organizations cannot rely on a compliance audit approach to fulfill the internal audit needs of an organization in an ever-changing operating environment. The compliance audit approach of performing internal audit is based on predetermined audit programs, questionnaires, and checklists. The approach is backward-looking and -thinking. The focus is on historical information, transactions, and activities and more of a ticking the box exercise. The primary objective is confirming whether the organization is adhering to laws, regulations, standards, policies, and procedures. The emphasis is on providing assurance that the organization continues to operate within set parameters, boundaries, rules, and guidelines and not on how new and emerging risks are being managed. The audits are often considered of little or no value to stakeholders because the improvement opportunities often become outdated and irrelevant from the fast pace of change. Stakeholders need information on what is happening currently and what to expect in the future. They are often less interested in historical information and past activities.

A compliance GIA-operating environment underutilizes the training, knowledge, and expertise of internal auditors. This is because of the heavy reliance on predetermined audit programs, questionnaires, checklists, and ticking the box-driven exercise. Organizations regularly hire internal auditors with public accounting and internal audit experience. However, opportunities to utilize and leverage the knowledge and experience that new hires bring to the organization are often limited. This also limits the opportunity for team members of GIA to utilize and develop their critical thinking, interpersonal, problem solving, analytical, and business acumen skills. This can lead to team members' boredom, complacency, and eventual loss or turnover of high-performing staff.

RBIA is a holistic and dynamic approach to performing internal audits. Risks from all aspects of the organization are considered. This includes the risk of non-compliance with financial, regulatory, and organizational compliance requirements. These are covered in the RBIA risk assessment. RBIA drives the alignment of GIA's activities with the strategy, objectives, and risk mitigation plan and activities of the organization. It paves the way for enhanced engagement, collaboration with stakeholders, and understanding of the business and operations. RBIA contributes to more effective and efficient allocation of GIA's resources. This is by assigning GIA's resources to the high-risk areas of the organization.

RBIA approach is more of a forward-looking and -thinking approach. The focus is more on the current and future activities of the organization. RBIA approach is also more flexible and adaptive to meet the challenges and demands of a fast-paced, constantly changing, and disruptive operating environment. Improvement opportunities from RBIA are usually more relevant and valuable to stakeholders. This is because the improvement opportunities are usually aligned with the strategy and the business, operating, reporting, and compliance objectives of the organization. RBIA is also more collaborative as shown below in Table 7.1.

TABLE 7.1
Comparison of RBIA and Compliance Audit Approach

Subject	RBIA	Compliance
Level of understanding of the business and operations	High	Low
Allocation of GIA's resources	Risk driven	Compliance driven
Level of alignment with the objectives and risk mitigation plan and activities of the organization	High	Low
Identification of emerging risks	Proactive	Reactive
Root cause analysis	More likely	Not or less likely
Problem solver or fault finder	More focus on problem solving	Fault finder
Engagement and collaboration with stakeholders	High	Low
Audit plan	Dynamic	Static and cyclical
Audit program	Dynamic and risk based	Predetermined audit programs, questionnaires, and ticking the box
Creativity and innovation	Encouraged	More about maintaining the status quo
Adaptive to an ever-changing operating environment	More adaptive	Less adaptive
Utilizing and leveraging the knowledge and experience that new hires bring to the organization	More likely to be utilized	Less likely to be utilized
Opportunities for continuous learning and professional development of staff	More opportunities	Less opportunities

STRATEGIC AND TRANSFORMATIONAL NATURE OF RBIA

The transformation of GIA from a compliance audit to an RBIA approach for performing internal audit is a strategic initiative. It is strategic as it is a transformation to a risk-driven operating environment as well as the following:

- Requires rethinking, and reshaping how internal audits are performed
- Change from a compliance culture to a risk-based GIA culture
- Requires senior management and the audit committee support
- Impacts the governance of the organization as the audit committee relies on information GIA provides in performing their governance oversight responsibilities
- Impacts stakeholders across the organization
- Usually requires additional investment

The transformation to an RBIA-operating environment is a journey and not a walk around the block due to the time it takes for the changes to stick. It is a complex and challenging type of change because of the following:

- Rethinking and reshaping of GIA's culture, including values, customs, and norms
- Usually impacts the mindset, and attitude of team members, including the way they think engage, communicate, and work with others within and external to GIA
- Usually takes years to stabilize and normalize

The transformation to RBIA is a change from ticking the box to proactively engaging and collaborating with stakeholders on risks. It provides an opportunity for the leaders and team members of GIA to learn and share their expertise and knowledge of risks and the business. This includes providing advice, including insight and foresight, to stakeholders. This enables stakeholders to make more informed decisions.

SUPPORT FOR THE RBIA INITIATIVE

The transformation to RBIA addresses most of the complaints associated with a compliance audit approach of performing internal audit, including the following:

- Resources are less likely to be allocated to the high-risk areas of the organization
- Limited interaction and engagement with stakeholders
- Limited knowledge and understanding of the organization's operations and business
- Focus is on ticking the box of predetermined checklists and questionnaires
- Too much time spent on stale or historical and low value information and data
- Lack of empathy for the challenges that stakeholders encounter daily
- Telling stakeholders things that they already know and nothing new
- GIA is perceived as a culture of fault finders instead of problem solvers

- GIA's function is a waste of resources
- Concerns and questions regarding the value of GIA to the organization

The CAE needs to be able to articulate what is driving the initiative. This may include trends in the industry and profession, technological innovation, or simply the desire to improve GIA's effectiveness, efficiency, and value to the organization. The CAE must also be able to share, at a minimum, the following information:

- Justification
- Objective
- Support for the initiative
- Leadership of the initiative
- Impact of the initiative, including what is expected to change or remain the same
- Potential risks and rewards
- Estimated cost and return on investment (ROI)
- Funding source
- Key performance indicators (KPI)
- Deliverables and timelines

The CAE must informally share and test the appetite of trusted stakeholders on the idea of transforming GIA to the RBIA approach of performing internal audit. The approval of the initiative is unlikely if the CAE does not have the support of trusted stakeholders. Trusted stakeholders in this case include the CAE's manager, the leaders of GIA, the CEO, and chairperson of the audit committee. The CAE should also share and obtain input from the organization's external auditor. Senior management and the audit committee often ask the external auditor for their advice on matters of this nature. The sharing must be done before time and resources are invested in developing the business case for the RBIA initiative. The importance of trusted stakeholders support is as follows:

- The leaders and team members of GIA: The CAE must obtain the buy-in and support of the leaders of GIA before pursuing the support of other trusted stakeholders. Their buy-in and support is a question that is likely to be asked by the CAE's manager, the CEO, and audit committee. Additionally, the support of the team members must be obtained prior to embarking on the implementation of the initiative.
- CAE's manager: The CAE's manager is usually a member of the senior management team and the sponsor of the RBIA initiative. The CAE's manager support is critical in obtaining the approval as well as assisting in securing the resources for the RBIA initiative.
- The chief executive officer (CEO): The CEO's support sets the tone at the top as well as the organization's commitment to the initiative. It is also an indication of the importance and value of the initiative to the organization. Additionally, the CEO's support enhances the likelihood of GIA obtaining the approval and the required resources for the initiative. The CEO's support is also critical in getting the employees of the organization to support the initiative.

- Audit committee: The support of the audit committee plays a key role in setting the tone at the top of the organization for the initiative. It is also an indication of the importance and value of the initiative to the organization.

Preliminary support of members of the senior management team is usually required to expedite the approval process of a strategic or major initiative. The CAE must share and obtain preliminary input, feedback, and support from members of the senior management team whose support is needed for the initiative. This includes support in identifying and securing the required resources and satisfying any compliance requirements for the RBIA initiative. Senior management whose support may be required includes the following:

- Chief financial officer (CFO): To address the availability of funding for the initiative
- Chief human resources officer (CHRO) or chief people officer (CPO): To address staffing concerns such as redundancies, budget cuts, redeployment, severance packages, among other things
- Chief legal officer (CLO): To ensure compliance with local labor laws, assist with contractual agreements and negotiations with unions, if applicable
- Chief operating officer (COO): To ensure alignment with operation strategy and objectives
- Chief risk officer (CRO): To discuss support, sharing, and coordination of activities
- Chief technology officer (CTO): To address information technology (IT) matters such as system security, connectivity, integration, reliability, availability, and accessibility

Sharing the idea of the transformation of GIA with trusted stakeholders and members of the senior management team is an important first step in the RBIA journey. This is to obtain their preliminary feedback and support. This paves the way for a more favorable and less challenging approval process for the business case and project plan. This is because most, if not all, of the important questions regarding the initiative will be addressed during the preliminary phase of collaborating with trusted stakeholders and members of the senior management team. It paves the way for a smoother process for the approval of the initiative by senior management and the CEO. Obtaining their preliminary buy-in and support improves the likelihood that the initiative will be approved.

The owner of the change initiative must also share and obtain the buy-in and support of stakeholders most impacted by the change. Staff and stakeholders at the regional and local office levels are usually the ones most impacted. They are usually closest to the activities and know what will work best in their operating environment. Additionally, they are usually the ones responsible for implementing, using, maintaining, monitoring, and reporting on the status of the initiative. The global or corporate office should be careful not to take an attitude that they know what is best for team members and stakeholders in the field. That attitude only makes matters worse. Team members and stakeholders' support can easily be eroded if their input is ignored. The loss of their support could delay or derail the implementation of the initiative.

Engaging, collaborating closely, and incorporating, to the extent possible, team members and stakeholders input into the project plan and implementation process are critical to the successful implementation of the initiative. Their support strengthens and enhances the likelihood that the changes will stick. It also empowers and gives them a sense of part ownership of the initiative. Their support includes the following:

- Implementers: Responsible for ensuring that the RBIA is completed and implemented as planned
- Users: Team members and stakeholders using the system to do their work, including the following:
  - Performing risk assessment
  - Planning and performing audits
  - Performing data analytics
- Maintainers: Responsible for keeping the system updated and current
- Monitors: Responsible for ensuring that the system is operating as expected, and effectively
- Reporters: Responsible for periodically reporting on compliance and effectiveness of the system

The CAE must ensure that steps are taken to maintain the support of key stakeholders. Maintaining the support of key stakeholders, particularly those most impacted by the RBIA initiative, requires keeping them engaged and motivated. Actions that can be taken to keep team members engaged and motivated include the following:

- Sharing and welcoming input from stakeholders on the change initiative
- Including key stakeholders in the change initiative's decision-making process
- Ongoing communication of the status of activities and progress of the initiative
- Providing timely response to feedback, questions, concerns, and complaints
- Providing timely, honest, and consistent messaging as staff roles may change or be eliminated
- Creating a culture where team members are empowered to make decisions on their own
- Encouraging the timely sharing of failures and mitigation plans and activities
- Reconfirming the objectives and value of the initiative to the organization
- Providing subject matter experts and contact persons at the global, regional, and local office levels
- Recognizing and rewarding team members and stakeholders for achieving their objectives

THE BUSINESS CASE

The support of trusted stakeholders and members of the senior management team is the green light for the CAE to develop the business case for the initiative. The CAE should network with and learn from other CAEs who have made the change to RBIA. There is no need to reinvent the wheel when CAEs at other organizations have successfully made the transformation to RBIA.

The business case is the mechanism for getting the initiative officially approved. It can be either a one- or multipage document depending on the organization's approval process. A preliminary project plan, if available, may be attached to the business case. The business case usually includes the following:

- Initiative or project title
- Owner or requestor
- Sponsor
- Justification
- Strategy and objectives
- Project management team
- Current state, proposed changes, and expected future state
- Options or alternative solutions
- Risks and rewards
- Source of funding
- Cost/benefits of the initiative, including ROI
- KPIs
- Timeline and deliverables
- Required approvals

The manager of the requestor of the change initiative and certain members of the senior management team's approval may be required before the business case is submitted for final approval. Senior management's approval may include the following:

- CFO
- CHRO or CPO
- CLO
- COO
- CTO

The CEO and, if applicable, the chairperson of the audit committee usually give final approval of the business case.

MANAGING THE TRANSFORMATION TO RBIA

Effectively managing the transformation to RBIA requires the support of key stakeholders. It also requires prioritizing and effectively managing the areas and activities that are most important in ensuring the success of the initiative. The areas and activities include the following:

- The plan
- Communication
- Execution
- Risk

- Change management
- Monitoring
- Reporting
- Post-implementation review

The Plan

The plan is the roadmap for effectively managing the transformation process. This is because the plan paves the way and minimizes risks to the successful implementation of the initiative. The plan should not be developed in isolation. Effective planning will ensure that the transformation process is collaborative and includes input from team members and stakeholders most impacted by the initiative. Effective planning includes the following:

- Developing strategy and objectives
- Identifying and assessing risk
- Determining the following:
    - Organization's structure, policies, processes, and procedures
    - Required resources to implement the transformation
    - Required coordination and collaboration to keep stakeholders informed
    - Required monitoring and periodic reporting on the status of the transformation
    - Strategy for communicating the transformation
    - Deliverables and timeline
    - KPIs
- Assigning roles, responsibilities, authority, and accountability

Communication

Communication is one of the most important elements for ensuring clarity, agreement, and alignment with the strategy and objectives of the initiative. The announcement of the RBIA initiative to the organization is the official starting point of the communication process. The communication of the announcement usually comes from senior management, and, if required, the chairperson of the board and/or the audit committee, to all staff of the organization. The senior management in this case is the CEO, the CAE's manager, and the CAE. This sets the tone at the top of the organization of the importance and support for the initiative. This also contributes to the support and cooperation of management and staff across the organization for the initiative. Staff are usually more receptive to the message when it comes from senior management. Support from the chairperson of the board or the audit committee enhances the importance of the initiative to the organization. The announcement should include the following:

- Justification
- Objective
- Risks and rewards

- Roles, responsibility, and accountability
- What will change, remain the same, or be eliminated
- Deliverables and timelines
- Contact person(s) for questions and information about the initiative

Communication ensures that messages are effectively communicated to stakeholders. The success of the RBIA initiative depends on how well it is communicated to team members and stakeholders from the beginning to the completion of the initiative. Well-communicated messages are usually those that are delivered in the simplest of forms due to the diverse culture and language in a global organization. It is important that the message is clear and understood by all stakeholders. This is to ensure that everyone is on the same page. The risk of miscommunicating and misunderstandings is high in a global organization where the culture and language are diverse.

Effective communication is a three-way and ongoing activity going up, down, and across the organization. It requires confirming and periodically reconfirming the understanding of messages. It is particularly important for team members and stakeholders in the field at the regional and local office levels. This minimizes the risk of lost messages, confusion, mission drift, and ensures that official messages, including any updates, remain intact. Confirming and reconfirming mission critical messages help to keep the initiative on track and at the forefront of team members' thinking and activities. Timely, clear, concise, and easy to understand messages are key elements of effective communication as well as the following:

- Recapping of messages by recipients
- Confirming receipt of messages
- Reconfirming periodically mission's critical messages, including benefits of the transformation
- Listening to input from staff and stakeholders especially those impacted and closest to the activities
- Providing timely, transparent, and honest response to questions and feedback
- Timely sharing of failures, including delays, and cost overruns with key stakeholders
- Timely sharing of modifications to the transformation and plan with key stakeholders

Miscommunications and misunderstanding of messages can be costly. Although not intentional, miscommunications and misunderstandings of messages can be as damaging as someone sabotaging the initiative. The CAE must ensure that communication of the objectives of the initiative is clear, concise, and easy to understand for everyone across the organization. Miscommunication and misunderstanding of messages can lead to missed opportunities in a fast-paced, constantly changing, and disruptive operating environment. The cause of miscommunication and misunderstanding includes the following:

- Ambiguous messages
- Misinterpretation of messages

- Distorted or lost messages
- Diverse culture and language barriers
- Use of multiple modes of communication mediums and devices

Ongoing communication is critical for team members and stakeholders to stay connected, current, and informed. This will keep the project management team, team members, and stakeholders engaged and focused on the transformation initiative. It is particularly important for team members and stakeholders in the field that are most impacted by the initiative. This includes implementers, users, maintainers, and monitors of the change. They play a key role in the success of the initiative. They can make or break the success of the initiative. Periodic status reports, meetings, and project monthly or quarterly newsletters are effective ways of keeping stakeholders informed and engaged.

Execution

Effective change management requires effective execution of the RBIA initiative. Effective execution is converting the plan into action or setting the plan into motion. The key objective of the execution phase is the successful implementation of the initiative. This includes obtaining the buy-in and support of team members and stakeholders using and benefiting from the outcome or results of the change. The outcome or results include new or updated structures, systems, policies, processes, and procedures. Obtaining the buy-in and support of team members and stakeholders in the field at the regional and local office levels are particularly important in the execution phase. They are usually closest to the action and activities of the initiative. They are usually more knowledgeable of the local context and operating environment and know what works best. It also empowers and gives them a sense of part ownership of the RBIA initiative.

The effective execution of the automation requires a competent and experienced manager, preferably a Certified Internal Auditor (CIA), to lead and oversee the project team. The team should include the required subject matter expertise to effectively implement the change. Leading and overseeing the initiative include monitoring, directing, supporting, and motivating the team. Ongoing communication is required to keep the initiative at the forefront of the thinking and activities of team members and stakeholders. It also includes timely sharing of events to avoid surprises and providing periodic reports on the progress of the initiative, including what is working well and what needs to be changed or stopped.

There are required steps that must be taken to ensure the successful execution and implementation of the plan. The steps include the following:

- Obtain and document a detailed understanding of stakeholder' requirements of the RBIA initiative
- Confirm and prioritize stakeholders' requirements
- Develop and document specifications for prioritized stakeholders' requirements
- Confirm specifications are in alignment with stakeholder' requirements
- Design the system (Note: assumption is that the RBIA approach will be automated).

- Confirm system design is in accordance with the specifications
- Perform stress test of the system
- Develop migration plan and strategy
- Develop electronic user manual
- Test the functionality of the system
- Train and coach stakeholders
- Roll out and implement system, including policies, processes, and procedures
- Perform follow-up or post-implementation review

Risk

Effective risk management is required to provide reasonable assurance of the successful implementation of the RBIA initiative. Risks are known and unknown activities or events that present a threat to achieving the objectives of the RBIA. This may include obstacles, challenges, and roadblocks. Risks must be effectively managed to a reasonable level to enable the achievement of the objectives of the RBIA initiative. This requires timely identifying, assessing, mitigating, monitoring, and periodically reporting on the status of the RBIA initiative to stakeholders. Identifying risks includes brainstorming sessions with key stakeholders, thinking out of the box, and the inclusion of what if scenarios. Assessing risks includes evaluating and prioritizing them.

Team members and stakeholders must be aware of the risks to effectively mitigate, monitor and to periodically report on the status of risks to the implementation of RBIA. The risks include the following:

- Lack of buy-in and support by key stakeholders
- Lack of understanding of the RBIA initiative
- Resource constraints such as inadequate skilled staff and technology
- Staff taking a wait-and-see attitude by holding out or sitting on the fence to see if the change works
- Suppressing information regarding the change initiative
- Spreading misinformation about the change initiative
- Downplaying or ignoring the change initiative
- Deprioritizing and delaying the competition of required tasks and deliverables of the change
- Misalignment and mission drift
- Resisting to learn, improve, and grow from failures

The CAE and leaders of GIA must be proactive in managing risks to the RBIA initiative. This is because the operating environment is constantly changing and disruptive and so is risk. This requires ongoing communications and monitoring as well as the following:

- Ensuring there is clarity of authority, responsibility, and accountability
- Providing adequate resources, including competent management team and subject matter experts

- Simplifying the transformation process since complexity is a driver of risk
- Including input from stakeholders most impacted by the initiative in the decision-making process
- Providing timely status updates to stakeholders, including changes, and risks to the initiative
- Providing timely, transparent, and honest response to stakeholders' questions and feedback
- Managing expectations, failures, and resistance to the change initiative
- Agreeing on realistic deliverables and timelines
- Providing adequate training

Change Management

The transformation from a compliance to RBIA GIA-operating environment is a major disruptive undertaking and change. It usually requires a change in the mindset of team members and stakeholders. It includes the way they think, engage, communicate, and work and often requires the retraining of team members. Emotions usually run high in these situations. The emotions give rise to fear, concerns, and uncertainties, including stress and anxiety of team members across the organization. The fear and concerns also include the following:

- Losing power or control
- Becoming redundant and losing one's job
- Being transferred to another department
- Learning new ways of doing things
- Stepping out of one's comfort zone
- Finding a new job

There is always going to be some resistance to a change initiative that needs to be effectively managed. Resistance can easily derail a change initiative if not effectively managed. There will be early adopters as well as resistors within and external to GIA. The fear of doing things differently can be traumatic and uncomfortable for team members and stakeholders. Those resisting the change at times may engage in activities to undermine and derail the initiative. The activities may include one or more of the following:

- Sabotaging the RBIA initiative
- Taking a wait-and-see attitude by holding out or sitting on the fence to see if the change works
- Ignoring the change
- Making excuses continuously for why things are not getting done
- Resisting to learn, improve, and grow from failures
- Blaming others for failures, including mistakes, delays, and cost overruns

The CAE and the project leader of the initiative must collaborate with team members and stakeholders resisting the change. They must collaborate with resistors of the initiative on finding common ground where there are disagreements. Those resisting the change must be given an opportunity to share their feedback and concerns. The CAE and the project leader of the initiative must be open to and listen to team members and stakeholders' feedback and concerns. This is particularly important for team members and stakeholders most impacted and closest to the activities. Their feedback and concerns should be considered and incorporated where feasible in the project plan. The most effective decision where there is a failure to find common ground on disagreements is usually mutual separation. This is because ongoing resistance will be a constant risk to the success of the change initiative. The CAE must collaborate with human resources and legal to mitigate risks of claims of wrongful termination and monetary damages against the organization.

The CAE must set the expectation of the possibility of failure during a major initiative. There are going to be failures undertaking a strategic or major initiative. It is not a matter of whether there will be failures; it is a matter of when. The CAE must manage expectations by sharing with team members and stakeholders upfront of the possibility of failure and mitigation plans. This will reduce the fear, surprise factor, the "I told you so," and the noise from the skeptics of the project should a failure occur. The project management team must learn and act quickly to address failures before they become disasters. A failure could be the end of an initiative or project. The cause of failures includes the following:

- Change in user requirements such as the addition, adjustment, or deletion of a process or activity
- Defective project design, including not in alignment with the user requirements and specifications
- Modifications to the original project plan
- Changes in the operating environment, including technology, laws, and regulations
- Inadequate resources, including inadequate funding, staffing, expertise, and technological tools
- Incompetence or mismanagement of the project, including lack of expertise and negligence
- Outdated policies, processes, and procedures
- Fatigue and burnout of team members

The CAE must ensure that the controllable activities are effectively managed. This includes the following:

- Selection of the project management team
- Securing required resources
- Users need assessment and requirements
- Design and documentation
- Testing
- Training
- Rollout and implementation

Additionally, there should be contingencies, redundancies, and flexibility built into the project plan to allow for quick adjustment to changes in the operating environment.

The CAE and project leader of the initiative must learn and act quickly to address failures. Failure is a major risk to the successful implementation of an undertaking whether small or large. A failure could be the end of an initiative or project. The CAE must take the necessary steps to minimize the risk of failure. This includes quickly learning and addressing failures before they turn into a disaster. Failure can be costly and may include the following:

- Cancelation of the project
- Reduction in the scope of the project
- Reduction in funding for the project
- Budget cuts in other areas to cover project cost overruns
- Restart of the project
- Reassignment or replacement of the project management team

There is pushback at times on the timely sharing of failures with key stakeholders. Failures may include missed deadlines, setbacks, mistakes, delays, and cost overruns. This is often caused by the fear of the consequences from the delivery of bad news, including the following:

- Cancelation of the initiative
- Negative impact on performance evaluation
- Cut back on the funding of the initiative
- Replacement of the project management team
- Reassignment of the project team

The best practice for handling failures is to timely share the event with key stakeholders. This is to avoid surprises, quickly learn from the experience, and take corrective action to keep the initiative on track. The truth will surface sooner or later. Later can be a costly risk to the CAE and leaders of GIA. The risks include damage to the integrity, credibility, and reputation of GIA. As a reminder, there are going to be failures in any major undertaking. The potential risks should be shared upfront with stakeholders and expectations effectively managed throughout the execution and implementation process.

Monitoring and Reporting

Monitoring is to ensure that the transformation to the RBIA approach of performing internal audit is progressing as planned. This includes effectively, efficiently, and in compliance with required laws, regulations, standards, policies, and procedures. Periodic reports are required to keep stakeholders informed of the status of the RBIA initiative. Periodic reports assist the CAE and leaders of GIA in making more informed decisions regarding the implementation of the RBIA initiative.

Post-Implementation Review

A post-implementation review is necessary to ensure that the RBIA approach to performing internal audit is operating as planned. This includes operating effectively, efficiently, and in compliance with required laws, regulations, standards, policies, and procedures. The review provides an opportunity for the CAE and leaders of GIA to timely address any gaps in the approach to minimize subsequent risk.

THE RBIA IMPLEMENTATION ROADMAP

Effectively managing the transformation process requires a documented roadmap to guide the implementation of the initiative. The key steps of the transformation process are as follows:

Step I: Test the appetite of key stakeholders for the RBIA initiative – The CAE should obtain preliminary or informal support for the initiative from key stakeholders. This should be done before committing significant resources to developing a business case.

Step II: Prepare the business case – The business case is a high-level document that is designed to obtain the official approval for the initiative. It contains a summary of the key elements of the initiative.

Step III: Communicate the initiative – Once the initiative is approved, a joint announcement from the CAE, CEO, and, if required, the chairperson of the board or the audit committee is sent to all employees of the organization.

Step IV: Develop detailed project plan – The project plan is the roadmap for an effective execution and successful implementation of the RBIA initiative. Steps V–XIIX are key elements of the project plan.

Step V: Obtain and document users' requirements – This is where stakeholders are engaged to provide input regarding their requirements. This is a critical step in the successful implementation of the RBIA initiative. Implementers and users will continue with business as usual if the system is not working or valuable to them. This is where users internal and external to GIA are consulted to obtain input of their current and future needs. This requires engaging and collaborating closely with users to determine what is most important to them. It is also an opportunity for the CAE to set expectations on what the system will be able to deliver. The needs should be categorized into must have, like to have, and nice to have.

- Must have: Functionality needed to perform basic tasks such as the tracking of audit results, including audit findings, recommendations, and actions taken by management.
- Like to have: Functionality required to enhance the basic tasks such as creating a database of audit results.
- Nice to have: This is geared more to, for example, aesthetics of system than the functionality.

In this phase, a detailed understanding of the current state, what needs to be changed, disrupted, or eliminated, and the future needs are obtained and documented.

Step VI: Confirm and prioritize user requirements – This is to ensure the understanding of the users' requirements and priorities are captured accurately.

Step VII: Develop specifications – This is where the requirements of stakeholders are converted into technical specifications for the design of the system and processes. It is important to have at least one member of GIA's IT team on the project team to ensure among other things that the technical specifications are in accordance with user requirements.

Step IIX: Confirm technical specifications – This is to ensure that the specifications are in accordance with user requirements. This is an important step because this is the last chance to change or correct the system specifications before coding. Once the system is coded, it is costly to undo.

Step IX: Design the system and processes – This is where the coding or programming of the technical specifications of the system occurs. In-house or external expertise is usually required during this phase to ensure compatibility and connectivity of the RBIA software and tools. This will enable GIA to interface and connect with other relevant organizational systems to work more effectively and efficiently. This includes risk management and compliance systems, databases, and data warehouse. The CAE should ensure that the system is documented whether developed or acquired. The CAE should also ensure that program source code is secured and accessible. Maintenance of the system can be costly if there is no documentation or access to the program source code should there be a problem. This minimizes the risk of a fatal failure should the service provider sells or goes out of business.

Step X: Confirm the design of the system and processes – This is to ensure that the design of the system and processes are in accordance with the technical specifications.

Step XI: Stress test the system – This is to ensure that the system can perform under significant stress without crashing. This usually includes a unit and systemwide test.

Step XII: Migration of the system – This is where files and data are prepared for transferring from an existing system such as a manual or hybrid, standalone or home-grown system to the new system. Cleansing, organizing, and preparing the data to migrate to the new system is a critical step in the migration phase. This includes cleaning up data sets, fields, cells, and files to ensure compatibility and alignment with the new system. This is to avoid inconsistencies, unusable information and data, and corruption of the new system. As the old saying goes, garbage in garbage out.

Step XIII: Develop electronic user manual – This is required for testing, maintaining the system, and training users of the system. This is to assist in ensuring that the system is used as intended.

Step XIV: Test the functionality of the system – The system must be tested to ensure that it is functioning as intended. It is also to identify and eliminate any gaps in the system, processes, and procedures. The testing can be in the form of either piloting, parallel runs, or a sample of test or mock audits at certain offices.

Step XV: Training – During this phase, it is critical that stakeholders, including implementers, users, maintainers, and monitors are trained. Stakeholders need to be trained on how the system works before it goes live or becomes effective. This includes training in new policies, processes, and procedures.

Step XVI: Rollout – This is where the development of the process and/or system is completed and ready to be implemented. The rollout should be properly planned, communicated, and supported by subject matter experts and coordinators located in each office. There are several options available to organizations for rolling out new systems, policies, processes, and procedures, including the following:

- Piloting – This is where the system is implemented at a sample of offices to ensure that it is working effectively and efficiently.
- Parallel run – This is where the old and the new systems operate simultaneously until the new system is stabilized.
- Gradual phased-in – This is where the system is implemented in phases.
- All in approach – This is where the full implementation of the system takes place at the same time across the organization.

The pilot, parallel run, and the gradual phased-in approach minimize the risk of a catastrophic loss to the organization from a fatal failure of the system. It is advisable not to discard the old system, data, and files until the new system is stabilized and working as expected. It is also important to assess the risk and reward of each approach to determine which approach works best for the organization before making that decision.

Step XVII: Implementation – This is where RBIA goes live or becomes effective or operational.

Step XIIX: Post-implementation review – This is where a follow-up review is performed to determine if the system is functioning as expected as well as effectively and efficiently. This review should be performed by a team member who was not a member of the RBIA project team.

MAKING THE CHANGE SUSTAINABLE

The transformation to RBIA GIA-operating environment and making the changes stick is a journey due to the length of time it takes for the changes to stabilize and normalize. A transformation often results in a change in culture, including values, customs, and norms of an organization. This usually requires a change in the mindset of team members. The changes usually impact the way team members think, engage, communicate, and work with others within and external to GIA. Patience, commitment, and perseverance are required as the changes usually take years to adopt, stabilize, and normalize.

The RBIA initiative must remain at the forefront of how team members and stakeholders operate. It is easy for team members to continue or return to business as usual if the rollout of the change is not effectively managed. The rollout of the change must be well planned, communicated, and implementers and users trained, and supported throughout the rollout process. There should also be periodic status meetings and reports to update team members and stakeholders on the progress of the initiative. This includes updates on what is working well, what needs to be changed or stopped.

The change should be communicated in a manner that is easy to understand, memorize, and embrace. Simplifying and breaking down the key elements of the change into memorable one liner make it easier and more likely to be long-lasting. A complex change initiative process is a risk to the successful implementation of the change. How the change is communicated and rolled out across the organization is critical to the successful implementation. Rollout includes transparency, clarity, and understanding of the objectives, risks, and rewards of the change.

There are steps that senior management, managers, and supervisors can take to make the change sustainable. The steps include the following:

- Appointment of change management champions to support departments, functions, and offices
- Create and share a one-page memoizable flyer of the key elements of the change
- Post and display key elements of the change on the organization's website and communal areas
- Create a help desk where team members and stakeholders can call in with questions
- Provide refresher training
- Make the change initiative status update a standing agenda item at team meetings
- Make the change a part of team members KPI
- Recognize and reward team members for outstanding performance
- Hold leaders accountable for the implementation of the change initiative
- Create global dashboard of the status of the change initiative and make it accessible to stakeholders
- Publish monthly global newsletter on the status of the change initiative
- Send global alerts or blast of the achievement of major milestones of the change initiative

VALUE OF RBIA TO THE ORGANIZATION

The transformation of RBIA creates and enhances GIA value to its team members and the organization and its stakeholders. The value to the organization includes the following:

- Takes a holistic approach to risk assessment that includes risks from all aspects of the organization
- Assists in the allocation of resources to high-risk areas that are most important to stakeholders
- Fosters and requires increased engagement and collaboration with stakeholders

The value of RBIA to team members of GIA includes the following:

- Provides a sense of personal satisfaction from knowing that GIA's RBIA work contributes to the achievement of the objectives and success of the organization

- Provides an opportunity for team members to engage with business owners and learn more about their operations instead of finding or looking for faults
- Enhances and strengthens team members business acumen and soft skills
- Promotes keeping current with technical, industry and professional trends, and innovations
- Enhances team members ability to connect the dots, interpret, and translate the results of data analytics into valuable and actionable advice
- Enhances stakeholders' appreciation and value of GIA to the organization
- Requires alignment with the strategy, objectives, and risk mitigation plan and activities of the organization
- Facilitates more effective and efficient allocation of GIA's resources
- Enhances promotional opportunities of team members to other areas of the organization because of their broader and comprehensive perspective of the business and operations of the organization

CHAPTER SUMMARY

The transformation to RBIA approach of performing internal audit is one of the most valuable contributions that a CAE can make to an organization. It is a strategic and transformational approach performing internal audit. The transformation is to a risk-driven operating environment. It is a change from ticking the box to proactively engaging and collaborating with stakeholders. The transformation to RBIA creates and enhances GIA's value to the organization and its stakeholders as well as team members of GIA. It also provides an opportunity for the leaders and team members of GIA to learn from stakeholders and expand their business acumen. The stakeholders are often subject matter experts for their area(s) of responsibilities. A compliance audit approach underutilizes the knowledge and expertise of internal auditors.

Organizations cannot rely on a compliance audit approach to fulfill the internal audit needs of an organization in an ever-changing operating environment. They need a holistic and dynamic internal audit approach. RBIA is a holistic and dynamic approach of performing internal audit. Risks from all aspects of the organization are considered. RBIA is also more of a forward-looking and -thinking approach.

Sharing the concept of the RBIA initiative with key stakeholders by the CAE is the beginning of the journey to transform GIA to RBIA approach of performing internal audit. The CAE must informally test the appetite of key stakeholders to obtain their input, feedback, and support for the initiative. This is particularly important to stakeholders in the field at the regional and local office levels. Team members and stakeholders at the regional and local office levels are usually the ones responsible for implementing, using, maintaining, monitoring, reporting, and complying with the policies, processes, and procedures of the initiative. They often know what will work best in their operating environment. The success of the initiative is usually in their hands.

Effectively managing the transformation to RBIA requires the support of key stakeholders. It also requires prioritizing and effectively managing the areas and activities that are most important in ensuring the success of the initiative. Adopting, normalizing, and stabilizing the transformation to RBIA and making the changes stick is a journey due to the length of time it takes for the changes to stabilize and normalize. It usually requires a change in the culture, including the values, customs, and norms of the organization. This includes a change in the mindset of team members as well as the way they think, engage, communicate, and work with others within and external to GIA. Patience is required as the change in the culture of the organization usually takes years to adopt, stabilize, and normalize. The CAE must ensure that steps are taken to maintain the support of key stakeholders.

8 Automation of Internal Audit Operations

INTRODUCTION

A manual or a hybrid-driven global internal audit (GIA) operation is a risk to its survival and sustainability in a dynamic operating environment. Leveraging technology is the only way that a GIA operation can survive and remain ready, resilient, and relevant. Technological innovations and big data are driving organizations to evolve and transform their operations. The automation of GIA's operations is the foundation for a technology-driven GIA-operating environment. It will be the gateway to a wide range of opportunities for GIA to leverage technology to enhance its effectiveness, efficiency, and value to the organization.

Chief audit executives (CAEs) operating in a manual or a hybrid-driven operating environment must change for the survival and success of GIA. They must evolve, automate, and transform GIA's operation into an electronic operating environment. The change is a strategic and transformational undertaking that requires the support of senior management and the audit committee. It requires reimagining GIA's operation, including consolidating, streamlining, and integrating GIA's operations and activities. The automation process must be effectively managed to achieve the objectives of the automation.

The purpose of this chapter is to provide advice and guidance on why a manual or a hybrid-driven GIA operation is a risk to the survival, sustainability, and success of GIA. Topics covered include the following:

- The end of manual or hybrid-driven GIA operation
- Strategic and transformational nature of the automation
- Obtaining and maintaining the support for the automation
- The business case
- Managing the automation implementation process
- The implementation roadmap
- Making the change sustainable
- Expert advice
- Build, buy, lease, or fee for service agreement
- Value of the automation to GIA and the organization

Key learnings from the chapter include the following:

- Reasons a manual or a hybrid GIA operation will not survive in a dynamic operating environment

DOI: 10.1201/9781003207559-8

- Understanding the strategic and transformational nature of the automation
- Importance of the business case and stakeholders' participation in the decision-making process
- Importance of prioritizing and effectively managing the key areas and activities of the automation
- Understanding the implementation process and steps to take in making the change stick
- Benefits of leasing or a fee for service agreement, including software-as-a-service (SAAS)
- Contribution to GIA's readiness, resilience, relevance, and value to the organization

THE END OF MANUAL OR HYBRID-DRIVEN GIA OPERATION

A manual or hybrid-driven GIA operation is a risk to its survival and sustainability in a fast-paced, constantly changing, and disruptive operating environment. It is an operation that usually comprises siloed, fragmented, standalone, and home-grown applications and spreadsheets. Technological innovations and big data have accelerated the pace of change in the operating environment. This has forced organizations to change to survive, remain relevant, competitive, and successful.

There are many reasons why a manual or a hybrid-driven GIA operation cannot survive in an ever-changing operating environment. They include the following:

- Rigid
- Slow accessibility and adapting to change
- Prone to errors
- Lacks integration and connectivity
- Not conducive to data mining and analytics
- Inconsistent processes and procedures
- Not conducive to continuous monitoring, learning, and improvement
- Not environmentally friendly

The CAE and leaders of GIA must evolve and transform GIA operation from a manual or a hybrid to an automated operating environment. This needs to be done for GIA to improve its effectiveness, efficiency, and value to the organization. There is no value in manually doing the same thing, the same way each day when it can be done more effectively, efficiently, and less costly electronically. This is of particular importance when the tasks and activities are voluminous, routine, and repetitive. It is a waste of time and resources that could be redeployed to more strategic activities that matter most to stakeholders. The key differences between a manual or a hybrid and an automated-driven GIA-operating environment are summarized in Table 8.1 below.

TABLE 8.1
Differences between Manual or Hybrid and an Automated GIA Operation

Subject	Manual or Hybrid	Automated
Audit approach	Reactive, backward looking, compliance driven, and troubleshooting role	Proactive, forward looking, and risk driven
Data mining and analytics	Slow and limited	Quick and robust
Access to data and information	Slow	Quick
Value to the organization	Less valuable	More valuable
Data privacy and protection	Less secured	More secured
Productivity	Less productive	More productive
Quality of work	More prone to errors	Less prone to errors
Risk of outsourcing of the operation	High	Low
Environmentally friendly	Less friendly (paper documents)	More friendly (e-documents)

The automation of GIA is the gateway to a wide range of opportunities to enhance GIA's effectiveness, efficiency, and value to the organization. This includes the readiness, resilience, relevance, and value of GIA to the organization and stakeholders. The key activities of GIA's operation that are likely to be automated include the following:

- Audit management:
    - Risk assessment
    - Audit planning and supervision
    - Audit fieldwork
    - Audit findings and recommendations
    - Reporting
    - Issues tracking
    - Filing and storage
- Audit administrative activities:
    - Time and expense budgets
    - Staff time budgets
    - Staff time sheets and expense reports
    - Staff evaluations
    - Customer survey results
    - Job descriptions

The system usually has a centralized database where the information is stored. The information can be quickly accessed 24 hours daily/seven days weekly (24/7) where access to the internet is available. The stored information includes the following:

- Audit universe
- Risk assessment
- Audit plan
- Audit programs
- Audit reports

- Audit findings and recommendations
- Management response, including action taken and pending

STRATEGIC AND TRANSFORMATIONAL NATURE OF THE AUTOMATION

The change from a manual or a hybrid to an automated GIA-operating environment is a strategic and transformational undertaking. It is a journey and not a walk around the block due to the time it takes for the changes to stick. Patience, commitment, and perseverance are required as the changes usually take years to adopt, stabilize, and normalize. The automation is strategic because of the following:

- Requires reimagining GIA's strategy, objectives, and operating environment
- Requires senior management and the audit committee support
- Requires additional investment in GIA
- Contributes to the governance of the organization
- Impacts GIA's staff and stakeholders across the organization

The automation of GIA's operation is a transformational undertaking. This is because it usually:

- Requires revisiting, rethinking, and the reshaping GIA's culture, including the values, customs, and norms
- Requires a change in staff mindset and attitude
- Impacts the way staff think, engage, communicate, and work with others within and external to GIA

The CAE must research and learn from others who have experience automating a GIA operation. There is no need to reinvent the wheel if others have successfully automated their GIA operation. This must be done before beginning the journey of making the case for the automation. Those who would be helpful in providing information to build the case for the initiative include the following:

- CAEs at other organizations who have automated their GIA operation
- Service providers for literature and demonstration of their application or software
- External auditor as senior management and the audit committee often ask for their input and advice

OBTAINING AND MAINTAINING SUPPORT FOR THE AUTOMATION

The CAE must informally test the appetite of trusted stakeholders on the concept of automating GIA's operation to obtain their feedback, and preliminary buy-in and support. The approval of a strategic or major organizational change often depends on their buy-in and support. Trusted stakeholders in this case include the leaders of

GIA, CAE's manager, chief executive officer (CEO), and the chairperson of the audit committee. Testing the appetite of trusted stakeholders must be done before time and resources are invested in developing the business case. The CAE must be able to articulate what is driving the initiative. It may be driven by the CAE's desire to improve GIA's effectiveness, efficiency, and value to the organization or to address change in the operating environment, including the following:

- Technological innovations
- Regulatory requirements
- Trends in the industry and the profession

The CAE must prepare and be ready to share the key elements of the automation with stakeholders. This includes the following:

- Justification
- Objective
- Support for the initiative
- Leadership of the initiative
- Impact of the initiative, including what is expected to change or remain the same
- Potential risks and rewards
- Estimated cost and return on investment (ROI)
- Funding source
- Key performance indicators (KPIs)
- Deliverables and timelines

Sharing the concept of the automation of GIA with key stakeholders is the beginning of the journey to transform GIA into an electronic operating environment. Key stakeholders include the leaders of GIA, the CAE's manager, senior management, CEO, and chairperson of the audit committee. Sharing the concept with key stakeholders paves the way for a smoother process for the approval of the automation business case. Obtaining their preliminary buy-in and support for the automation improves the likelihood of its approval. The success or failure of a strategic or major organizational change often depends on the level of support it receives from key stakeholders.

The CAE must share and obtain preliminary buy-in and support from certain members of the senior management team. It is usually required to expedite the approval process of a strategic or major organizational change initiative. This includes support in identifying and securing the required resources and satisfying any compliance requirements for the automation. Senior management whose support may be required includes the following:

- Chief Financial Officer (CFO): To address the availability of funding for the initiative.
- Chief Human Resources Officer (CHRO) or Chief People Officer (CPO): To address staffing concerns such as redundancies, budget cuts, redeployment, severance packages, among other things.

- Chief Legal Officer (CLO): To ensure compliance with local labor laws, assist with contractual agreements and negotiations with unions, if applicable.
- Chief Risk Officer (CRO): To discuss support, sharing, and coordination of activities.
- Chief Technology Officer (CIO): To address information technology (IT) matters such as system security, connectivity, integration, reliability, availability, and accessibility.

The CAE must also share and obtain the buy-in and support of staff and stakeholders most impacted by the automation. Staff and stakeholders at the regional and local office levels are usually the ones most impacted. They are usually closest to the activities and know what will work best in their operating environment. Additionally, they are usually the ones responsible for implementing, using, monitoring, maintaining, and reporting on the status of the initiative. Engaging, collaborating closely, and incorporating, to the extent possible, their input into the project plan and process are critical to the successful implementation of the automation. Their support strengthens and enhances the likelihood that the changes will be long-lasting and achieve the objectives of the automation. Their support can easily be eroded if their input is ignored. The global or corporate office should be careful not to take an attitude of "they know what is best for staff in the field". That attitude only makes matters worse. The loss of their support could delay or derail the automation.

The CAE must ensure that steps are taken to maintain the support of key stakeholders. Maintaining the support of key stakeholders, particularly those most impacted by the automation, requires keeping them engaged and motivated. Actions that can be taken to keep staff and stakeholders engaged and motivated include the following:

- Sharing and welcoming input from stakeholders on the change initiative
- Including key stakeholders in the change initiative's decision-making process
- Ongoing communication of the status of activities and progress of the initiative
- Providing timely, honest, and consistent messaging as staff roles may change or be eliminated
- Creating a culture where staff are empowered to make decisions on their own
- Encouraging the timely sharing of failures and mitigation plans and activities
- Providing timely response to feedback, questions, concerns, and complaints
- Reconfirming the objectives and value of the initiative to the organization
- Providing subject matter experts and contact persons at the global, regional, and local office levels
- Recognizing and rewarding staff and stakeholders for achieving their objectives

THE BUSINESS CASE

The preliminary support of key stakeholders is the green light for the CAE to develop the business case for the automation. It paves the way for expediting the formal approval process. The business case is the mechanism for getting the automation approved. It can be either a one- or multipage document depending on the organization's approval process. A preliminary project plan, if available, may be attached to the business case. The business case usually includes the following:

- Initiative or project title
- Owner or requestor
- Sponsor
- Justification
- Strategy and objectives
- Project management team
- Current state, proposed changes, and expected future state
- Options or alternatives solutions
- Risks and rewards
- Source of funding
- Cost benefits of the initiative, including ROI
- KPI
- Timeline and deliverables
- Required approvals

The manager of the requestor of the change initiative and certain members of the senior management team's approval may be required before the business case is submitted for final approval. Senior management's approval may include the following:

- CFO: To address the availability of funding for the initiative.
- CHRO or CPO: To address staffing concerns such as redundancies, budget cuts, redeployment, severance packages, among other things.
- CLO: To ensure compliance with local labor laws, assist with contractual agreements and negotiations with unions, if applicable.
- Chief operating officer (COO): To ensure alignment with operation strategy and objectives.
- CRO: To discuss support, sharing, and coordination of activities.
- CIO: To address IT matters such as system security, connectivity, integration, reliability, availability, and accessibility.

Final approval of the business case is usually given by the CEO and the chairperson of the audit committee, if applicable.

MANAGING THE AUTOMATION IMPLEMENTATION PROCESS

Effectively managing the automation of GIA requires prioritizing and managing the areas and activities that are most important in driving the success of the initiative.

The areas and activities that are most important in driving the success of the automation are as follows:

- The plan
- Communication
- Execution
- Risk
- Change management
- Monitoring and reporting
- Post-implementation review

The Plan

The plan is the roadmap for effectively managing and guiding the transformation and automation of GIA's operation to an electronic operating environment. This is because the plan paves the way and minimizes risks to the successful implementation of the automation. The plan should not be developed in isolation. Effective planning will ensure that the transformation process is collaborative and includes input from staff most impacted by the automation. Effective planning includes the following:

- Developing objectives and strategy
- Identifying and assessing risk
- Determining the following:
  - Organization's structure, policies, processes, and procedures
  - Required resources to implement the transformation
  - Required coordination and collaboration to keep stakeholders informed
  - Required monitoring and periodic reporting on the status of the transformation
  - Strategy for communicating the transformation
  - Deliverables and timeline
  - KPI
- Assigning roles, responsibilities, authority, and accountability

Communication

The announcement of the automation initiative to the organization is the official starting point of the communication process. The communication of the announcement usually comes from senior management, and, if required, the chairperson of the audit committee, to all staff of the organization. Senior management in this case is the CEO, the CAE's manager, and the CAE. This sets the tone at the top of the organization of the importance and support for the automation. This also contributes to the support and cooperation of management and staff across the organization for the initiative. Staff are usually more receptive to the message when it comes from senior management. Support from the chairperson of the board or the audit committee enhances the importance of the automation to the organization. The announcement should include the following:

- Justification
- Objective
- Risks and rewards
- Roles, responsibility, and accountability
- What will change, remain the same, or be eliminated
- Deliverables and timelines
- Contact person(s) who staff and stakeholders can call in to with questions

The success of the automation initiative depends on how well it is communicated to staff and stakeholders from the beginning to the implementation. Well-communicated messages are usually those that are delivered in the simplest of forms. This is due to the diverse culture and language in a global organization. It is important that the message is clear and understood by all stakeholders. This is to ensure that everyone is on the same page. The risk of miscommunicating and misunderstandings is high in a global organization where the culture and language are diverse.

Effective communication is a three-way and ongoing activity going up, down, and across the organization. It requires confirming and periodically reconfirming the understanding of messages. It is particularly important for staff and stakeholders in the field at the regional and local office levels. This minimizes the risk of impacted staff and stakeholders of not receiving messages. It also minimizes the risks of confusion, mission drift, and ensures that the original message and updates remain intact. Confirming and reconfirming mission critical messages help to keep the initiative on track and at the forefront of staff thinking and activities. Clarity and understanding of messages are key elements of effective communication as well as the following:

- Recapping of messages by recipients
- Confirming receipt of messages
- Reconfirming mission critical messages periodically, including the benefits of the automation
- Listening to input particularly from stakeholders most impacted and closest to the activities
- Providing timely, transparent, and honest response to questions and feedback from stakeholders
- Timely sharing of failures, including mistakes, delays, and cost overruns with key stakeholders
- Timely sharing of adjustments and modifications to the transformation with key stakeholders

Miscommunication and misunderstanding of messages can be costly at times, which can derail the automation initiative. Although not intentional, miscommunications and misunderstandings can be as damaging as someone sabotaging the initiative. The CAE must ensure that communication is clear, concise, and easy to understand for everyone across the organization. Miscommunication and misunderstanding of messages can lead to missed opportunities in a rapidly and constantly changing and disruptive operating environment. The reasons include the following:

- Ambiguous messages
- Misinterpretation of messages
- Distorted or lost messages
- Diverse culture and language barriers
- Use of multiple modes of communication mediums and devices

Ongoing communication with stakeholders minimizes the risks of miscommunication and misunderstandings of the objectives of the automation. Communication is up, down, and across the organization. It is required for staff and stakeholders to stay engaged, connected, current, and informed. This will assist in keeping the project management team, staff, and stakeholders focused on the automation initiative. It is particularly important for staff and stakeholders in the field most impacted by the changes. This includes implementers, users, maintainers, monitors, and reporters of the change. They play a key role in the success of the initiative. Periodic status reports, meetings, and project newsletters are effective actions in keeping stakeholders engaged, connected, current, and informed.

Execution

Management of the automation requires effective execution. Effective execution is converting the plan into action or setting it into motion. The key objective of the execution phase is the successful implementation of the automation. This includes obtaining the buy-in and support of staff and stakeholders implementing, using, maintaining, monitoring, reporting, and complying with the requirements of the automation. The outcome may include new or updated structures, systems, policies, processes, and procedures. Obtaining the buy-in and support of staff and stakeholders in the field at the regional and local office levels is particularly important in the execution phase. Staff and stakeholders in the field are usually closest to the activities and action of the initiative. They are also more knowledgeable of the local context and operating environment and usually know what works best in their environment. Their buy-in and support strengthen and enhance the likelihood that the changes will stabilize and normalize to enable the successful implementation of the initiative. It also empowers and gives them a sense of part ownership of the automation.

The effective execution of the automation requires a competent and experienced manager, preferably a Certified Internal Auditor (CIA), to lead and oversee the project team. The team should include any required subject matter expertise to effectively implement the change. Leading and overseeing the automation include monitoring, directing, supporting, and motivating the team. Ongoing communication is also required to keep the automation at the forefront of the thinking and activities of staff and stakeholders. This includes providing periodic updates and reports on the status of the progress of the automation such as what is working well, what needs improvement, and what needs to be stopped.

There are required steps that must be taken to ensure the successful execution and implementation of the plan. The steps include the following:

- Obtain and document detailed understanding of stakeholder' requirements of the automation
- Confirm and prioritize stakeholders' requirements
- Develop and document specifications for prioritized stakeholders' requirements
- Confirm specifications are in alignment with stakeholder' requirements
- Design the system
- Confirm system design is in accordance with the specifications
- Perform stress test of the system
- Develop migration plan and strategy
- Develop electronic user manual
- Test the functionality of the system
- Train and coach stakeholders
- Roll out and implement the system, including policies, processes, and procedures
- Perform post-implementation review

Risk

Risks are known and unknown activities or events that present a threat to achieving the objectives of the automation. Simply put, risks are anything that will prevent GIA from achieving the objectives of the automation. Risks must be effectively managed to a reasonable level to enable the achievement of the objectives. This requires timely identifying, assessing, mitigating, monitoring, and reporting on the status of risks to the automation to key stakeholders. Identifying risks includes brainstorming sessions with key stakeholders, thinking out of the box, and the inclusion of what if scenarios. Assessing risks includes evaluating and prioritizing them.

Effective risk management minimizes risks and provides reasonable assurance of the successful implementation of the automation. Team members and stakeholders must be aware of the risks to effectively manage and mitigate them. The risks include the following:

- Lack of buy-in and support by key stakeholders
- Lack of understanding of the automation
- Lack of skills, expertise, and technological tools
- Misalignment and mission drift
- Staff taking a wait-and-see attitude by holding out or sitting on the fence to see if the change works
- Suppressing and spreading misinformation about the automation
- Downplaying or ignoring the change
- Deprioritizing and delaying the completion of required tasks and deliverables
- Resisting to learn, improve, and grow from failures

There is pushback at times on the timely sharing of failures with key stakeholders. Failures may include missed deadlines, setbacks, mistakes, delays, and cost overruns. This is often caused by the fear of the consequences from the delivery of bad news, including the following:

- Cancelation of the initiative
- Impact on performance evaluation
- Cut back on the funding of the initiative
- Reassignment of the project team
- Replacement of the project management team

Ongoing communication, monitoring, and reporting are required to effectively manage risks to the automation. This is because risk is constantly changing in an ever-changing operating environment. Effectively managing risks to the automation include the following:

- Ensuring there is clarity of authority, responsibility, and accountability
- Providing adequate resources, including competent management team and subject matter experts
- Simplifying the transformation process since complexity is a driver of risk
- Including input from stakeholders most impacted by the initiative in the decision-making process
- Agreeing on realistic deliverables and timelines
- Managing expectations, failures, and resistance to the change initiative
- Providing timely status updates to stakeholders, including changes and risks to the initiative
- Providing timely, transparent, and honest response to stakeholders' questions and feedback
- Providing adequate training

Change Management

The transformation from a manual or a hybrid-driven to an automated GIA-operating environment is a major strategic and disruptive undertaking. This is because the undertaking often requires a change in the mindset of staff and stakeholders. This includes the way staff think, engage, communicate, and work. It often requires the retraining of staff. Emotions usually run high in these situations. The emotions give rise to uncertainties, stress, and anxiety of GIA staff across the organization. The emotions also give rise to fear and concerns of GIA staff, including the following:

- Losing power or control
- Becoming redundant and losing one's job
- Being transferred to another department
- Learning new ways of doing things
- Stepping out of one's comfort zone
- Finding a new job

There is always going to be some resistance to change that must be effectively managed. Resistance can easily derail a change initiative if not effectively managed. There will be early adopters of the change as well as those who will take a wait-and-see attitude. There are also those within and external to GIA who will resist the change. The fear of doing things differently can be traumatic and uncomfortable for team members and stakeholders. Those resisting the change at times may engage in activities to undermine and derail the initiative. The activities may include one or more of the following:

- Sabotaging the automation initiative
- Suppressing and spreading misinformation about the automation
- Making excuses continuously for why things are not getting done
- Resisting to learn, improve, and grow from failures
- Blaming others for failures, including delays and cost overruns

The CAE and the project leader of the automation initiative must collaborate with staff and stakeholders resisting the change. They must collaborate with resistors on finding common ground where there are disagreements. Those resisting the change must be given an opportunity to share their feedback and concerns. The CAE and the project leader of the initiative must be open to and listen to staff and stakeholders' feedback, emotions, and concerns. This is particularly important for staff and stakeholders most impacted and closest to the activities. Their feedback and concerns must be considered and incorporated where feasible in the project plan. Mutual separation is usually the most effective decision where there is failure to find common ground over disagreements. This is because ongoing resistance will be a constant risk to the success of the automation initiative. The CAE must collaborate with human resources and legal to mitigate risks of claims of wrongful termination and monetary damages against the organization.

The CAE must ensure that there is a plan in place to maintain and strengthen the support for the automation. The plan will help to reduce skepticism and risks to the initiative. The plan should include ongoing communications of the status of the automation as well as the following:

- Provide timely, transparent, honest, and consistent messaging
- Reconfirm the objectives and benefits of the automation, including the following:
  - Senior management and the audit committee support
  - Purpose, objectives, and value to the organization
  - Justification for the project
  - What is expected to change or remain the same
- Provide timely response to feedback, questions, and complaints
- Provide periodic project status update meetings and reports
- Encourage quick ownership of failures and learn, share, and grow from the experience
- Recognize and reward staff and stakeholders for achieving their objectives

The CAE must set the expectation of the possibility of failure during a major change initiative. There are going to be failures in any major change initiative. It is not a matter of whether there will be failures. It is a matter of when. The CAE must set the expectation of the possibility of failure, especially during an IT project. This requires sharing with staff and stakeholders upfront the possibility of failure and mitigation plans. This will reduce the fear, surprise factor, and negativity from the skeptics of the project should a failure occur. A failure could be the end of an initiative or project. The cause of failures includes the following:

- Defective project design, including not in alignment with the user requirements and specifications
- Changes in the operating environment, including technology, laws, and regulations
- Inadequate resources, including inadequate funding, staffing, expertise, and technological tools
- Incompetence or mismanagement of the project, including lack of expertise and negligence
- Outdated structures, policies, processes, and procedures
- Staff fatigue and burnouts

The project leader of the initiative must learn and act quickly to address failure. Failure is a major risk to the successful implementation of any undertaking whether small or large. A failure could be the end of an initiative or project. The project leader must take the necessary steps to minimize the risk of failure. This includes quickly learning and addressing failures before they become a disaster. Failure can be costly and may result in any of the following:

- Cancelation or cutback on the initiative
- Cutting funding for the initiative
- Cutting budget in other areas to cover project cost overruns
- Restarting the project
- Scaling back of the project where only a fraction of the project is pursued
- Reassigning or replacing the project management team
- Becoming redundant and losing one's job

The best practice for managing the risk of failures is to be transparent, honest, and timely share the status and activities of the automation with key stakeholders. This is to avoid surprises. The truth will surface eventually. Later can be a costly risk to the CAE and leaders of GIA. The risks include damage to the integrity, credibility, and reputation of the CAE and GIA. The potential risks should be shared upfront with stakeholders and expectations effectively managed throughout the execution and implementation process.

Monitoring and Reporting

Monitoring is done to ensure that the automation initiative is progressing as planned. This includes effectively, efficiently, and in compliance with required laws, regulations, standards, policies, and procedures. Periodic reports are required to keep stakeholders informed of the status of the automation. Periodic reports assist the CAE and leaders of GIA in making more informed decisions regarding the automation.

Post-Implementation Review

A post-implementation review is necessary to ensure that the automation is operating as planned. This includes operating effectively, efficiently, and in compliance with required laws, regulations, standards, policies, and procedures. The review provides an opportunity for the CAE and leaders of GIA to timely address gaps in the planning and implementation process to minimize subsequent risk.

THE IMPLEMENTATION ROADMAP

A roadmap detailing the phases of the implementation process must be prepared and shared with key stakeholders. Key stakeholders in this case include team members of GIA, implementers, users, maintainers, monitors, and reporters particularly those in the field at the regional and local offices. The phases are as follows:

Phase I: Obtain and document users' needs and requirements – This is where users internal and external to GIA are consulted to obtain input of their current and future needs. This requires engaging and collaborating closely with users to determine what is most important to them. It is also an opportunity for the CAE to set expectations on what the system will be able to deliver. The needs should be categorized into must have, like to have, and nice to have.

- Must have: Critical for performing basic tasks, including issues tracking
- Like to have: Not critical for performing basic tasks such as adding extra tools to the requirement
- Nice to have: Not critical or necessary (e.g., the aesthetics of the system) for performing basic tasks

Phase II: Prioritize and confirm users' needs and requirements – This is to ensure the understanding of the users' needs and requirements are captured accurately. This includes an understanding of the current state, proposed changes, and expected future state.

Phase III: Analysis and identification of tasks and activities to automate – This is to determine what manual processes and activities can and will be automated. This step requires an understanding of the data sets, fields, cells, files, reports as well as the consistency and usability of the data. Areas to consider include the following:

- Audit administration
- Risk assessment
- Audit planning and budget
- Audit schedule
- Audit fieldwork
- Audit supervision
- Review and approval of fieldwork
- Audit report

- Audit issue tracking
- Time and expense reports
- Centralized depository of audit reports
- Database of audit findings, recommendations, management response, and action(s) taken
- Access and system security
- Access to stakeholders

Phase IV: Prioritization of users' requirements – This is where the CAE and leaders of GIA discuss and agree on the needs that the automation will address, including contingencies, redundancies, and flexibility to allow for quick adjustment to rapid changes in the operating environment.

Phase V: Develop technical specifications – This is where the user requirements are converted into specifications for the design of the system and processes. It is important to have at least one GIA IT member of staff on the project team to ensure among other things that the technical specifications are in accordance with user requirements.

Phase VI: Confirm technical specifications – This is to ensure that the specifications are in accordance with user requirements. This is an important step because this is the last chance to change or correct the system specifications before the specifications are coded. Once the specifications are coded, it is costly to undo.

Phase VII: Design the system – This is where the coding or programming of the technical specifications of the system occurs. In-house or external expertise is usually required during this phase to ensure compatibility and connectivity of the automation software and tools. This will enable GIA to interface and connect with other relevant organizational systems to work more effectively and efficiently. This includes enterprise risk management (ERM) and compliance systems, databases, and data warehouse. The CAE should ensure that the system is documented whether developed or acquired. The CAE should also ensure that program source code is secured and accessible. Maintenance of the system can be costly if there is no documentation or access to the program source code should there be a problem. This minimizes the risk of a fatal failure should the service provider sells or goes out of business.

Phase IIX: Confirm the design of the system – This is to ensure that the design of the system is in accordance with the technical specifications.

Phase IX: Stress test the system – This is to ensure that the system can perform under significant stress without crashing. This usually includes a unit and systemwide test.

Phase X: Migration of the system – This is where files and data are prepared for transferring from an existing system such as a manual or hybrid, standalone or home-grown to the new system. Cleansing, organizing, and preparing the data to migrate to the new system is a critical step in the migration phase. This includes cleaning up data sets, fields, cells, and files. Data sets, fields, cells, and files need to be compatible and aligned to avoid inconsistencies, unusable information and data, and corruption of the system. As the old saying goes, garbage in garbage out.

Phase XI: Develop electronic user manual – This is required for testing, maintaining, and training users of the system. This is to assist in ensuring that the system is used as intended.

Step XII: Test the functionality of the system – The system must be tested to ensure that it is functioning as intended. This is also to identify and eliminate any gaps in the system, processes, and procedures.

Phase XIII: Training – Operators and users must be trained before the system goes live.

Phase XIV: Rollout – This is where the development of the system is completed and ready to be implemented. The rollout should be carefully planned, communicated, and supported by subject matter experts and coordinators located in each office. The CAE, including the leaders of GIA, must decide on the strategy for the rollout of the system. There are options available, including the following:

- Pilot: System implemented at a sample of offices to ensure it is working as planned and effectively
- Parallel run: Old and new systems operate simultaneously until the new system is stabilized
- Gradual phased-in: System implementation is done in phases
- All in approach: Full implementation of the system occurs at the same time across the organization

The pilot, parallel run, and the gradual phased-in approach minimize the risk of a catastrophic loss to the organization from a fatal failure of the system. A pilot at a sample of field offices and at the corporate office before going live is a good practice. This is to correct gaps or bugs and kinks in the system. It is best to address the gaps before going live with the system. The gaps will surface over time and become disruptive. Parallel run of the new and old systems allows for fallback to the old system should the new system crash or a fatal failure occur once the system goes live. The old files must be maintained in accordance with the organization's record retention policy and not discarded until the system is stabilized, working as expected, and available for at least one external audit cycle. It is also important to assess the risk and reward of each approach to determine which approach works best for GIA before making that decision.

Phase XV: System Implementation – This is where the automation goes live and becomes operational.

Phase XVI: Post-implementation review – This is to ensure that the system is functioning as expected as well as effectively and efficiently. Ongoing follow-up reviews should continue until the system is stabilized.

MAKING THE CHANGE SUSTAINABLE

The transformation of GIA to an automated operating environment and making the changes stick is a journey due to the length of time it takes for the changes to stabilize and normalize. A transformation often, as mentioned earlier, results in a change in culture, including values, customs, and norms of an organization. This usually requires a change in the mindset of staff. Patience, commitment, and perseverance are required as the changes usually take years to adopt, stabilize, and normalize.

The automation of GIA must remain at the forefront of the thinking and activities of staff to make the changes stick. It is easy for staff to continue or return to business as usual if the rollout of the change is not effectively managed. The rollout of the change must be well planned, communicated, executed, and implementers and users trained, and supported throughout the rollout process. There must also be periodic status meetings and reports to update staff and stakeholders on the status of the initiative. This includes updates on what is working well, what needs to change, or stopped. A post-implementation review is also required to ensure that the implementation of the change is operating as planned as well as effectively and efficiently.

The automation initiative should be communicated in a manner that is easy to understand, memorize, and embrace. Simplifying and breaking down the key elements of the automation into memorable one liner make it easier and more likely to be long-lasting. A complex change initiative process is a risk to the successful implementation of the change. How the change is communicated and rolled out across the organization is critical to the successful implementation of the automation. It includes transparency, clarity, and understanding of the objectives, risks, and rewards of the change.

There are steps that senior management, managers, and supervisors can take to make the changes stick. The steps include the following:

- Appointment of change management champions to support departments, functions, and offices
- Create and share a one-page memoizable flyer of the key elements of the change
- Post and display key elements of the change on the organization's website and communal areas
- Provide contact person(s) for stakeholders to call in with questions
- Provide refresher training
- Make the automation status update a standing agenda item at staff meetings
- Make the objectives of the automation a KPI for all staff
- Recognize and reward staff for outstanding performance
- Hold leaders accountable for the implementation of the initiative
- Create global dashboard of the status of the change initiative and make it accessible to stakeholders
- Publish periodic global newsletter on the status of the automation initiative
- Send global alerts or blast of the achievement of major milestones of the automation

EXPERT ADVICE

Obtaining expert advice or a second opinion on major decisions is always advisable when undertaking a strategic or major change initiative. The automation of GIA is a major and highly technical undertaking that requires expert advice and guidance. The advice can be either obtained in-house from GIA's IT Audit team, the organization's IT department or from a consultant. GIA's IT Audit or the IT department may have the required expertise to provide an in-house option. The cost benefit of internal or external expert support should be explored. The in-house expertise, although is likely to be more knowledgeable of the organization, may have competing priorities. The in-house knowledge of the subject matter may also be limited or outdated. The external expert is likely to be more current in knowledge and subject matter. GIA's leadership, including at least one representative from GIA's IT Audit, must play an active role on the project management team. This is to ensure that the agreed upon requirements and specifications are met and delivered.

BUILD, BUY, LEASE, OR FEE FOR SERVICE AGREEMENT

The dynamic nature of the operating environment is a key factor in the financing decision of GIA's automation initiative. The financing decision will be whether to build, buy, lease, or enter into a fee or a software-as-a-service (SAAS) agreement with a service provider for the automation. The CAE and leaders of GIA focus must be on a system that is user-friendly, current, flexible, adaptable, scalable, and portable. These features are important to have to effectively meet the needs of an ever-changing operating environment. The features also enhance GIA's readiness, resilience, relevance, and value to the organization.

Building things from scratch is exciting and requires a creative and innovative mindset. However, the risks of building from scratch often outweigh the benefits. This is because building a system from scratch often tends to focus on what stakeholders would like to have rather than on what is needed. The build option is also usually costly and a source of delays in systems development projects. It is best to start off with building a basic system that addresses the core needs of GIA, stakeholders, and the organization. The core needs would include what staff need or must have to effectively perform their responsibilities and address the needs of stakeholders. The system should also include built-in redundancies and contingencies. This will enable GIA to quickly adjust and adapt to future changes in the operating environment. The risks of building a system from scratch include the following:

- Inadequate user requirements: Key stakeholders such as implementers, users, maintainers, and monitors, particularly those in the field, were not consulted for input on the automation initiative. What is most important to them must be considered in the decision making or project prioritization process.
- Significant upfront cash investment: Hardware and software development costs, while depreciable, are usually a significant investment for an organization. Such investments are at times postponed by organizations until it is mandatory or something major happens.
- Ineffective system design: This includes inadequate system security and data privacy and protection controls.
- Turnover of key project staff: The loss of key project staff and expertise can significantly delay an automation project.
- Delays and cost overruns: They are often a common event in major system development projects that must be effectively managed.

- Lack of system documentation: Costly maintenance issues due to lack of system documentation.
- Obsolescence: System becomes obsolete before the project is completed due to technological innovation. This is because of the emergence of more effective and efficient systems during the build.
- Economic downturn: Additional funding could be denied and/or deferred during an economic downturn. The project could also be scaled down, cut back, or cancelled.
- Inflexible, unscalable, and unportable: This is usually because of the narrow focus and rigidity of building a system from scratch.
- Limited life cycle: This is usually because of the introduction of new and more effective and efficient systems and applications mostly driven by technological innovations.
- Maintenance: The cost of maintaining the system over time often outweighs the benefits. This is usually due to a scarcity of parts and expertise. Technology service providers usually stop supporting the outdated version of a system after a period. This is usually after a new and more effective and efficient system replaces the old.

Buying an off-the-shelve system mitigates certain risks compared to building a system from scratch. This includes the following:

- Ineffective system design
- Turnover of key project staff
- Delays and cost overruns
- Lack of system documentation
- Economic downturn

There are areas where building and buying a system share similar risks. The similar risks include the following:

- Significant upfront cash investment
- Obsolescence
- Limited scalability and portability
- Limited life cycle
- Unsupportable system

Leasing or a fee for service agreement, including SAAS, is the growing trend in technology services. This option is attractive to stakeholders, especially in an ever-changing operating environment. Technology services such as SAAS and the Cloud mitigate certain risks associated with building or buying a system off the shelf. The risks mitigated include the following:

- Significant upfront cash investment
- Obsolescence
- Limited scalability and portability

- Ineffective system design
- Turnover of key project staff
- Delays and cost overruns
- Limited life cycle
- Unsupportable system
- Lack of system documentation

There are also risks associated with leasing or a fee for service agreement, including SAAS. A fee for service or SAAS agreement is typical of a web or cloud-based service. The CAE must conduct a due diligence review of the technology service provider before entering into a service agreement. Reliable sources of a service provider's performance and exposure to risks include the following:

- Past and current customers
- Quality assurance review report
- The external auditor annual audit report
- The external auditor management letter comments

The CAE must ensure that GIA receives a copy of the most recent quality assurance review report from the service provider. The risks associated with leasing or a fee for services agreement include the following:

- Ability of the service provider to support the organization wherever it operates
- Solvency and financial stability of the service provider
- Qualification to deliver the service, including training, experience, and expertise
- Compliance with applicable laws and regulations
- System and data integrity
- Data protection and privacy
- Access to program and source code
- System availability, accessibility, and reliability

The benefits available from leasing or a fee for service agreement, including SAAS, are more attractive than a build or buy option. This is because the ownership and management of IT risks, for the most part, shift to the technology service provider. The benefits include the following:

- Low initial cash investment: There is no major purchase of hardware or software required such as servers. There are different negotiable pricing arrangements. The pricing arrangements usually include an annual license fee and a monthly usage and service fee. The monthly usage and service fee may be based on the number of users and/or transactions, service, and maintenance fee.
- Access to current technology: Service provider will be forced to keep up and offer new and current technology to remain competitive.
- Automatic system upgrades: Automatic upgrades are usually available for new versions and patches.

- Accessibility: The system is available 24/7 usually where the internet is available.
- Usually scalable and portable: Restrictions on adding locations and significantly increasing activities are unlikely.
- Maintenance: Usually provided by the service provider, including system upgrades and patches.
- Cybersecurity risk: The responsibility is shared with the service provider.

VALUE OF THE AUTOMATION OF GIA TO THE ORGANIZATION

The transformation of GIA's operation from a manual or a hybrid to an automated-driven operating environment is just the beginning of enhanced value creation, preservation, and protection journey of GIA. The following is a summary of key benefits of the automation to GIA and the organization as shown below in Table 8.2.

TABLE 8.2
Summary of Key Benefits of Automation to GIA and the Organization

GIA	Organization
• Enhances the effectiveness and efficiency of GIA and potential cost savings in the future from staff redundancies • Enables and enhances GIA's agility • Enables team members of GIA to be more proactive • Provides secured centralized database of audit reports, findings, recommendations, management response, and action(s) taken • Enables the performance of more robust data mining and analytics • Enables supervisors to observe the performance and status of fieldwork online and in real time in the Cloud • Enables supervisors to provide feedback as the work progresses instead of waiting until the work is completed • Enables the integration and connectivity with other relevant organizational systems and databases, such as risk management, finance, accounting, and compliance • Enables quick access and sharing of information and data • Enables the use of other advanced technology such as Machine Learning, Robotics, Data Visualization, Artificial Intelligence, Internet of Things, and ChatGPT	• Enhances potential cost savings to the organization in the future from staff redundancies • Notifies stakeholders electronically as soon as a finding is deemed valid to share for feedback, agreement, and suggested corrective action • Provides access to audit findings and recommendations to stakeholders 24/7on a need-to-know basis • Provides a valuable source of information for data mining, analytics, and trend analysis • Enables the integration and connectivity with other relevant organizational systems and databases, such as risk management, finance, accounting, and compliance • Enables quick access and sharing of information and data

CHAPTER SUMMARY

A manual or a hybrid-driven GIA operation is a risk to its survival and sustainability in a dynamic operating environment. The CAE and leaders of GIA must evolve and transform from a manual or a hybrid to an automated operating environment. Automation is the gateway to a wide range of opportunities to enhance GIA's effectiveness, efficiency, and value to the organization. The CAE must research and learn from others who have experience automating a GIA operation.

Automation of GIA is a strategic and transformational undertaking that requires the support of key stakeholders. The CAE must informally test the appetite of trusted stakeholders on the idea of automating GIA's operation. The preliminary support of senior leaders of support functions is usually required to expedite the approval process of a strategic or major organizational change initiative. The approval and success of the automation are unlikely if the CAE does not have the preliminary support of key stakeholders. The CAE must also share and obtain support from staff and stakeholders most impacted by the automation, particularly those at the regional and local office levels. They often know what will work best in their operating environment. Additionally, the CAE must also ensure that steps are taken to maintain the support of key stakeholders.

Effectively managing the automation of GIA requires prioritizing and effectively managing the areas and activities that are most important in driving the success of the initiative. The areas and activities that are most important in driving the success of the automation include the following:

- Plan
- Communication
- Execution
- Risk
- Change management
- Monitoring and reporting
- Post-implementation review

Stabilizing and normalizing the transformation of GIA to an automated operating environment and making the changes stick is a journey. It is a journey due to the length of time it takes for the changes to stabilize and normalize. This is because it often results in a change in culture, including values, customs, and norms of the organization. It usually requires a change in the mindset of staff, including the way staff think, engage, communicate, and work with others. Patience is required as the change in the culture of the organization usually takes years to adopt, stabilize, and normalize. Additionally, the change must be communicated in a manner that is easy to understand, memorize, and embrace. This is necessary for the initiative to remain at the forefront of the thinking and activities of staff to make the change sustainable.

The dynamic nature of the operating environment is a key factor in the financing decision of GIA's automation initiative. The options include build, buy, and lease or a fee for service agreement. Building anything from scratch is exciting and requires a creative and innovative mindset. Buying an off-the-shelve system mitigates certain key risks of building a system from scratch. There are areas where building and buying a system share similar risks. Leasing or a fee for service agreement, including SAAS, is the growing trend in technology services. The benefits are usually more attractive to stakeholders than the build or buy option.

The transformation of GIA's operation from a manual to an automated-driven operating environment is just the beginning of the value creation and preservation journey of GIA. The automation of GIA's operation is the foundation for a technology-driven GIA-operating environment. It will be the gateway to a wide range of opportunities for the CAE to use technology to enhance GIA's effectiveness, efficiency, and value to the organization.

9 Establishment of an Enterprise Risk Management Program

INTRODUCTION

Establishment of an enterprise risk management (ERM) program is a signal to staff and stakeholders of the board of directors (herein after the board) and management's commitment to effectively manage risks to the organization. The establishment of the program is a journey due to the length of time it takes for the changes to stabilize and normalize. It is integral to the development of an organization's risk culture as it paves the way for stakeholders to proactively engage and collaborate on mitigating risks. Managing risk must become the responsibility of everyone affiliated with the organization to maximize the value of the ERM program to the organization.

The oversight of an organization's ERM program is one of the most important board governance and management responsibilities. One of the first steps in adopting an organization's ERM program is the development of a risk management policy (RMP) and risk appetite statement (RAS). The agility, effectiveness, and efficiency of the organization's ERM program are enhanced with the implementation of governance, risk, and compliance (GRC) software. This is necessary to effectively manage the myriad of risks and related internal controls across the organization. It also paves the way for an integrated ERM system and approach to effectively manage risks. Managing risk is a dynamic and ongoing activity. Gone are the days of annual risk assessment.

The purpose of this chapter is to provide advice and guidance on the importance and value to an organization of adopting an ERM program. Topics covered include the following:

- Overview of COSO ERM – Integrated Framework
- The ERM journey
- Responsibility and accountability for risk
- RMP and RAS
- Key elements of an effective ERM program
- Managing the ERM implementation process
- Making the change sustainable
- ERM in action
- Role of internal audit

DOI: 10.1201/9781003207559-9

- Integrated ERM system
- Value of ERM to the organization

Key learnings from the chapter include the following:

- Contribution of COSO to ERM
- Reasons ERM is a journey and not a walk around the block
- Value of the RMP and RAS
- Understanding the key elements of an effective ERM program
- Value of internal audit to the organization's ERM program
- Importance of obtaining and maintaining support for the ERM initiative
- Importance of prioritizing and effectively managing the key areas of the ERM initiative
- Value in adopting an integrated ERM system and approach to manage risk
- Importance of making the change sustainable

OVERVIEW OF COSO ERM – INTEGRATED FRAMEWORK

The Committee of Sponsoring Organizations (COSO) of the Treadway Commission, a joint venture of five private-sector professional organizations, was created in 1987. The mission was to develop and provide integrated guidance on internal controls. The five private-sector professional organizations are as follows:

- American Accounting Association
- American Institute of Certified Public Accountants
- Financial Executive International
- Institute of Internal Auditors (IIA)
- Institute of Management Accountants

COSO Enterprise Risk Management – Integrated Framework was published in 2004. The purpose of the publication was to help entities better protect and enhance stakeholder value.[1] COSO updated the 2004 Framework in June 2017 and renamed it "COSO Enterprise Risk Management (ERM) - Integrating with Strategy and Performance." It addresses the evolution of enterprise risk management and the need for organizations to improve their approach to managing risk to meet the demands of an evolving business environment.[2] It also highlights the importance of considering risk in both the strategy-setting process and driving performance.[3] The Framework consists of five interrelated components, which are supported by 20 principles. The description and relationships of the five components and 20 principles are illustrated in Figure 9.1 below.

The COSO ERM – Integrated Framework provides an enterprise-wide and holistic approach to risk management (RM). It is a roadmap for the implementation of an integrated and agile ERM program. Managers can use it to effectively manage risk. Additionally, it sets the standards and paved the way for organizations to comply with the 2001 Sarbanes-Oxley Act. The Act was created in response to the gaps in GRC in corporate RM. The gaps were evident in the failures of Fortune 500 companies, including Tyco, Enron, World Com, and Computer Associate.

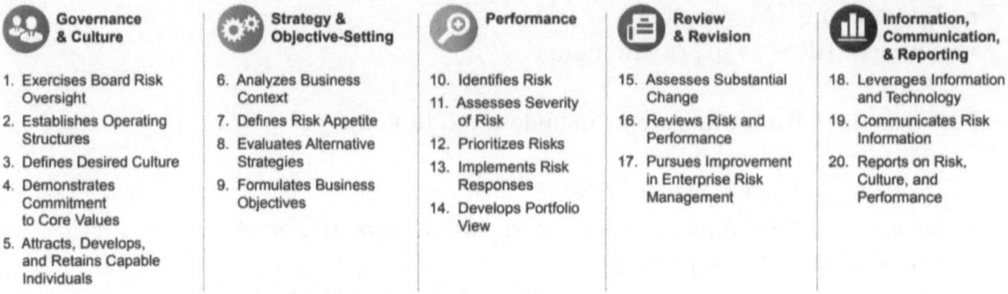

FIGURE 9.1 COSO Enterprise Risk Management – Integrating with Strategy and Performance.[4] (Permission granted by COSO)

The benefits of applying the framework to boards, management, and other internal and external stakeholders of the organization include the following:

- Provides a structured approach for managing and evaluating the effectiveness of an ERM program
- Provides reasonable assurance that resources are allocated to high-risk areas and core activities
- Signifies the board and senior management's commitment to managing risks to the organization
- Provides guidance to boards and management on effectively performing their responsibility for risk
- Enhances stakeholders' confidence and trust in the management of risks to the organization
- Ensures risk is considered in strategy setting and evaluation of performance[5]
- Assists organizations in anticipating and mitigating risks to strategy and performance[6]

THE ENTERPRISE RISK MANAGEMENT (ERM) JOURNEY

The establishment of an ERM program is a journey due to the length of time it takes for the changes to stabilize and normalize. It usually takes three to five years to implement and requires a change in the mindset and culture, including the values, customs, and norms of an organization. A change in the mindset and culture also takes years for an organization to adopt, stabilize, and normalize. It requires patience, understanding, focus, perseverance, and commitment. However, the COVID-19 Pandemic has proven that strategic and transformational change can be done much quicker when there is a will and commitment. For example, the major change from working in an office to working from home, virtual meetings, wearing a mask, developing, and approving a vaccine for use in less than a year are strategic and transformational changes. The development and approval of a vaccine for use normally take years and decades in some cases to develop for use. People, organizations, and governments across the globe had to quickly respond and adapt to the change to stay healthy, safe, and survive during the COVID-19 Pandemic.

The decision to establish an ERM program is usually made at the highest level of an organization. This is because it is integral to the governance of an organization. The establishment of an RM program is also required by law in many countries. Regulatory and standard setting bodies emphasize the importance and necessity for organizations to institute a structured RM program. They include the Security and Exchange Commission (SEC) and the Basel Committee on Banking Supervision (BCBS). The SEC oversees and regulates publicly traded companies in the United States. The BCBS is a series of international banking regulations known as the Basel Accord. The Basel Accord emphasizes the importance of implementing systematic and organized RM practices within banking and financial institutions.

The decision to establish an ERM program is usually a mutual agreement and commitment of the board and senior management of the organization. It includes the adoption, implementation, management, and oversight of the program. The board and senior management's commitment set the tone at the top of the organization of the importance and support for the program. This contributes to the support and cooperation of management and staff across the organization for the program. Management and staff usually join the journey when the message comes from the board and senior management.

The board and senior management support are critical to the successful establishment of an organization's ERM program. They must ensure that the program is provided with the required resources to enable it to operate effectively and efficiently. This includes the establishment of an RM function and support for the development and implementation of an RMP and RAS. The responsibility of the function includes the following:

- Providing assurance and advice to the board to assist in the performance of their governance oversight responsibilities for RM
- Providing assurance and advice to management and process owners to assist them in performing their RM responsibilities
- Providing guidance, tools, and risk awareness training to stakeholders
- Collecting, coordinating, and updating the organization's risk dashboard and profile
- Providing periodic RM reports to stakeholders

The implementation of an ERM program is strategic. It is strategic because it is integral to the governance of the organization as well as the following:

- Requires rethinking and reshaping how the organization manages risk
- Impacts the governance of the organization as the audit and/or risk management committee relies on the assurance and advice that RM provides in performing their oversight responsibilities for governance
- Requires senior management and board approval
- Cross-cutting activity that impacts and applies to all employees in an organization
- Assists stakeholders in making informed decisions
- Usually requires additional investment

The implementation of an ERM program is also transformational. It is transformational because of the following:

- Usually requires a rethinking, and reshaping of culture, including values, customs, and norms
- Usually requires a change in the mindset of staff and stakeholders
- Impacts the way staff think, engage, communicate, and work with each other

RESPONSIBILITY AND ACCOUNTABILITY FOR RISK

Managing risk must become the responsibility of everyone affiliated with the organization. The effectiveness of an organization's ERM program requires the participation of everyone. It is everybody's business, including the board, senior management, managers, employees, and volunteers. Senior management includes the CEO and his or her direct reports. Risks exist everywhere and there is some level of risk in every decision that is made at all levels of an organization. The risks need to be effectively managed, including identified, assessed, mitigated, monitored, and reported periodically. While senior management is responsible and accountable for the implementation and maintenance of an organization's ERM program, the ultimate accountability for risk rests with the board of the organization.

The oversight of an organization's ERM program is one of the most important board governance roles and management responsibilities of an organization. The board, in collaboration with the CEO and the senior management team, is responsible for the governance of the organization. This includes developing the mission, vision, strategic plan, governance structure, and policies of the organization. The board's oversight responsibilities are usually delegated to a sub-committee of the board to facilitate effective oversight of governance programs. While having a separate risk committee may be considered optimal, it is not unusual to see the oversight role performed by an audit and risk sub-committee. The specific form and composition of the oversight committee depend on industry standards and practices. In some industries, audit and risk committees are combined, while in others, it is a requirement that the risk committee exclusively concentrates on risk matters without taking on other oversight roles. To ensure effectiveness, members of the risk committee must possess the requisite industry experience and qualifications. This enables the committee to effectively scrutinize, ask thought-provoking questions, and advise management on RM decisions.

The board governance oversight role of an ERM program requires engaging periodically or as needed, listening, learning, sharing, and providing guidance to the CEO and senior management. Engaging with senior management also includes the following:

- Ensuring that the organization has an effective RMP and RAS
- Participating in enterprise risk assessment and brainstorming sessions as needed instead of annually
- Ensuring that the RM function is placed at a level in the hierarchy of the organization where the CRO has the authority to perform independently and objectively
- Ensuring that the function is resourced with competent staff and technological tools

- Receiving periodic reports and presentations from leaders of assurance functions on the status of the ERM program, including the following:
  - New and emerging risks
  - Effectiveness of the ERM program
  - Compliance with the RMP and RAS
- Following up on the implementation of outstanding recommendations

Listening, learning, sharing, and providing guidance to the CEO and senior management include asking relevant and thought-provoking questions. This includes the following:

- Does the organization have an RMP and RAS?
- Does the organization have a risk profile and dashboard?
- Are there any significant increase or decrease in new and emerging risks, opportunities, and mitigation plans and activities?
- What is working well, needs to be improved or changed?
- Is risk assessment a standard requirement of management's decision-making process?
- Is the ERM risk database timely updated with the results of internal audits?
- What risks keep you awake at night?
- Are resources adequate to effectively manage risks to the achievement of the objectives of the organization?
- Are procedures developed and implemented by managers to comply with the RMP and RAS?
- How can we help you?

The CEO is accountable to the board for the establishment and overall effectiveness and efficiency of the organization's governance programs, including the ERM program. The CEO usually delegates the responsibility for developing, implementing, and maintaining governance programs to members of the senior management team. Senior management is responsible for developing, implementing, and maintaining effective governance programs for their area(s) of responsibility. This includes governance structures, management policies, processes, and procedures to ensure compliance with board policies. Senior management may, in turn, delegate the responsibility to managers in their reporting line. They satisfy their responsibility by providing oversight over the development, implementation, maintenance, and effectiveness of the program by managers. Senior management is also responsible for reporting periodically to the CEO on the status of their governance programs. The information is incorporated into the CEO's periodic report on the organization's governance programs to the board.

Managers are responsible for developing and implementing processes and procedures to ensure compliance with board policies. The processes and procedures must include the local context and operating environment in which the organization operates. This is because of differences in local laws and regulations, customs and norms, and economic conditions compared to the home country of the organization. For example, a manager's authorization limit of $50K in a developed country may be too high in a developing country. Compliance with local laws and regulations takes priority over compliance with board policies. However, managers must obtain approval for modifications or exceptions to board policies to align with the local context and operating environment.

Managers must conduct risk assessment of their area(s) of responsibility on an ongoing basis. This is because risk is continuously changing. Conducting risk assessment on an ongoing basis is necessary for managers to stay current and be proactive in addressing changes in risks, including existing, new, and emerging risks. Delays in addressing new and emerging risks can significantly impact the organization in avoiding disasters or missing opportunities. The risk assessment process includes identifying, evaluating, and prioritizing the risks to manage. The risk assessment can be done in brainstorming sessions with stakeholders. Managers should be required to report periodically or as needed to their supervisors and senior management on the status of risks to their area(s) of operation.

Clarity over roles, responsibilities, and accountability for providing oversight and assurance enhances the quality, effectiveness, and efficiency of the organization's ERM program. This includes the reliability, accuracy, and consistency of the information being provided to stakeholders by the leaders of assurance functions. Clarity also eliminates confusion and the assumption that required activities are being performed by others when in fact they are not being performed by anyone. The IIA's Three Lines Model is an excellent depiction of the roles that the governing body, management – The First Line, support functions – The Second Line, and internal audit – The Third Line play in an organization. The model offers a structured framework of the roles, responsibility, and accountability of the board, management, and assurance functions in organizations.

The IIA's Three Lines Model is illustrated below in Figure 9.2.

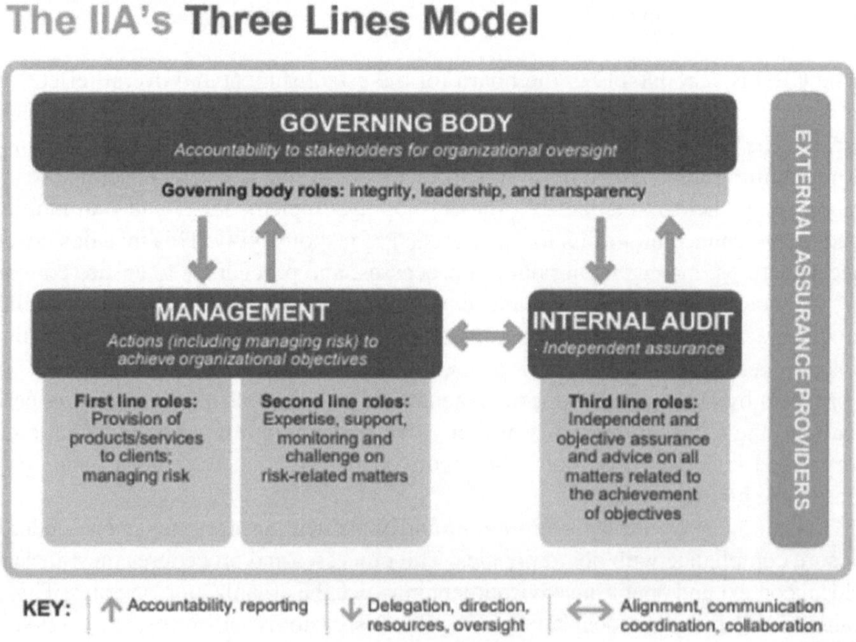

FIGURE 9.2 The IIA Three Lines Model – An Update of the Three Lines of Defense.[7] (Permission granted by The IIA)

RISK MANAGEMENT POLICY AND RISK APPETITE STATEMENT

The board, in collaboration with the CEO and senior management, is responsible for ensuring the development and adoption of the governing policies of the organization. The oversight of the development of board policies is often delegated to a sub-committee of the board. Senior management often drafts board policies for the board's review and approval. The board may also engage consultants to draft board policies for their review and approval. The sub-committee of the board usually collaborates with senior management on finalizing board policies. Once finalized, senior management or the board sub-committee prepares a board resolution for the adoption of the policy by the full board.

One of the first steps in adopting an organization's ERM program is the development of an RMP and an RAS. This is to assist in providing reasonable assurance that risks to the organization are being effectively managed by management. The risks must be managed in accordance with the organization's RMP and RAS. The RMP provides high-level guidance on what is expected of stakeholders taking risks on behalf of the organization. This includes the board, senior management, managers, and employees of the organization. The RMP brings clarity to the ERM program. It also serves as a common ground for stakeholders to understand and align with the program. It would be chaotic trying to implement an ERM program without first developing the RMP. An RMP is also a signal to stakeholders of the board and senior management's commitment and support for the program. The RMP typically contains the following:

- Sponsor and owner
- Effective date and applicability
- Purpose
- Roles, responsibility, authority, and accountability
- Specific or key guidance on what is expected
- Definitions
- Revised date
- History of changes

An organization must manage its risk appetite to curb greed and the temptation of stakeholders crossing the red line. The RAS provides the boundaries for decision making. It assists in ensuring that stakeholders' risk-taking aligns with the risk appetite and tolerance of the organization. Alignment is often conveyed through tolerance levels established for specific risks. Terms like "zero," "low," "moderate," and "high" risk appetite are commonly used in qualitative RASs. When the RAS is expressed in quantitative terms, it defines specific limits beyond which the organization and its employees must not venture.

The concept of risk appetite can often be challenging to grasp, particularly for stakeholders without a background in RM, audit, or finance. Therefore, it is essential for the RM function to organize awareness training sessions aimed at fostering a shared understanding of the ERM program and other RM concepts across the organization. Emphasis on awareness becomes even more pronounced for organizations in the early stages of implementing an ERM program. The sessions may need to be more frequent in the early stages of the program compared to organizations with well-established and a mature ERM program.

Providing stakeholders' guidance and awareness training on the risk appetite of the organization protects the organization from stakeholders engaging in transactions that can bring the organization to its demise. As mentioned earlier, risk is the business of everyone affiliated with the organization. Therefore, it is important for all stakeholders to know the boundaries and where to draw the line when it relates to the level of risk to take on behalf of the organization. It should be noted that there are organizations that may be reluctant to document and/or disclose their risk appetite. This is to minimize the risk of loss to the organization from abuse of the disclosure of the organization's risk appetite. For example, fraudsters abusing the automatic write-offs of shortages of cash or shrinkage of inventory under $5 as it may not be cost-effective for the organization to investigate.

An organization usually has four choices to make regarding its risk appetite. The organization may either choose to manage, share, accept, or avoid risks as follows:

- Manage the risk by identifying, assessing, mitigating, monitoring, and periodically reporting on the status to stakeholders
- Share the risk by acquiring insurance coverage or partnering with other organizations as the risk would be too much for the organization to assume on its own should the risk materialize
- Accept where the likelihood and impact of the risk are low
- Avoid the risk by not engaging in a transactions or activities that exposes the organization to significant risks such as fraud

The effectiveness of the implementation of the RMP and RAS depends on how well it is communicated and shared. This includes the following:

- Communicating the RMP and RAS in a manner that is easy to understand, memorize, and embrace
- Sharing and distributing the RMP and the RAS to all employees
- Training, including lunch and learning sessions
- Including the RMP and RAS in new board and employee orientation program

The board must periodically review and reapprove board policies. This is to ensure that the policies are still relevant. The board sub-committee or senior management usually make policy change recommendations to the board for review and approval. A relevant policy today may not be relevant tomorrow in a dynamic operating environment.

KEY ELEMENTS OF AN ERM PROGRAM

The agility, effectiveness, and efficiency of an ERM program are enhanced when the leader of RM reports to the highest possible level of senior management in the organization. It empowers and enhances RM's leadership authority to effectively perform its responsibilities. It is also an indication of the importance of the ERM program to the organization. Additionally, it is an indication of the board and senior management's support and commitment for the program. There will be fewer direct and indirect reporting lines or hurdles to cross to elevate and share important issues with senior management and the board. This also eliminates the risk of important issues being suppressed, modified, manipulated, downplayed, ignored, or deemed insignificant. It is always better to receive information firsthand rather than second- or thirdhand.

The agility of an ERM program is critical to the effectiveness, efficiency, survival, and sustainability of the organization. Agility enhances the ability of stakeholders to quickly think, pivot, respond, and adapt to change or do things differently. Additionally, it assists in minimizing risks to its business, operating, reporting, and compliance objectives and capitalizes on opportunities in a competitive and fast-paced operating environment.

Technological innovations and tools assist in enhancing the agility, effectiveness, efficiency, and value of the organization's ERM program. The tools enable stakeholders to quickly think, pivot, respond, and proactively adapt to change. Information is readily available for stakeholders to quickly access for data mining, analytics, and trend analysis. The results assist in driving the agility and proactiveness of stakeholders. This includes mitigating risks, making more informed decisions, and capitalizing on opportunities that come along with change and risk. Technological tools include GRC software, data analytics (DA), machine learning (ML), robotics (BOTS), robotics process automation (RPA), and artificial intelligence (AI). The enhancements include the following:

- Provides a single source of RM activities
- Increases the speed and ease how information is collected, analyzed, and available to stakeholders
- Makes information easy to access, understand, and utilize
- Reduces the complexity and enhance transparency across the organization
- Identifies hidden issues such as ineffective use of resources on low-risk areas instead of on the core

There are certain tools that must be present in an ERM's toolkit, including the following:

- GRC software: This is an integrated software that enables leaders of assurance functions to work collaboratively. This enables them to effectively assist stakeholders mitigate risk to the organization and make more informed decisions.
- Risk profile: List of the top or significant risks to an organization that the board and senior management should focus on or have on their radar. The focus usually ranges between the top five and 20 risks to an organization and includes the following:
  - Compliance with laws and regulations
  - Cybersecurity
  - Data security and privacy

  - Financial
  - Fraud
  - Geopolitical
  - Information technology
  - Operational
  - Reputation
  - Safety and security
  - Strategic
  - Succession plan
  - Terrorism
- Risk dashboard: The risk dashboard usually contains a description of the strategy and business, operating, reporting, and compliance objectives as well as the following:
  - Risks, including inherent risks
  - Risk rankings
  - Mitigation plan and activities
  - Residual risks
  - Residual risk mitigation plan and activities
- Risk heat maps: Used to show the ranking or status of a particular risk whether the risk is high, medium, or low. The status is based on the likelihood or frequency and impact or severity of the risk.
- Risk traffic lights: Used to show the direction of a particular risk whether it is trending up or down.
- Risk arrows: Used to show the change or movement of a particular risk where an increase is represented by the upward arrow; no change is represented by a flat line, and a decrease in a particular risk is represented by a downward arrow. ERM tools make it easy for stakeholders to quickly obtain, understand, and utilize information provided by RM to assist in making more informed decisions.

The key requirements of an agile, effective, and efficient ERM program includes the following:

- Support of senior management and the board
- Participation of the board and management at all levels of the organization
- Existence of the following:
  - RM committee
  - RMP and RAS
  - Competent ERM leadership and team
  - RM subject matter expert or point person is at each office
  - Risk profile and dashboards for all the reporting entities within the organization
  - Centralized ERM risk database
  - ERM process gate keepers and subject matter experts to review, analyze, and classify risk information submitted for entry to the ERM system and alerting relevant stakeholders on a need-to-know basis

- Provision of the required resources to support the organization's ERM program
- Require risk assessment as a step in the organization's decision-making process
- Require managers to conduct risk assessment and develop a risk profile and dashboard for their area(s) of responsibility
- Utilize risk heat map and risk traffic lights in reporting on the status of risks

MANAGING THE ERM IMPLEMENTATION PROCESS

Effective management of the ERM program implementation process requires that it be effectively planned. This requires prioritizing and effectively managing the areas and activities that are most important in driving the success of the program. The areas and activities include the following:

- Plan
- Communication
- Execution
- Risks
- Resistance
- Expectation and failures
- Monitoring
- Reporting
- Post-implementation review

The following is an overview of each of the preceding (refer to Chapters 7 and 8 for more details).

- The plan is the roadmap for effectively managing the implementation of the ERM program. It paves the way and minimizes risks to the successful implementation of the program. Effective planning ensures that the implementation process is shared, collaborative, and includes input from staff most impacted by the program. This includes the buy-in and support of staff and stakeholders implementing, using, maintaining, monitoring, reporting, and complying with the requirements of the program. Staff and stakeholders, particularly those at the regional and local offices, buy-in and support can easily get lost or eroded if their input is ignored.
- Communication is one of the most important elements for ensuring clarity, agreement, and alignment with the objectives of the ERM program. Effective communication of messages requires confirming and periodically reconfirming mission critical messages. Miscommunicating and misunderstanding of the objectives of the program, required coordination, and cooperation can be costly. The risk of miscommunication and misunderstandings is minimized by ongoing communication. Ongoing communication is critical for staff and stakeholders to stay connected, current, and informed.

- Effective execution is converting the plan into action. The key objective of the execution phase is the successful implementation of the program. This requires a competent and an experienced manager to lead and oversee the execution. It must be led by a professional who possesses a strong background and understanding of how an ERM program operates. This includes professionals with risk, change, and project management experience and possesses a certification in RM or a related field such as auditing or finance. Executing includes directing, supporting, and motivating the team. It also includes monitoring and reporting periodically on the status of the activities and progress of the implementation.
- Risk must be effectively managed to provide reasonable assurance of the successful implementation of the ERM program. Risks to the program must be identified, assessed, mitigated, monitored, and the status reported periodically.
- There is always going to be some resistance to change. There will be early adopters and supporters as well as skeptics who will take a wait-and-see attitude. There are others who will oppose the change and try to sabotage it. The leader of the ERM program must collaborate with staff and stakeholders resisting the change. The leader must also ensure that there is a plan in place to maintain and strengthen the support for the program. The plan should include obtaining expert advice or a second opinion on major decisions.
- The leader of the ERM program must set the expectation of the possibility of failure. This requires sharing with staff and stakeholders upfront the possibility of failures and mitigation plans. Failures during the journey of a strategic or major initiative or project are not a matter of if but when. This may include missed deadlines, setbacks, mistakes, delays, and cost overruns. The leader of the ERM program must learn and act quickly to address failures before they become disasters.
- Monitoring is done to ensure that the implementation of the program is progressing as planned as well as effectively, efficiently, and in compliance with required laws, regulations, policies, and procedures.
- Reporting periodically is required to keep stakeholders informed of the status of the implementation of the program.
- Post-implementation review is necessary to ensure that the program is operating as expected as well as effectively and efficiently.

MAKING THE CHANGE SUSTAINABLE

The transformation to an ERM program and risk culture is a journey due to the time it takes for the changes to stick. Patience and understanding are required as the change in the culture of an organization takes years to adopt, stabilize, and normalize. It often results in a change in culture, including values, customs, and norms of an organization. It usually requires a change in the mindset and attitude of staff. The changes usually impact the way staff think, engage, communicate, and work with team members and stakeholders.

The transformation to an ERM program must remain at the forefront of staff and stakeholders' thinking and activities to make the changes stick. It is easy for staff and stakeholders to continue or return to business as usual if the rollout of the program is not effectively managed. The rollout must be well planned, communicated, and staff and stakeholders trained, and supported throughout the rollout process. There should also be periodic status meetings and reports to update staff and stakeholders on the progress of the implementation. This includes updates on what is working well, what needs to change, or stopped.

The transformation must be communicated in a manner that is easy to understand, memorize, and embrace. Simplifying and breaking down the key elements of the program into memorable one liner make it easier and more likely to be long-lasting. A complex transformation process is a risk to the successful implementation of the program. How the program is communicated and rolled out across the organization is critical to the successful implementation. It includes transparency, clarity, and understanding of the objectives, risks, and rewards.

There are steps that management can take to make the changes stick. The steps include the following:

- Appointment of change management champions to support departments, functions, and offices
- Create and share a one-page memoizable flyer of the key elements of the ERM program
- Post and display key elements of the program on the organization's website and communal areas
- Create a hotline where staff and stakeholders can call in with questions
- Provide refresher training
- Make the status update of the program a standing agenda item at team meetings
- Make the adoption of the ERM program a key performance indicator (KPI) for all staff
- Recognize and reward staff for outstanding performance
- Hold leaders accountable for the implementation of the program
- Create global dashboard of the status of the program and make it accessible to stakeholders
- Publish monthly global newsletter on the status of the implementation of the program
- Send global alerts to stakeholders of achievements of major milestones of the implementation

ERM IN ACTION

Effective RM is an ever-changing and ongoing management activity. Gone are the days of annual risk assessment. Organizations cannot delay risk assessment to an annual or periodic exercise in an ever-changing operating environment as risk is also ever-changing. The internal and external operating environments must be monitored constantly for new and emerging risks as well as changes in existing risks. This will ensure that resources are allocated to the risks that pose the greatest threat to the objectives of the organization.

The ERM operating process is a multiple-step activity. The process must be user-friendly to ensure that everyone affiliated with the organization can participate. The design of the ERM process must include clear and easy-to-understand instructions. It must also be interactive and populated with pop-up screens to make it easy for everyone to use. The process should also include built-in automated procedures to ensure compliance with the RMP and RAS. The preceding is necessary for ERM to be the business of everyone affiliated with the organization. The ERM process includes the following:

Step I: Obtain, document, and confirm understanding of the mission, vision, strategy, and objectives of the organization or the reporting entity.

Step II: Identify risks, including inherent risks, to the organization.

Step III: Assess the risks by evaluating the likelihood and impact and prioritize risk mitigation based on available resources.

Step IV: Revisit and assess the relevance and effectiveness of existing internal controls in mitigating prioritized risks.

Step V: Keep existing or implement internal controls to mitigate prioritized risks to an acceptable level in accordance with the organization's risk appetite and tolerance.

Step VI: Assess residual risks and the effectiveness of existing internal controls in mitigating the risks.

Step VII: Keep existing or implement internal controls to mitigate prioritized residual risks to an acceptable level.

Step IIX: Monitor the movement of risks and the effectiveness of the mitigation plans and activities, including being on the alert for new and emerging risks and opportunities to improve and add value to the organization.

Step IX: Update on an ongoing basis the risk profile and dashboard of the organization and its reporting entities based on the movement in the rankings and trend of risks.

Step X: Periodically report on the status of the effectiveness of mitigation plans and activities, including new and emerging risks, and opportunities.

ROLE OF INTERNAL AUDIT

The chief audit executive (CAE) is responsible for performing independent and objective audits of the organization's ERM program. The audits provide stakeholders with assurance and advice, including insight and foresight, regarding the effectiveness of the program. This assists the board and senior management in performing their governance oversight and management, responsibilities, respectively, for the program. The areas that GIA provides assurance and advice on include the following:

- Effectiveness of the rollout and implementation of the RMP and the RAS
- Effectiveness of the organization's ERM program
- Independence and objectivity of the program

- Effectiveness of policies, processes, and procedures to ensure compliance with the RMP and RAS
- Modifications and exceptions to the RMP and the RAS are properly approved
- Accessibility and reliability of the information in the ERM's database
- Emerging risks and improvement opportunities
- Adequacy and use of ERM resources

GIA's audits assist in preserving the integrity and credibility of the ERM program. GIA's independent and objective audit of the ERM program provides assurance and advice on the integrity and credibility of the program and the information it produces. Reliability and quick and easy access to risk information are of utmost importance to stakeholders in an operating environment where risk is constantly changing. Stakeholders rely on the information to assist them in making informed decisions to mitigate risks to the achievement of the objectives of the organization. This is also to capitalize on opportunities to enhance value creation and preservation arising from new risks.

ERM's leadership must leverage GIA's audit results to enhance the reliability of the information in ERM's risk database. This includes the accuracy, currency, and usefulness of the information. ERM's process and procedures should include a step where GIA's audit findings, recommendations, management mitigation plans, and activities are timely uploaded to ERM's risk database. This must be done in real time once there is agreement with management on the findings and recommendations. This is particularly important in a fast-paced operating environment where the risk is constantly changing.

INTEGRATED ERM SYSTEM

The implementation of an integrated ERM system and approach for managing risk in a global organization provides one of the greatest values to an organization. It plays a vital role in building an effective organization's risk culture. It also enhances the holistic approach of the ERM program by making it easy for everyone to participate in mitigating risks to the organization. This is by allowing stakeholders to quickly access and share information and perform DA anywhere in the organization. This provides reasonable assurance that risks up, down, and across the organization are being managed. It also enhances the following:

- Risk awareness across the organization
- Engagement and collaboration on risks across the organization
- Alignment and agreement on significant risks to the organization's strategy and objectives
- Use of common language and risk terminology
- Standardization and consistent application of policies, processes, and procedures
- Transparency of staff contribution to the achievement of the objectives of the organization

An integrated system and approach to managing risks enhances the agility, effectiveness, and efficiency of an organization's ERM program. The enhancements include the following:

- Provide quick and easy access to risk information
- Assist stakeholders to quickly, think, pivot, and respond to risk
- Enable stakeholders to mine and analyze data across the organization within seconds and minutes
- Provide single source of reliable risk assessment for the organization
- Eliminate the duplication of risk assessment and assurance activities
- Drive the standardization of policies, processes, and procedures
- Enhance consistency in the processing and reporting of risk across the organization
- Enhance the quality of risk information and reports
- Ensure that the risk database is updated online and in real time
- Signal to internal and external stakeholders that the board and management are committed to effectively managing risks and preserving value
- Minimize complexity

A key element of an integrated ERM system is the risk database. It is the centralized repository of the myriad of risks and activities across an organization. The database usually contains the following information:

- Sponsors
- Risk owners
- Strategy and business, operating, reporting, and compliance objectives
- Risks to strategy and objectives
- Inherent risks
- Risk ranking or rating based on the impact and likelihood of the risk to the organization
- Mitigation plan and activities
- Residual risks

The integrated ERM system database is a fountain of knowledge and intelligence for the ERM program and stakeholders. It is the warehouse of the tens of thousands of risks and mitigation plans and activities identified by managers, staff, and stakeholders at all levels of the organization. The information is available for data mining and analysis by stakeholders. Senior leaders of assurance functions and decision makers anywhere in the organization where the internet is available can quickly access and use the information for making more informed decisions.

The knowledge and intelligence gained from the information include valuable insights and foresight into new and emerging risks, trends, and opportunities. The information enables management and stakeholders to be proactive in anticipating and quickly acting to mitigate risks to the strategy and objectives of the organization. It also assists management in making more informed decisions regarding the creation, preservation, and protection of organizational value. The information in the database is also a key source for determining the effectiveness of the organization's ERM's risk mitigation plans and activities, including the following:

- What mitigation controls are working well
- What mitigation controls are no longer effective, relevant, or need to be improved
- Assist in identifying new and emerging risks and trends

ERM tools such as the organization's risk profile, risk matrix, heat map, dashboard, and an integrated risk database enhance risk awareness and education at all levels of an organization. The common enemy to the achievement of an organization's business, operating, reporting, and compliance objectives is clear for everyone to see. Risk awareness will help to unite and motivate staff and stakeholders to work collaboratively to minimize risk, the common enemy.

An ERM system enhances the agility, effectiveness, and efficiency of an organization's assurance functions. This is by leveraging the information and data in the ERM system risk database. The leaders and team members of assurance functions must leverage the information in the database to enhance the quality of assurance services and to assist in:

- Providing clarity over roles and responsibilities for risk and assurance activities
- Minimizing confusion over the prioritization of risks
- Eliminating duplication of work
- Minimizing gaps in the performance of tasks
- Improving and enhancing consistency of reporting on risk
- Enhancing the focus on what is most important to stakeholders
- Reducing cost from the use of multiple to shared systems and applications

VALUE OF ERM TO AN ORGANIZATION

The COVID-19 Pandemic is a clear indicator that wherever there are risks, there are also opportunities. The focus of an organization's ERM program must not only be on risk but also on opportunities for value creation, preservation, and protection. For example, during the COVID-19 Pandemic, there were manufacturers who diversified their production to address the demand for hand sanitizers, ventilators, and face coverings. There were alcohol manufacturers making hand sanitizers, an auto manufacturer producing ventilators, and clothing manufacturers making face coverings.

The transformation of an organization to an ERM culture paves the way for stakeholders to proactively engage and collaborate. It is also an opportunity for stakeholders to broaden their knowledge and understanding of the organization as well as the following:

- Mission, vision, strategy, objectives, risks, and mitigation plan and activities
- What risks are most important to the organization and stakeholders
- What is working well and what needs to be improved or changed
- What keeps key stakeholders awake at night
- What stakeholders expect from ERM
- Any known emerging issues and risks

The benefits of an ERM program coupled with an integrated system and approach includes the following:

- Indicates to internal and external stakeholders that the board and management are committed to effectively managing risk and preserving value
- Enhances the agility of stakeholders
- Enhances agility, creativity, and innovation
- A single source and holistic database of information on risks to the organization
- Easy and quick access to the organization's risk information
- Enhances the effectiveness and efficiency of internal assurance function services
- Enables proactive internal audits and investigations
- Source of internal knowledge and intelligence
- Enhances the ability of the leaders of assurance functions and stakeholders to anticipate and paves the way for providing insight and foresight
- Enable the performance of robust DA and trend analysis
- Eliminates the multiple applications and risk assessments performed in an organization
- A key member and contributor to the assurance services functions of the organization, including the following:
    - Global internal audit
    - Compliance
    - Information security
    - Quality assurance
    - Investigations

CHAPTER SUMMARY

The transformation of an organization to an ERM program is integral to and paves the way for the development of an organization risk culture. It also paves the way for stakeholders to proactively engage and collaborate on risk. The transformation and implementation of an ERM program is a journey due to the length of time it takes for the changes to stabilize and normalize.

The decision to establish an ERM program is usually made at the highest level of the organization. It is a strategic and transformational undertaking that requires the board and senior management's buy-in, and support for the successful establishment of the program. To maximize the value of ERM, managing risk must become the responsibility of everyone affiliated with the organization. The ERM program is one of the most important board governance oversight roles and management responsibility of an organization. It requires engaging periodically or as needed, listening, learning, sharing, and providing guidance to senior management. This includes asking relevant and thought-provoking questions.

The COSO ERM guidance publications provide an enterprise-wide and holistic approach to RM. The guidance highlights the need for organizations to improve their approach to managing risk to meet the challenging demands of an ever-changing operating environment. The guidance also highlights the importance of considering risk in both the strategy-setting process and driving performance.[8] They also set the standards and paved the way for organizations to comply with the 2001 Sarbanes-Oxley Act.

One of the first steps in adopting an organization's ERM program is the development of an RMP and RAS. An organization must manage its risk appetite to curb greed and the temptation of staff and stakeholders crossing the red line. The effectiveness of the implementation of the RMP and RAS depends on how well it is communicated and shared. It is enhanced when the function reports to the highest possible level of senior management in the organization.

Management of the ERM initiative requires effective planning, communication, and execution of the initiative. Staff and stakeholders buy-in and support can easily get lost or eroded if their input is ignored. It also requires the effective management of risks, expectations and failures, and resistance to the ERM initiative. This requires a competent and experienced leader to oversee and lead the project team.

The transformation to a risk-culture operating environment is a journey due to the length of time it takes to stabilize and normalize the changes. The change initiative must remain at the forefront of staff and stakeholders' thinking and activities to make the changes stick. Change must be communicated in a manner that is easy to understand, memorize, and embrace.

Effective RM is an ever-changing and ongoing management activity. It requires the adoption of an ERM program coupled with an integrated system and approach. This approach provides one of the greatest values of an ERM program to a global organization. It enhances the agility, effectiveness, and efficiency of the program and value of assurance services to the organization. Additionally, an integrated ERM system and approach provides a fountain of knowledge and intelligence to an organization. Its integrated risk database is a comprehensive and single source of risk information. It is the repository of the organization's RM activities. The effectiveness of an organization's assurance service function is enhanced by leveraging the information in the risk database.

The ERM operating process is a multiple-step activity. The process must be user-friendly to ensure that everyone affiliated with the organization can participate. The design of the ERM process must include clear and easy-to-understand instructions. It must also be interactive and populated with pop-up screens to make it easy for everyone to use. The process should also include built-in automated procedures to ensure compliance with the RMP and RAS.

NOTES

1 COSO Enterprise Risk Management, Integrating with Strategy and Performance, Executive Summary, June 2017 Update, @WWW.COSO.org
2 Ibid
3 Ibid.
4 Ibid.
5 Ibid.
6 Ibid.
7 The IIA's Three Lines Model, An Update of the Three Lines of Defense.
8 COSO Enterprise Risk Management, Integrating with Strategy and Performance, Executive Summary, June 2017 Update, @WWW.COSO.org

10 Internal Controls as Stakeholders' Best Friend

INTRODUCTION

An organization's system of internal control is a vital element of the governance of an organization. It is one of the most important oversight and management responsibilities of the board of directors (hereinafter the board), senior management, and leaders of assurance functions. Setting the tone at the top of the organization of the value and importance of internal controls is critical in the implementation and maintenance of an effective system of internal control. An organization with an effective system of internal control is more likely to be successful than those that do not have one. It is the number one gatekeeper and mitigator of risks to the achievement of the objectives of an organization. Internal controls should be embraced and become the best friend of management and the board. It is what gives internal and external stakeholders comfort that risks to their interests are effectively managed.

The Committee of Sponsoring Organization (COSO) of the Tredway Commission defines internal controls as "a process carried out by an entity's board of directors, management, and other personnel, designed to provide reasonable assurance with respect to the achievement of objectives in operations, financial reporting, and risk with applicable laws and regulations."[1] There are usually thousands of internal controls to mitigate risks to achieving the objectives of the organization. Internal controls must also be in alignment with the strategy, objectives, and risks to the organization to be effective. It is integral to an organization's enterprise risk management (ERM) program.

The fast-paced, constantly changing, and disruptive operating environment have increased the challenges in developing, implementing, and maintaining an effective system of internal control. Organizations must leverage technology to enhance the agility, effectiveness, and efficiency of their system of internal control. This is necessary to mitigate the myriad of risks in the countries where the organization operates.

The purpose of this chapter is to provide advice on the significant role that internal controls play in mitigating risks to the achievement of the objectives and the success of an organization. Topics covered include the following:

- Overview of COSO Internal controls – Integrated Framework
- Stakeholders' best friend
- Roles and responsibilities
- Key elements of the design of an effective system of internal control
- Role in risk management
- Reporting on internal controls
- Reliance on internal controls by stakeholders

DOI: 10.1201/9781003207559-10

- Leveraging technology
- Impact of technological innovations and tools on internal controls
- Challenges of maintaining effective internal controls
- Value to the organization

Key learnings from the chapter include the following:

- Benefits of applying the COSO Internal controls – Integrated Framework in the design and evaluation of internal controls
- Reasons why internal controls should be stakeholders' best friend
- Roles and responsibilities of the board, management, and the CAE
- Important role that internal controls play in board governance oversight responsibilities
- Role of internal controls in the provision of assurance services
- Important role internal controls play in an organization's ERM program
- Importance of aligning internal controls with the strategy and objectives of the organization
- Reliance on internal controls by internal and external stakeholders
- Importance of leveraging technology to enhance the effectiveness of internal controls
- Impact of technological innovations and tools on internal controls
- Value of an effective system of internal control to an organization
- Challenges of maintaining effective internal controls

OVERVIEW OF COSO INTERNAL CONTROLS FRAMEWORK

COSO, a joint venture of five private-sector professional organizations, was created in 1987. The mission was to develop and provide integrated guidance on internal controls. The professional organizations are as follows:

- American Accounting Association
- American Institute of Certified Public Accountants
- Financial Executive International
- Institute of Internal Auditors
- Institute of Management Accountants

COSO released its first official guidance on internal controls "the COSO Internal Controls - Integrated Framework" in 1992. The target of the guidance was publicly traded companies in response to the rise in corporate fraud and corruption during the 1970s. However, private and non-profit organizations saw the value of adopting the framework to improve the effectiveness and efficiency of their system of internal control and risk management programs. The original framework was updated in May 2013. The focus was to enable organizations to "effectively and efficiently develop and maintain systems of internal controls that can enhance the likelihood of achieving the entity's objectives and adapt to changes in the business and operating environments."[2] The updated Framework also included guidance on the importance of non-financial and internal reporting.

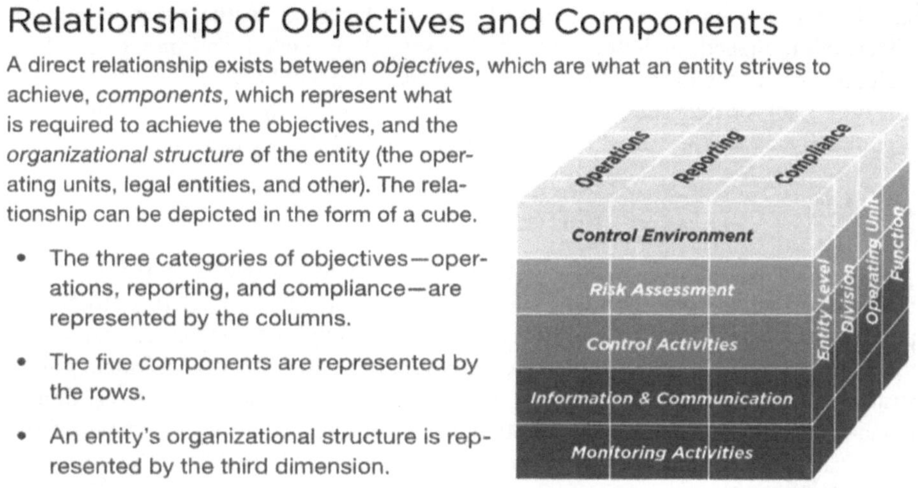

FIGURE 10.1 COSO CUBE. (Used by Permission.)

The COSO Internal controls – Integrated Framework is widely recognized for designing, implementing, and evaluating internal controls.[3] The Framework comprises interrelated objectives, components, and the organizational structure of the entity.[4] The components are supported by 17 principles. The principles are flexible, allow for judgment, and provide the requirements for effectively designing, implementing, conducting, and evaluating the effectiveness of internal controls.[5] The objectives, components, and relationships are illustrated above in Figure 10.1.[6]

The benefits to the board, management, and other internal and external stakeholders of the organization in applying the framework include the following:

- Provides a structured and disciplined approach for developing and maintaining an effective and efficient system of internal control no matter the industry or size of the organization
- Provides reasonable assurance of the achievement of an organization's business, operational, reporting, and compliance objectives
- Assists the board and senior management in performing their governance oversight and management responsibilities, respectively, for internal controls
- Enhances stakeholders' confidence in the organization's system of internal control

STAKEHOLDERS' BEST FRIEND

Internal controls should be embraced and become stakeholders' best friend. This includes the board, senior management, and managers. Senior management includes the CEO and his or her direct reports. An organization's system of internal control is the number one gatekeeper and mitigator of risks to the achievement of the business, operating, reporting, and compliance objectives of an organization. It gives stakeholders reasonable assurance and comfort that risks to the organization are effectively managed, including identified, assessed, mitigated, and monitored. This includes risks at the global or corporate, regional, and local office levels of an organization. Lack of internal controls is a disaster waiting to happen. It is a risk to an organization as well as board members and officers of the organization.

ROLES AND RESPONSIBILITIES

The board entrusts management with the resources and authority to manage the organization and achieve its objectives. Internal controls, including governance structures, policies, processes, and procedures, are required to provide reasonable assurance that the objectives of the organization are achieved. This includes the mission, vision, strategy, and the business, operating, reporting, and compliance objectives. Senior management is responsible and accountable for ensuring that the resources of the organization are safeguarded and used in accordance with the authority given by the board. Safeguarding resources includes developing, implementing, and maintaining effective internal controls to mitigate risks to the resources of the organization. This includes mitigating the risk of fraud, waste, and abuse.

The system of internal control is a key element of the governance of an organization. The establishment of the controls is one of the most important board, CEO, and senior management responsibilities. This includes the development, implementation, and maintenance of the system. The board is responsible for providing oversight of internal controls, which is usually delegated to the audit committee. The board and senior management have a fiduciary responsibility for the implementation and effectiveness of the organization's system of internal control.

The CEO is accountable to the board for the establishment and overall effectiveness of the organization's system of internal control. Additionally, the CEO and the Chief Financial Officer (CFO) of publicly traded companies in the United States are required to evaluate and report on the effectiveness of the organization's system of internal control to the Security and Exchange Commission (SEC) annually. However, the ultimate responsibility for the organization's system of internal control rests with the board.

Setting the tone at the top of the organization is critical to the successful implementation and sustainability of an effective system of internal control. It plays a key role in shaping the culture and control environment of an organization. The chairperson of the audit committee and chief executive officer (CEO) must set the tone that the organization is committed to an effective system of internal control. They must communicate their support to employees at all levels of the organization. Employees of the organization are more likely to support the system of internal control when it is communicated by the CEO and the chairperson of the board or audit committee.

As mentioned above, the CEO is accountable to the board for the establishment and overall effectiveness of the organization's system of internal control. The CEO usually delegates the responsibility for developing, implementing, and maintaining the organization's system of internal control to senior management. Senior management typically delegates this responsibility to their managers. This is because organizations usually have thousands of risks and internal controls disbursed across the countries where they operate. It is not realistic for the CEO and senior management to directly manage all the risks and internal controls across the organization. However, they satisfy this responsibility by providing oversight over the establishment and effectiveness of the internal control that their managers have implemented to mitigate risks to the organization.

Managers are responsible and accountable for developing, implementing, and maintaining effective internal controls for their area(s) of operations. The manager of each entity of the organization must perform a risk assessment of their area(s) of responsibility. This is to identify, evaluate, prioritize, and determine the required internal controls to mitigate risks to the organization. They are also responsible for periodically reporting to senior management and/or the CEO on the state of internal controls for their area(s) of operation. Developing, implementing, and maintaining the organization's system of internal control include the following:

- Understanding: Required to ensure that there is clarity and understanding of the strategy, business, operating, reporting, and compliance objectives of the organization.
- Identifying: Required to determine where internal controls are needed to mitigate risks to the strategy and objectives.
- Assessing: Required to analyze, evaluate, and prioritize risks to manage.
- Designing: Required for developing effective and efficient system of internal control to mitigate risks to an organization.
- Testing: Required to ensure that internal controls are working as expected.
- Training: Stakeholders need training to ensure that they understand how to use and comply with internal controls.
- Implementing: Required for the system of internal control to become effective and operational.
- Monitoring: Required to ensure that the system of internal control is working as expected, effectively, and efficiently to mitigate risk to the organization.
- Reporting: Required to periodically update stakeholders on the status of effectiveness and compliance with internal controls.
- Maintaining: Required to ensure that internal controls are current, relevant, and effective in mitigating risks to the achievement of the objectives of the organization and its stakeholders.

The key activities of senior management, the CEO, and the board's oversight role for the organization's system of internal control include the following:

- Obtaining assurance on the effectiveness and efficiency of the organization system of internal control and compliance with laws and regulations, policies, and procedures
- Participating in periodic enterprise risk assessment or brainstorming session at least annually or as needed
- Monitoring compliance with the organization's system of internal control
- Following up on the implementation of recommendations
- Offering advice and guidance

Questions that those performing oversight roles should consider asking include the following:

- Are resources adequate to effectively implement and maintain the organization's system of internal control?
- Are the resources, including technological tools, adequate to mitigate significant risks to the organization?
- Is there any significant increase, decrease, new, or emerging risks, opportunities, and mitigation activities?
- What is working well, needs improvement or should be stopped?
- Are internal controls aligned with the risks to the entity and the organization?
- What risks keep you awake at night?
- How can we help you?

KEY ELEMENTS OF THE DESIGN OF AN EFFECTIVE SYSTEM OF INTERNAL CONTROL

An effective system of internal control needs the audit committee and senior management buy-in and support. Their buy-in and support are critical to the effectiveness of the internal controls. Senior management buy-in and support are also needed to ensure that adequate resources are allocated to the internal controls program. The effectiveness of the organization's system of internal control depends on the level of resources, including expertise, and technological tools that are allocated to the program.

The design of an effective system of internal control must be based on risks to the achievement of the mission, vision, strategy, and the objectives of the organization. It must include risks that are most important to the organization and stakeholders at all levels of the organization, including the global or corporate, regional, and local office levels. The design must also take into consideration the risk appetite and tolerance of the organization. This is critical to the effectiveness and value of internal controls to the organization. Management should utilize a risk assessment tool to assist in prioritizing risks to manage. The priority must be on mitigating significant risks to the organization since it is not cost-effective or realistic to mitigate all risks, including inherent risks, to an organization.

Obtaining an understanding of the activities and related risks that the internal controls are expected to mitigate is a key element of the design process. This includes an understanding of the following:

- Business, operating, reporting, and compliance objectives of the entity and the organization and related risks
- Current and future states of the organization
- Priorities and what matters most to stakeholders
- What is working well, needs improvement, or needs to be stopped
- Inherent and residual risks
- Technological innovations impact on internal controls
- Opportunities for improving the effectiveness of internal controls

The design of a system of internal control must provide reasonable assurance regarding the achievement of objectives of the organization to be effective. The system of internal control cannot remain static in a fast-paced, constantly changing, and disruptive operating environment. It must be agile, flexible, and adaptable. This requires regular or ongoing risk assessment and risk-based reviews of the organization's key internal controls to ensure that they are still relevant, effective, and adding value to the organization. Key factors to be considered in the design of an effective system of internal control include the following:

- Inclusion of key stakeholders in the design process
- Clarity of roles and responsibilities
- Alignment with the strategy, objectives, and risks of the organization
- Alignment with the organization's risk appetite and tolerance limits
- Compliance with laws, regulations, policies, processes, and procedures
- Agility, flexibility, and adaptability of internal controls
- Risks the internal controls will mitigate
- Treatment of inherent and residual risks
- Inclusion of audit trail for tracking and monitoring transactions and activities
- Opportunities for automation and continuous monitoring and auditing
- Impact of technological innovation on internal controls
- Simple rather than complex design
- Realistic and cost-effective processes and procedures
- Risk and rewards
- Impact on staff and morale
- Value to the organization

The design of an effective system of internal control must include the participation of stakeholders impacted by the activity. This includes staff and stakeholders at the regional and local office levels of the organization. They are usually closest to the activity and include trainers, implementers, users, monitors, and reporters. Staff and stakeholders at the regional and local office levels of an organization often know what will work best in their operating environment. The inclusion of input from stakeholders who are closest to the activity will increase the likelihood of greater buy-in, support, ownership, and a smoother implementation of internal controls.

ROLE IN RISK MANAGEMENT

An organization system of internal control is integral to an organization's ERM's program. It is the source of the measures and tools to support the risk mitigation plans and activities of the organization. The measures and tools include the following:

- Planning
- Strategy
- Objectives

- Organizational structure
- Policies, processes, and procedures
- Key performance indicators
- Documentation
- Training
- Supervising
- Reviewing and approving
- Monitoring
- Reporting

Internal controls must be aligned or linked to the risk mitigation plan and activities of the organization. There should be a specific or related internal control for each risk in the organization's risk mitigation plan. It is common for an internal control to mitigate multiple risks in an organization.

Management must determine how it wants to mitigate risks based on the organization's risk appetite and tolerance limit. This includes the cost and value to the organization of the mitigation effort. Four key questions must be considered when deciding how to manage risks:

- What risk to mitigate?
- What risk to share?
- What risk to avoid?
- What risk to accept?

REPORTING ON INTERNAL CONTROLS

Periodically reporting on the effectiveness and efficiency of the system of internal control is a key element of the governance of an organization. The board, management, and other stakeholders such as investors, donors, creditors, insurers, and regulators have an interest in the effectiveness and sustainability of an organization's system of internal control. A comment that is often made when there is a gap in internal controls that leads to a major issue is where were the auditors when we needed them?

The scope of the system of internal control covers all aspects of the organization, including the following:

- Accounting
- Administration
- Compliance
- Finance
- Governance
- Information systems
- Operations
- Risk management
- Regulatory
- Strategy

Reviewing, evaluating, and periodic reporting on the effectiveness of internal controls must be an ongoing activity. Risks are constantly changing and so too should internal controls. This is to ensure that internal controls are still relevant and effective in mitigating risks to the achievement of the objectives of the organization. The prioritization and focus of the review and evaluation of internal controls must be driven by risk assessment and what is most important to the organization and its stakeholders.

A key responsibility of the leaders of assurance functions is to provide periodic reports to stakeholders on the effectiveness of the organization's governance programs. The leaders of assurance functions providing the information include global internal audit (GIA), compliance, internal investigation, and information security. The CAE is responsible for overseeing and directing the performance of independent and objective risk-based audits of the organization's operations. This is to provide periodic reports to stakeholders on the effectiveness and efficiency of the organization's system of internal control. The organization's external auditor, third-party reviewers, regulators, and other external assurance service providers also perform reviews and evaluation of internal controls. Senior management, the CEO, and the board rely on the information from assurance service providers to assist them in performing their governance responsibilities for internal controls. Additionally, the CEO and CFO have a legal responsibility to evaluate and report on the effectiveness of internal controls to the SEC annually.

The review and evaluation of internal controls over operations and administration, including compliance and information systems, are equally as important as the testing of internal controls over financial reporting. Significant deficiencies or a material weakness in operations or administration tend to eventually materialize in the financial statements of the organization. This often significantly impacts the top and bottom lines, stock price, and new investments to the organization.

RELIANCE ON INTERNAL CONTROLS BY STAKEHOLDERS

There are internal and external stakeholders who have an interest in the organization's system of internal control. Interest of internal stakeholders includes the following:

- The board and senior management have a fiduciary responsibility for the implementation and effectiveness of the organization's system of internal control. They are interested in the effectiveness of internal controls to mitigate risks to the strategy and the achievement of the objectives of the organization. As mentioned earlier, the CEO and CFO have a legal responsibility to evaluate and report on the effectiveness of the internal controls to the SEC annually.
- Managers are interested in whether internal controls are operating as expected and effectively mitigating risks to the organization.
- Leaders of assurance functions are interested in the organization's system of internal control because it is the basis for providing assurance and advice, including insight and foresight, to stakeholders.

- GIA is interested in the implementation and maintenance of the organization's system of internal control. This is the basis for GIA to evaluate and provide assurance and advice into the effectiveness of the organization's system of internal control in mitigating risks to the objectives of the organization. GIA is usually the only support function in the organization that is mandated to operate independent of management and perform objective internal audits of the organization's system of internal control.

Interest of external stakeholders includes the following:

- External auditors are interested in the organization's systems of internal control with particular interest in internal controls over financial reporting. This is to determine whether they can rely on the organization's internal controls over financial reporting to assist in expressing their opinion on the reasonableness of the organization's financial statements.
- Investors, donors, creditors, insurers, and stock and bond rating agencies are interested in the effectiveness of the organization's system of internal control to mitigate risks to their investment, interest, and the reputation of the organization.
- Regulators are interested in the organization's compliance with laws and regulations. They are also interested in whether they can rely on the organization's system of internal control to plan the timing and scope of their work.

Additionally, external stakeholders are usually interested in the results of GIA's tests of internal controls to determine the timing and scope of their work. They usually reperform tests of a sample of GIA's work to determine if they can rely on the results. This is added value to the organization when GIA's work is relied on by external stakeholders. It minimizes duplication of work, reduces the stress and demand on administrative and operations staff time, and potential cost savings on the external audit fees. It is also an indicator of the quality of GIA's work and value to the organization.

LEVERAGING TECHNOLOGY

Global organizations must leverage information technology to enhance the agility, effectiveness, and efficiency of their system of internal control. Technology assists in mitigating the myriad of risks across the world in the countries where the organization operates. Similarly, the entities of the organization, including functions, departments, business units, regional and local offices, usually have hundreds and thousands of internal controls to mitigate risks to their operation. The number of internal controls and risks usually depends on the size and complexity of the organization's operations. While many of the risks and internal controls are similar, the system of internal control, manual, hybrid or automated, may vary from one entity and country to another. The systems may be home-grown and/or standalone and not integrated or able to interface with other systems.

Leveraging information technology enhances the agility, effectiveness, and efficiency of internal controls by streamlining, consolidating, and integrating internal controls across the organization. The enhancements include the following:

- Increasing the speed at which transactions are processed
- Unlocking and maximizing the use of big data to make more informed decisions
- Standardizing and streamlining policies, processes, and procedures
- Eliminating duplication of work
- Enabling continuous monitoring
- Providing quick and easy access to information for data analysis
- Reducing costs of maintaining multiple automated systems
- Minimizing or eliminating human errors

Technological tools include the following:

- Artificial intelligence (AI)
- Automation
- ChatGPT
- Data analytics
- Digitalization
- Internet of Things (IoT)
- Machine learning
- Robotics (BOT)

Technological innovations and tools are driving the survival, success, and sustainability of organizations in a fast-paced, constantly changing, and disruptive operating environment. They are enabling organizations to quickly navigate and analyze big data that are now available for making more informed decisions. The analysis is more robust, comprehensive, and done in seconds and minutes rather than hours and days. For example, routine and recurring tests of voluminous transactions that were once done by staff are now being done electronically. The test covers 100% of the population instead of a sample in a fraction of the time that it would take staff. This enables an organization to be more proactive, competitive, and successful.

IMPACT OF TECHNOLOGICAL INNOVATIONS

Technological innovations bring about new and valuable opportunities as well as risks. Technological tools are constantly changing to improve the effectiveness and efficiency of an organization's operations. They are speeding up the delivery and quality of goods and services across the globe, often at a cheaper price. The effectiveness and efficiencies are being driven by the simplification, consolidation, integration, and elimination of ineffective and redundant operations, functions, structures, policies, processes, and procedures.

Information systems controls are becoming a more dominant factor in the operations of an organization. This includes physical and application controls. The physical controls include security of the premises, building, and areas housing the hardware and software of the system. Application controls cover the processing of transactions, including the input, processing, and output.

One of the greatest risks of technological innovations and tools to an organization's system of internal control pertains to the segregation of duties. Segregation of duties is one of, if not, the most important elements of an effective system of internal control. The risks to segregation of duties from the simplification, consolidation, elimination, and integration of activities must be assessed. This is to ensure that effective internal controls are in place to mitigate new risks to segregation of duties from technological innovations and tools. It also ensures the removal or elimination of outdated or irrelevant controls. Segregation of duties can easily get lost in the process if not addressed in the specification, design, and development phases of internal controls. Segregation of duties controls includes the following:

- Programming from operations or production
- Dual signatories
- Requestor from approver
- Recording from reconciling
- Custody from authority to release
- Custody from the accounting

The CAE and leaders of GIA must play a key role assisting stakeholders with addressing risks from technology-driven changes. This includes system as well as changes in an organization's operations, functions, structures, policies, processes, and procedures. They must also participate in the review of the specifications, design, testing, and migration to the new system and/or application. GIA's IT Audit should also conduct its independent pre- and post-implementation reviews of the system and/or application. Internal controls over the activities of machine learning and robotics must also be examined to ensure that there is no risk of bias.

CHALLENGES MAINTAINING EFFECTIVE INTERNAL CONTROLS

The fast-paced, constantly changing, and disruptive operating environment has increased the challenges in maintaining an effective system of internal control. Management do not usually have the time to manage their regular responsibilities and address the existing, new, emerging, and constantly changing risks in the operating environment. The speed and rapid pace of change requires agility to quickly think, pivot, and act to address existing, new, and emerging risks. This includes revisiting existing risks and internal controls to evaluate the relevance and value of the controls to the organization.

Delays in addressing new and emerging risks expose the organization to fraud, waste, and abuse. Fraud is from fraudsters taking advantage of the lack of internal controls and the delay in developing and implementing controls. Fraudsters are aware that the implementation of internal controls is often delayed during major changes and/or disasters as is often the case in a fast-paced and constantly changing operating environment. Waste and abuse are usually from lack of internal controls and continuing to apply or comply with outdated or irrelevant internal controls.

There will be pushback at times by stakeholders on the need for internal controls. Their reasons include the following:

- Restricts competition
- Disruptive to the operations
- Takes time away from the core business
- Cost outweighs the rewards
- Low risk
- Lack of resources
- Staffing constraints

Non-compliance with existing internal controls can at times be more damaging than not having internal controls. Management exposes the organization to risk by not complying or ignoring internal controls such as policies, processes, and procedures that have been implemented to mitigate risks to the organization. The non-compliance or ignoring internal controls could be viewed by external stakeholders and regulators as a dereliction of the board and senior management governance responsibilities. This could result in reputational damage, penalties and fines, and legal liability to board members and officers of the organization.

Measures or actions that can be taken by management to mitigate challenges to an effective system of internal control include the following:

- Maintenance of the commitment at the top of the organization by the CEO and senior management for an effective system of internal control
- Periodic reminders to employees of the importance and value of an effective system of internal control to the organization
- Regular awareness training and education on internal controls
- Continuous auditing and monitoring
- More frequent testing of high-risk areas and key internal controls
- Ongoing or frequent risk assessment and brainstorming sessions
- Rooting out non-value adds internal controls
- Replacing trust with internal controls

VALUE TO THE ORGANIZATION

Organizations with an effective system of internal control are more likely to be successful than those that do not have one. The drivers of success include the following:

- Competent and experienced staff
- Clarity of roles and responsibilities
- Documented and standardized policies, processes, and procedures that:
  - Ensures transactions are processed consistently, accurately, and completely
  - Enhances the reliability of financial and non-financial reporting

    - Contributes to more effective data mining and analytics
    - Minimizes disruption of operations
- Cross-training of staff, which reduces the learning curve and disruption in operations should there be a gap in staffing

An effective system of internal control is a priceless asset of an organization. It is what gives internal and external stakeholders comfort that risks to their investment and/or interests are effectively managed and safeguarded. This includes the board, senior management, investors, donors, creditors, insurance carriers, regulators, and the organization's external auditor. Investors and donors would not want to invest, and creditors would not want to lend money or offer a line of credit to an organization with a reputation for having a weak system of internal control. As mentioned earlier, an organization's system of internal control is the number one gatekeeper and mitigator of risks to the objectives of the organization and its stakeholders. Any major weakness in the system of internal control is a risk to the success of an organization.

CHAPTER SUMMARY

Internal controls should be embraced and become stakeholders' best friend. This includes the board, senior management, and managers. The system of internal control is a key element of the governance structure of a responsible organization. The establishment of the organization's system of internal control is one of the most important board, CEO, and senior management responsibilities. It is the number one gatekeeper and mitigator of risks to the achievement of the organization's business, operating, reporting, and compliance objectives. It is also a key contributor to the leaders of assurance functions livelihood.

The board entrusts management with the resources and authority to manage the organization and achieve its mission and vision. Management is responsible and accountable for ensuring that the resources are safeguarded and used in accordance with the authority given by the board. Safeguarding resources includes identifying, developing, implementing, and maintaining effective internal controls. This is to mitigate risks to the achievement of the business, operating, reporting, and compliance objectives of the organization. Setting the tone at the top of the organization is critical to the successful implementation and sustainability of an effective system of internal control.

The board and management must also determine how it wants to mitigate risks based on the organization's risk appetite and tolerance.

An effective system of internal control needs the board and the CEO's buy-in and support. The chairperson of the board or audit committee and CEO must set the tone at the top for the organization's commitment to an effective system of internal control. Internal controls must also be in alignment with the business, operating, reporting, and compliance objectives, and risk mitigation plan and activities of the organization to be effective. Alignment is a key element of designing an effective system of internal control. This is integral to an organization's ERM program.

Reviewing, evaluating, and periodically reporting on the effectiveness of internal controls is a key element of the governance of an organization. It is an ongoing activity in an ever-changing operating environment. The prioritization and focus of the review and evaluation, including the testing of internal controls, must be driven by risk assessment. The review and evaluation of administration and operations, including compliance and information systems, are as equally as important as the testing of internal controls over financial reporting.

A key responsibility of the leaders of assurance functions is to provide periodic reports to stakeholders on the effectiveness of the organization's governance programs. The leaders of assurance functions providing the information include GIA, risk management, compliance, internal investigation, and information security. The CAE is responsible for overseeing and directing the performance of independent and objective risk-based audits of the organization's operations. Senior management, the CEO, and the board rely on the information to assist them in performing their management and governance oversight responsibilities, respectively, for internal controls. Additionally, the CEO and CFO have a legal responsibility to evaluate and report on the effectiveness of internal controls to the SEC annually.

There are internal and external stakeholders who have an interest in the organization's systems of internal controls. The internal stakeholders usually include members of the board, the CEO, senior management, managers, and the leaders of assurance functions, including GIA. The external stakeholders include the organization's external auditors, shareholders, investors, donors, creditors, insurers, stock and bond rating agencies, and regulators. There is also, more often now than in the past, interest by external stakeholders in the results of GIA's tests of internal controls in assessing the internal controls environment of the organization. The external stakeholders are usually interested in the results of GIA's tests of internal controls in determining the timing and scope of their work.

Organizations must leverage information technology to enhance the effectiveness and efficiency of internal controls. Technological innovations are driving the effectiveness, efficiency, sustainability, and success of organizations in a fast-paced, constantly changing, and disruptive operating environment. Leveraging technological innovations and tools to integrate, streamline, and consolidate internal controls across the organization enhances the effectiveness of the organization's system of internal control. However, technological innovations bring about valuable opportunities as well as risks. One of the greatest risks of technological innovations to an organization's system of internal control pertains to the proper segregation of duties. The leaders of GIA must play a key role assisting stakeholders with addressing risks from technology-driven changes.

The fast-paced, constantly changing, and disruptive operating environment has increased the challenges in maintaining an effective system of internal control. There will be pushback at times by stakeholders on the need for internal controls. Delays in addressing changes in the operating environment, including new and emerging risks, expose the organization to missed opportunities, fraud, waste, and abuse. An effective system of internal control is a priceless asset to an organization as it provides the measures and tools for mitigating risks to the achievement of the objectives of an organization. Organizations with an effective system of internal control are more likely to be successful than those who are without. Non-compliance with existing internal controls can at times be more damaging than not having them. Any major weakness in the system of internal control can be a risk to the organization and its stakeholders.

NOTES

1 COSO Internal Control – Integrated Framework, Executive Summary, May 2023 – WWW.COSO.org
2 Ibid.
3 Ibid.
4 Ibid.
5 Ibid.
6 Ibid.

11 Getting the Most from Assurance Functions

INTRODUCTION

The ongoing complexity, demands, and ever-changing risks in the operating environment have pushed organizations to invest and expand their assurances activities. This includes investment in specialized roles, services, and continuous monitoring tools. Additionally, the 2001 Sarbanes-Oxley Act in the United States elevated the importance of the role of governance, risk, and compliance in the governance oversight and management of organizations.

Technological innovations are disrupting and forcing organizations and their leaders to change or become obsolete. The leaders of assurance functions are no exception. The message is loud and clear for the leaders of assurance functions to evolve, abandon, and transform the traditional approach of providing assurance services to stakeholders. Adopting a combined assurance service program is one of the most effective ways for an organization to get the most from its assurance functions. It is a strategic and transformational undertaking that requires the support of senior management, particularly the leaders of assurance functions, and the board. Their support is critical to the successful adoption of a combined assurance service program. The adoption of the program will make it easier and more meaningful for the board to perform their governance oversight roles and responsibilities.

The purpose of this chapter is to provide advice and guidance on why the leaders of assurance functions must evolve and abandon the traditional approach of providing assurance services. Topics covered include the following:

- Role of assurance functions
- Abandoning the traditional approach of providing assurance services
- Requirements of a combined assurance service program
- Adopting a combined assurance service program
- Leveraging technology
- Mapping assurance
- Value of a combined assurance service program

Key learnings from the chapter include the following:

- Assurance function's role in the governance of an organization
- Reasons for abandoning the traditional approach of providing assurance services
- Importance of the support of key stakeholders

DOI: 10.1201/9781003207559-11

- Role of a combined approach in getting the most from the organization's assurance functions
- Leveraging technology to improve assurance services
- Value in mapping assurance function's service activities

ROLE OF ASSURANCE FUNCTIONS

The message is loud and clear for the leaders of assurance functions to evolve, abandon, and transform the traditional approach of providing assurance services. This is necessary for assurance functions to remain relevant, valuable, and for organizations to get the most from the functions. Stakeholders are demanding quality assurance services and information to effectively address the rapid pace of change, disruption, and risks in the operating environment. Quality information includes timely, accurate, reliable, and consistent assurance and advice, including insight and foresight, into the effectiveness of the organization's governance programs. The board and senior management rely on the leaders of assurance functions to provide quality information to assist them in effectively performing their governance oversight and management responsibilities, respectively. The information assists them in quickly responding and adapting to change and making more informed decisions.

The board and senior management need a single source of truth to effectively perform their governance oversight and management responsibilities, respectively. However, they are at times presented with assurance service reports that contain conflicting or inconsistent information. This includes similar topics or findings but different conclusions and recommendations. This erodes trust and cast doubt on the information being provided by the leaders of assurance functions. This is also a waste of senior management and the board's time sorting out reported differences in reports from the leaders of assurance functions. Overwhelming senior management and the board with multiple assurance service reports only add to the complexity and confusion around assurance functions services. The complexity has increased with digitalization and the abundance of big data that is now available to organizations 24/7.

The leaders of assurance functions must assist in making it easier and more meaningful for the board and senior management to perform their governance oversight and management responsibilities, respectively. Senior management is usually the CEO and his or her direct reports. The board governance oversight responsibilities are usually delegated to sub-committees of the board. This includes the following:

- Finance
- Governance
- Risks
- Compliance
- Audit
- Nomination
- Compensation

In some organizations, the oversight responsibility for audit, risk, and compliance is assigned to the audit committee.

The number of assurance functions has trended upward over the years. This is due in part to the 2001 Sarbanes-Oxley Act in the United States and the constant changes and disruption in the operating environment. The Act elevated the importance of governance, risk management, and compliance in the governance oversight of organizations. It was in the best interest of companies listed on stock exchanges to add and/or enhance the governance oversight roles in their organization. This was necessary to ensure compliance with the Act and to avoid penalties and fines by the United States Security and Exchange Commission (SEC). The complexity, disruption, constant changes, and risks in the operating environment have also increased the demands on organizations to effectively manage the changes and risks. Drivers of the complexity and demands include the following:

- Technological innovations
- New laws and regulations
- Global pandemics
- Geopolitical issues
- Environmental, social, and governance (ESG) issues

Assurance functions vary from organization to organization. The list below includes those that may be found in organizations:

- Compliance
- Data protection and privacy
- Information security
- Internal audit
- Investigation
- Payment card industry (PCI) security
- Quality assurance
- Risk management
- Sarbanes-Oxley compliance

The internal assurance service providers are as follows:

- The governing body or the board of directors – Accountable to shareholders.
- First Line – Management: Accountable to the board.
- Second Line – Management support, including specialists and subject matter experts.
- Third Line – Internal Audit: Accountable functionally to the audit committee and administratively, usually to the CEO or a member of the senior management team.

The IIA's Three Lines Model is a good illustration of the roles and responsibilities of the various assurance service providers in an organization is illustrated in Figure 11.1 below.

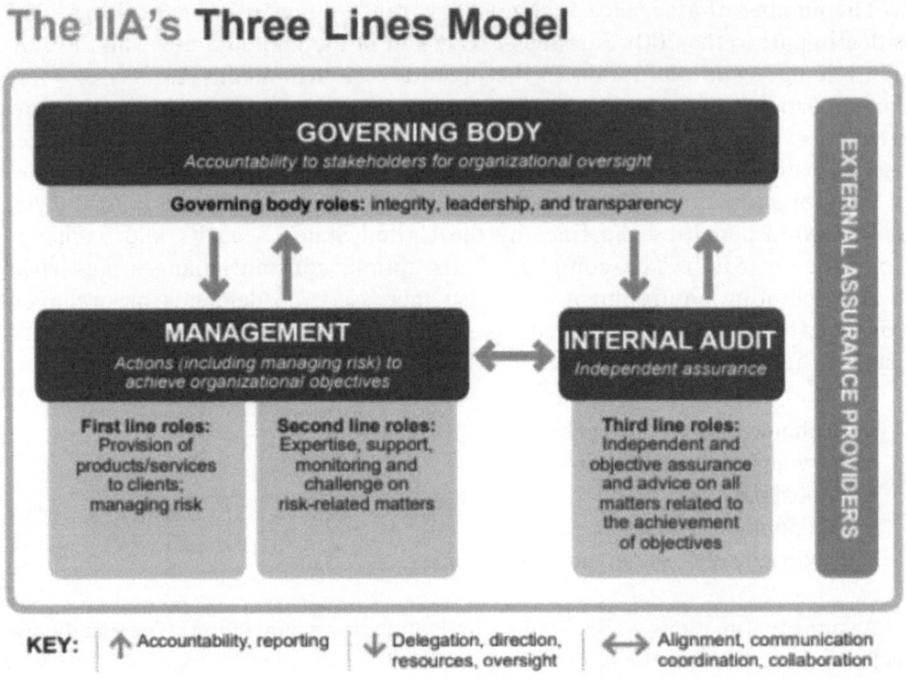

FIGURE 11.1 The IIA's Three Lines Model – An Update of the Three Lines of Defense.[1] (Permission granted by The IIA)

Global internal audit (GIA) is the only function that provides assurance services that fall under the Third Line bucket of the IIA's Three Lines Model. This is because GIA is the only function that is independent of management. Objectivity and independence of the day-to-day management of the operations of the organization is what typically qualifies a function to fall under the Third Line. GIA is not involved in the day-to-day operations of the organization except for its own operation. All the other assurance functions are an extension of management. They exist primarily to support management. Additionally, the Second Line functions are subject to audit by GIA based on risk. The audits are performed to determine the effectiveness and efficiency of the Second Line functions and programs to mitigate risk to the operations and objectives of the organization.

There is no time for bickering over who is responsible for providing assurance services in a fast-paced, constantly changing, and disruptive operating environment. The focus must be on getting the most from assurance functions to assist in the achievement of the business, operating, reporting, and compliance objectives of the organization. This is done by leveraging the work performed by various assurance functions to maximize the value to the organization and its stakeholders. The roles and responsibilities of assurance functions do overlap in certain areas, such as risk assessment, testing of compliance, and assurance reports. This is an opportunity for the leaders of assurance functions to collaborate and leverage each other's work to improve and enhance the quality of assurance services to the organization and its stakeholders.

The leaders of assurance functions must get comfortable with prioritizing what stakeholders need over their priorities. They must either adopt a stakeholder focus mindset or run the risk of losing their relevance and value to the organization. Assurance functions activities and priorities must be in alignment with the business, operating, reporting, and compliance objectives of the organization and its stakeholders. The leaders of assurance functions must invest time obtaining an understanding of the needs and what is most important to the organization and its stakeholders. They must know and understand what the assurance service priorities of stakeholders are and who is providing them. This is to avoid duplication of work and taking time away from the core business. As a reminder, assurance functions are support functions. Their priority must be to assist stakeholders achieve their business, operating, reporting, and compliance objectives.

ABANDONING THE TRADITIONAL APPROACH OF PROVIDING ASSURANCE SERVICES

The leaders of assurance functions must abandon their traditional approach of providing assurance services to stakeholders. The traditional approach of providing assurance services is ineffective and inefficient. It makes the provision of assurance services more complex than it should be. Abandoning the traditional approach is a change from working in silos with little or no interaction and the lack of sharing of information. Working in silos also contributes to the duplication of efforts and hoarding of information, which is a risk to an organization, particularly in an ever-changing operating environment. Senior management and leaders of assurance functions must revisit, rethink, and reshape the delivery of assurance services. This is required for the organization and its stakeholders to get the most from the functions.

There is a long list of evidence to support why the traditional approach of providing assurance services should be abandoned. The list includes the following:

- Siloed and uncollaborative approach
- Ineffective and inefficient assurance services
- Duplication of work
- Multiple systems, software, processes, and procedures
- Inconsistent information, findings, and recommendations
- Lack of coordination and sharing of assurance services plans and activities
- Lack of sharing of resources
- Diverting time away from the core business of the organization
- Stakeholders' assurance service fatigue
- Costly and wasteful services

There is always talk about quick wins, but quick wins must be measured based on what is most important to stakeholders. What stakeholders need most form assurance functions is timely and quality information on the effectiveness of the organization's governance programs, including the following:

- Alignment with strategy and objectives
- Effectiveness of governance structures, policies, processes, and procedures
- Effectiveness of internal controls in mitigating risks to the organization
- Compliance with laws, regulations, policies, and procedures
- New and emerging trends, risks, and opportunities

The leaders of assurance functions can collectively improve and enhance the effectiveness and efficiency of their operations. There are actions that they can take to improve and enhance the effectiveness and efficiency of their operations. The actions include the following:

- Adopting a stakeholder focus mindset
- Focusing on the needs and what is most important to the organization and its stakeholders
- Using common languages and terminologies
- Standardizing processes, procedures, and reports
- Sharing risk assessment, data mining, and analytics tools
- Collaborating closely and leveraging each other's assurance service work
- Collaborating and coordinating assurance service reports to stakeholders
- Utilizing a single-issue tracking system
- Leveraging technology to improve the effectiveness and efficiency of assurance functions

REQUIREMENTS OF A COMBINED ASSURANCE SERVICE PROGRAM

A combined assurance service program requires effective leadership and coordination. It will require a leader who is independent, objective, and understands the organization's assurance service requirements. The leader must also have an effective working relationship with stakeholders and knowledge of the organization business, operations, and functions. Additionally, the leader must spend time upfront with the leaders of the various assurance functions to obtain their buy-in and support. This is required to effectively plan and coordinate the activities of the various assurance functions across the organization.

The survival and success of the adoption of a combined assurance service program require the support of key stakeholders. The key stakeholders are the leaders of assurance functions, senior management, and the board or a sub-committee of the board, including audit, risk, and compliance sub-committees. Their buy-in and support are required to proceed with the initiative. Their buy-in and support are critical to the survival and success of the initiative, including the following:

- Setting the tone at the top of their commitment for the combined assurance service program
- Promoting the value of the program to the organization to management and employees

- Gaining the support for the program by management and employees across the organization
- Obtaining the necessary resources to support the program, including technological tools

It is important to obtain preliminary input from key stakeholders on the idea of adopting a combined assurance service program. Work must be done up front to obtain preliminary input, feedback, and secure the support of the leaders of assurance functions, senior management, and the board. They will have to be convinced that the combined assurance service program will enhance the value of the services to the organization and its stakeholders. It is particularly important to obtain the commitment of the leaders of assurance functions at the outset. This is because there is pushback and disagreements at times on the roles and responsibilities of the leaders of assurance functions. There are leaders who may view it as an attempt to take over their responsibilities and see it as a threat to their job security.

A combined assurance service program requires the leaders of assurance functions to engage and work collaboratively. It is critical in making the change from a traditional to a combined assurance service approach and improving the quality and value of assurance services to stakeholders. It requires coordinating and sharing assurance function plans, activities, and resources. It also includes sharing risk assessment, testing plans, schedules, and technological tools, and simplifying, consolidating, and leveraging the results of each other's work. This will enable the leaders of assurance functions to combine assurance functions activities and test results into a single report to senior management and the board.

The leaders of assurance functions engaging and working collaboratively will improve and enhance the quality of assurance functions service to the organization. This requires adopting a stakeholder-focused mindset. The focus is on what is most important to the organization and its stakeholders and is at the forefront of the leaders of the assurance functions plans and activities. It includes aligning their activities with the business, operating, reporting, and compliance objectives as well as the risk mitigation plan of the organization. This is necessary for the leaders of assurance functions to remain relevant and enhance the quality of their assurance services to the organization and its stakeholders. Additionally, it will enable the organization to realize the full potential and benefits of its assurance functions. Working collaboratively will also enhance the collective effectiveness, efficiency, and value of assurance functions services to the organization and its stakeholders.

There are internal and external assurance service providers. Internal service providers include the following:

- Internal audit
- Risk management
- Compliance
- Information security
- PCI
- Quality assurance

External assurance service providers include the following:

- The organization's external auditor
- Consultants
- Regulators
- Insurance carriers

GIA is considered the most reliable internal assurance service provider, while the organization's external auditor is considered the most reliable of the external service providers. The independence, expertise, training, licensure, certifications, and mandatory continuing professional education make these two groups stand out as the most reliable assurance service providers.

ADOPTING A COMBINED ASSURANCE SERVICE PROGRAM

The adoption of a combined assurance service program is one of the most effective ways to get the most from an organization's assurance functions. Getting the most from the organization's assurance functions requires abandoning the traditional approach of providing assurance services. A combined assurance service program will minimize the complexity and eliminate the siloed nature of the traditional approach of providing assurance services. The leaders of assurance functions have a unique opportunity for scaling up the effectiveness and efficiency of assurance services by adopting a combined assurance service program. This will improve and enhance the value of assurance functions to the organization and its stakeholders.

Adopting a combined assurance service program is a strategic and transformational undertaking. It is strategic because of the following:

- Requires rethinking, and reshaping how assurance services are performed and delivered
- Impacts the governance of the organization as the board rely on the services provided by the leaders of assurance functions in performing their oversight responsibilities for governance
- Requires senior management and the board support and approval
- Change in the method of providing assurance services
- Change in the norms and customs of assurance functions
- Impacts stakeholders across the organization
- Usually requires additional investment

It is transformational because it requires a change in the mindset and attitude of the leaders of assurance functions. It includes the way the leaders of assurance functions think, engage, communicate, and collaborate with each other and stakeholders.

The adoption of a combined assurance service program assists the organization and stakeholders in effectively managing the abundance of big data. The value of big data that is available within and external to the organization cannot

TABLE 11.1
Key Differences between a Traditional and Combined Assurance Service Function

Subject	Traditional	Combined
Plans and schedules	Separate	Shared and coordinated
System hardware & software	Separate	Shared
Risk assessment	Separate	Shared
Testing	Separate	Shared and coordinated
Findings and recommendations	Not always shared	Shared
Reporting	Separate/multiple	Single/combined
Issues tracking and reporting	Separate/multiple	Single/combined

be effectively realized under the traditional siloed approach of providing assurance services. An integrated approach is needed to capture the relevant information from across the organization in a centralized database. This will enable the timely mining and analysis of the information and sharing of the results with relevant stakeholders.

A summary of the key differences in the activities of a traditional and a combined assurance service function is provided above in Table 11.1.

The adoption of a combined assurance service program is one of the most effective ways to get the most from an organization's assurance functions.

LEVERAGING TECHNOLOGY TO IMPROVE ASSURANCE SERVICES

Technological innovations are disrupting and forcing organizations and their leaders to change or become obsolete. The leaders of assurance functions are not immune to the disruption. They must be able to quickly respond and embrace technological innovations and change to remain valuable to their organization. This is because technological innovation is a key driver of change, agility, effectiveness, and efficiency. The survival, sustainability, and livelihood of the leaders of assurance functions will depend on their ability to embrace technological innovations. This includes a change in how things are done.

The leaders of assurance services functions must embrace and leverage technology to improve assurance functions services to stakeholders. Leveraging technology enables the leaders of assurance functions to focus more on strategic matters, core business activities, and risks. This includes what is most important to key stakeholders. Stakeholders need faster and high-quality assurance services to make more timely and informed decisions. This includes timely addressing new and emerging issues and risks. It also includes capitalizing on the opportunities that come along with change. The leaders of assurance functions must also leverage technological innovations and tools to remain relevant and valuable to the organization and its stakeholders. Leaders who are not leveraging technology to improve their effectiveness, efficiency, and value to the organization will eventually become irrelevant and fade away.

Technological innovations and tools are reshaping the effectiveness and efficiency of the delivery of assurance services to stakeholders. Technological tools include automation, data analytics, machine learning, robotics, and artificial intelligence. Technological tools are taking over work that normally is done by humans and doing it more effectively and efficiently. This includes the delivery of higher quality, quicker, accurate, and cost-effective services to stakeholder as well as the following:

- Testing the entire population instead of a sample of transactions
- Monitoring and tracking compliance with laws and regulations, policies, and procedures
- Providing continuous monitoring and auditing
- Maximizing the use of big data

MAPPING ASSURANCE

Mapping assurance is a tool that links the activities of assurance functions to the objectives and risk mitigation plan and activities of the organization and its stakeholders. The objectives include the business, operating, reporting, and compliance. Mapping provides the framework for aligning the plans and activities of the various assurance functions with the objectives of the organization. This is to ensure that risks to the objectives are effectively managed. Assurance service activities that cannot be mapped to objectives must be evaluated to determine the value of the activity to the organization.

Mapping assurance brings transparency to the nature and quality of the assurance services being provided to stakeholders. This includes the timeliness, effectiveness, and efficiency of the assurance services. Mapping assurance assists senior management and the leaders of assurance functions with the following:

- Identifying the assurance activities being performed and by whom
- Clarifying and agreeing on responsibility and accountability
- Streamlining policies, processes, and procedures
- Assessing the value associated with the risks being mitigated
- Identifying and eliminating duplication of tasks
- Eliminating gaps and blind spots
- Identifying opportunities to improve the effectiveness and efficiency of assurance functions

There are steps that the leaders of assurance functions can take to align their activities with the objectives and strategy of the organization and its stakeholders. The steps include the following:

Step I: Conduct an inventory of assurance activities currently being performed by assurance service providers, including risk assessment, testing of internal controls and compliance, monitoring, and reporting the results periodically to stakeholders.

Step II: Identify and list the internal controls and compliance tests being performed.
Step III: Trace the internal controls to the risks the controls are designed to mitigate.
Step IV: Trace the risks being mitigated to the objectives of the organization.
Step V: Ensure that the objectives are in alignment with the strategy of the organization.

As mentioned earlier, assurance service activities that cannot be traced or mapped to objectives of the organization must be evaluated to determine the value of the service to the organization. This will assist in determining if there is a gap in internal controls or an insignificant or low-value assurance service activity. Assurance service activities that provide no value to the organization or its stakeholders should be eliminated. The resources are better redeployed to areas that are high-risk and/or most important to the organization and its stakeholders.

VALUE OF A COMBINED ASSURANCE SERVICE PROGRAM

The adoption of a combined assurance service program will make it easier and more meaningful for the board of the organization to perform their governance oversight role and responsibilities. The leaders of assurance functions have a unique opportunity to reduce unnecessary oversight work of senior management and the board of the organization. Overwhelming the board with multiple assurance services reports in the pre-reads for board meetings is not an effective use of their time. The reports, as mentioned earlier, at times contain similar topics and/or findings but different conclusions and recommendations. This diverts time and attention away from focusing on what is most important to the organization. This includes strategy, the core business, and high-risk areas and issues. The leaders of assurance functions must collaborate closely to eliminate multiple assurances service reports to senior management and the board. This includes coordinating their activities, and sharing, simplifying, and consolidating their assurance service reports. This will also mitigate stakeholders' fatigue from multiple assurance reviews of the same area.

Technology is a key driver of the success and value of a combined assurance service program to an organization. The standardization of policies, processes, and procedures, and technological tools are key elements of the driver of the effectiveness and efficiency of a combined assurance service program. The standardization includes the following:

- Definition and terminology
- Language
- System and software, including the following:
  - Technological tools such as data mining and analytics, robotics, machine learning, data visualization, and artificial intelligence
  - Databases
  - Issues tracking systems
- Risk assessment

- Assurance reports
- Rating scale

There are cost savings to the organization from adopting a combined assurance service program. The cost savings are likely to materialize overtime from the following sources:

- Elimination of multiple risk databases and applications
- Changing from multiple to a single system and application
- Sharing technological tools, including risk assessment, database, and data library
- Reduction in maintenance costs from the sharing of technological tools
- Reduction and/or redeployment of staff from the streamlining of processes, procedures, and the elimination of duplication of work

A recap of the key values of adopting a combined assurance service program includes the following:

- A single GRC system
- A single-risk assessment process, procedures, and database
- Sharing of assurance functions plans, schedules, and activities
- Consolidation of assurance service reports
- Common and standard language, rating scales, methodology, and reports
- Single source of assurance service information
- Single source of data analytics
- Elimination of duplication of work and effort
- Leveraging the work of other assurance functions

CHAPTER SUMMARY

The complexity, demands, and risks of an ever-changing operating environment have forced organizations to invest in specialized roles, services, and continuous monitoring tools and activities. The source of the growing complexity and risks include technological innovations, cybersecurity, changes in regulations, and geopolitical issues. Additionally, the 2001 Sarbanes-Oxley Act in the United States elevated the importance of the role of governance, risk, and compliance in the governance oversight of an organization. As a result, the number of assurance functions has trended upward over the years.

The message is loud and clear for the leaders of assurance functions to evolve, abandon, and transform the traditional approach of providing assurance services to stakeholders. This is necessary for the organization to get the most from its assurance functions. The board and senior management rely on the leaders of assurance functions to provide quality information to assist them in effectively performing their governance oversight and management responsibilities, respectively. The leaders of assurance functions must get comfortable with prioritizing what stakeholders need most over their own priorities.

Adopting a combined assurance service program is one of the most effective ways for an organization to get the most from its assurance functions. It is a strategic and transformational undertaking. It will require a change in the customs, norms, and mindset of the leaders of assurance functions, team members, and stakeholders. This includes the way the leaders of assurance functions think, engage, communicate, and collaborate with each other and stakeholders. The support of the board, senior management, and particularly the leaders of assurance functions are critical to the successful adoption of a combined assurance service program. The adoption of the program will make it easier and more meaningful for the board of the organization to perform their governance oversight roles.

Technological innovations are disrupting and forcing organizations and their leaders to change or become obsolete. The leaders of assurance functions are no exception. They must embrace change and leverage technology to improve their assurance services to the organization and its stakeholders. Technological innovations and tools provide an opportunity for reshaping the effectiveness and efficiency of the delivery of assurance services to stakeholders. Leveraging technology enables the leaders of assurance functions to focus more on strategy, core business activities, and high-risk areas and issues.

The leaders of assurance functions must utilize mapping assurance to fully realize the benefits of a combined assurance service program. Mapping assurance is a tool that links the activities of assurance functions to the objectives of the organization. It provides the framework for aligning the activities of the various assurance functions with the business, operating, reporting, and compliance objectives of the organization. It brings transparency to the nature of the assurance service being provided. Mapping assurance plays a key role in enhancing the quality of assurance services.

The survival and success of the adoption of a combined assurance service program require the support of key stakeholders. It is important to obtain preliminary input from key stakeholders on the idea of adopting a combined assurance service program. It requires the leaders of assurance functions to engage and work collaboratively. Engaging and working collaboratively will improve and enhance the quality of assurance functions service to the organization.

NOTE

1 The IIA's Three Lines Model, An Update of the Three Lines of Defense.

12 Clean Sheet of Paper Internal Audit Approach

INTRODUCTION

The clean sheet of paper internal audit (CSOPIA) approach is an inclusive, engaging, and collaborative approach to performing internal audit. It makes the notion of GIA being a member of the broader organizational team a reality. The approach is strategic, transformational, and incorporates agile and risk-based internal audit (RBIA) methodologies. Additionally, it is in alignment with the IIA's Global Internal Audit Standards.

The transition to the CSOPIA approach requires the buy-in and support of senior management, and the audit committee. The chief audit executive (CAE) and the leaders of GIA must be fully engaged in promoting and driving the support for the initiative. Soft or interpersonal skills and business acumen are essential to the successful implementation of the approach.

The CSOPIA approach is expected to be a win-win approach for leaders, team members, and stakeholders. It promises to enhance the relevance and value of GIA to the organization by prioritizing and focusing GIA's audits on what is most important to the organization and its stakeholders. The approach is also expected to strengthen team members' soft skills, business acumen, and improve the quality of the assurance and advice, including insight and foresight, that GIA provides stakeholders. It is also expected to strengthen relationships with stakeholders and likely enhance their appreciation of GIA's work. Additionally, the approach is expected to position the leaders and team members of GIA for promotional opportunities in other areas of the organization.

The purpose of this chapter is to provide advice and guidance on how the CSOPIA approach can be used to create and preserve GIA's value to the organization and its team members, particularly in an ever-changing operating environment. Topics covered include the following:

- Overview of the CSOPIA approach
- Requirements of CSOPIA
- Incorporation of agile and RBIA methodologies
- The CSOPIA process
- Expected effectiveness and efficiency of CSOPIA
- Role of CSOPIA in building relationships
- Expected benefits of CSOPIA to team members of GIA
- CSOPIA and the IIA's Global Internal Audit Standards

DOI: 10.1201/9781003207559-12

Key learnings from the chapter include the following:

- Understanding the CSOPIA approach and process
- Required skills to successfully implement the CSOPIA approach
- Important role CSOPIA plays in building and strengthening soft skills and business acumen
- Impact on the effectiveness and efficiency of GIA
- Role CSOPIA plays in building and strengthening relationships with stakeholders
- Role of CSOPIA in the development, advancement, and retention of team members

OVERVIEW OF THE CLEAN SHEET OF PAPER INTERNAL AUDIT (CSOPIA) APPROACH

The CSOPIA approach is an inclusive, engaging, and collaborative approach in performing internal audit. It requires the leaders and team members to engage and collaborate closely with stakeholders throughout the audit process. This is to ensure that audit plan and activities remain in alignment with the strategy, objectives, and risk management plan of the organization. Alignment is also necessary to arrive at value-added results and includes the following:

- Planning audits collaboratively with stakeholders
- Agreeing on high-risk areas and focus of the audit
- Sharing of findings with stakeholders as they arise
- Agreeing on audit findings and recommendations before the audit is finalized

The sharing of the audit findings as they arise is to ensure that the findings are valid, and the recommended actions are realistic, relevant, and valuable to the organization. This provides stakeholders an opportunity and time to be proactive in taking corrective action. It may also be one less audit finding to include in the audit report if the recommendation is implemented before the audit is completed.

The CSOPIA approach is strategic and transformational since it requires reimagining and reshaping how GIA performs internal audits. This will impact GIA's team members and stakeholders across the organization as it will require a change in culture, including customs and norms. It will also require the buy-in and support of senior management and the audit committee. The approach is transformational because it will require a change in the mindset of the leaders and team members of GIA and stakeholders. It will also impact the way leaders and team members think, engage, communicate, and work with stakeholders. The transition to the CSOPIA approach requires patience from all stakeholders as it usually takes years to undo and rebuild a culture.

The CSOPIA approach enhances the agility, relevance, and value of GIA to the organization and its stakeholders. It enables the leaders and team members to quickly pivot, respond, and adapt to change in a dynamic operating environment. This is because of the engaging and collaborating nature of CSOPIA's approach. It provides a forward-looking approach to performing internal audit where there is more focus on insight and foresight, and less on hindsight.

CSOPIA is a win-win approach for leaders, team members, and stakeholders. It includes the following:

- Ongoing engagement and collaboration with stakeholders to keep current and informed of the business and operations
- Focuses on key risks and what is most important to the organization and its stakeholders
- Enhances readiness and relevance of GIA to the organization
- Builds and strengthens team members soft skills and business acumen

REQUIREMENTS OF CSOPIA

The transition to the CSOPIA approach requires the buy-in and support of stakeholders. This includes the leaders and team members of GIA, senior management, and the audit committee. The effectiveness and success of the approach depend on their buy-in and support, particularly senior management, and the audit committee. It will require stakeholders' commitment to spend time engaging, conversing, and collaborating with the leaders and team members of GIA on matters of importance to them and the organization.

Ongoing engagement and collaboration with stakeholders are integral to the CSOPIA approach. The demand on GIA's team members and stakeholders' time is heightened in times of constant change and disruption in the operating environment. Keeping current with the activities of stakeholders' business and operations and the internal and external operating environment is paramount in such times. It enables the leaders of GIA to anticipate and provide timely insight and foresight to stakeholders on indicators of significant risks and improvement opportunities. This enables stakeholders to be proactive in mitigating risks to the objectives of the organization.

Senior management and the board, namely the audit committee, buy-in and support are critical to the success of the CSOPIA approach. It is an indication of the importance of the initiative and its value to the organization. Their buy-in and support also play a vital role with employees across the organization engaging and supporting the initiative. Additionally, the commitment by senior management and managers to spend time engaging and collaborating with the leaders and team members of GIA is critical to the success and value to the organization. Patience and understanding are required from stakeholders for the value of the CSOPIA approach to be fully realized. The buy-in and support of stakeholders also enhance the following:

- Engagement and collaboration
- Understanding and clarity of what is most important to stakeholders
- Alignment of the internal audit plan with the strategy and objectives of the organization
- Transparency

The leaders and team members of GIA must impress on stakeholders the need and value of ongoing engagement and collaboration as this is necessary to maximize the value to them. Value includes the following:

- Sharing valuable advice to timely assist stakeholders in making more informed decisions
- Ensuring that the focus is on what is most important to stakeholders and the organization
- Focusing more on the present and the future rather than on the past or historical information
- Linking audit findings and recommendations to strategy, objectives, and risks
- Sharing and obtaining feedback on audit findings and recommendations as they arise

Soft or interpersonal skills and business acumen are essential in the successful implementation of the CSOPIA approach. Soft skills include listening, empathizing, collaborating and along with business acumen are essential in having meaningful dialogue with stakeholders. Business acumen assists in ensuring that the conversation is of interest to stakeholders to gain their attention and support for the approach. The focus must be on what is most important to stakeholders' business and operations today and the future. The conversation may center around the state of the business and operations, the economy, technological innovations, government regulations, and related geopolitical matters. Stakeholders are mostly interested in advice, including insight and foresight, on the current and the future state of the business and operations.

The manager of a CSOPIA engagement must be knowledgeable of the business and the internal and external operating environment as this is necessary to effectively use this approach. Key skills, expertise, and knowledge required to effectively use the CSOPIA approach include the following:

- Interpersonal
- Business acumen
- Change and project management
- Knowledge and experience with information technology
- Audit, management, accounting, and finance
- Data analytics

The CAE, leaders, and team members of GIA must be fully engaged in promoting and driving support for the approach. They must actively promote the value of the approach to stakeholders within and outside of GIA. This is necessary to keep the initiative at the forefront of team members' thinking and activities and on the radar of stakeholders. It is also to obtain and maintain the buy-in and support of team members and stakeholders. The promotion must continue until the CSOPIA approach is adopted across the organization.

INCORPORATION OF AGILE AND RISK-BASED INTERNAL AUDIT METHODOLOGIES

The CSOPIA approach of performing internal audit incorporates agile and RBIA methodologies. It includes the best of the agile and RBIA audit approach, which leads to more effective and efficient internal audits. This is due in part to the engaging and collaborative nature of the CSOPIA approach, including the following:

- Focus on quickly delivering quality services to stakeholders
- Less time spent planning and documenting processes and procedures
- Enhanced focused on risk, solution, and what is most important to stakeholders
- Enhanced ability of team members to stay informed of stakeholders' business and operations

THE CSOPIA PROCESS

The objective of the CSOPIA approach is to streamline and assist in expediting the audit process and making it more inclusive and collaborative. Key elements of the conversation and strategy must be captured on a clean sheet of paper, preferably on an electronic device provided by the organization such as a personal computer, mobile phone, or iPod. Recording the conversation is also an option if the stakeholder consents to it. A good practice is to have a designated team member not leading the conversation take notes so that the flow of the conversation is not interrupted.

Obtaining an understanding and capturing stakeholders' knowledge and perspective of the business and operations are the starting point of the CSOPIA process. This includes an understanding of the strategy, objectives, risks mitigation plan, and activities. The following steps are required to effectively perform a CSOPIA:

Step I: Preparation for a CSOPIA requires the audit team to obtain an understanding of the stakeholder(s) business, operations, applicable regulations, and risks. Sources of information in preparation for the audit include the business plan, minutes of meetings, management reports, risk dashboards, and relevant prior audit reports.

Step II: Meet, virtually or in person, and obtain an understanding of stakeholders' knowledge and perspective of their business and operations. This includes an understanding of the strategy, business, operating, reporting and compliance objectives, and risk mitigation plan and activities. Key elements of the conversation and collaboration must be captured as mentioned earlier electronically. The following are some of the key topics and items that should be covered during the meeting:

- Overview of the organization's strategy, objectives, and risks
- Changes since the last audit
- Stakeholders' concerns and challenges
- What is most important to stakeholders

- Agreement on high-risk areas, including those disclosed in the organization's risk register
- GIA's role

Step III: Share and confirm understanding and takeaways from the meeting in Step II.

Step IV: Develop the audit plan in collaboration with stakeholder, including the scope, timing, and nature of the audit based on high-risk areas agreed on in Step II above.

Step V: Share, obtain feedback, and agreement from stakeholders on the internal audit plan. It is important that the audit plan is in alignment with the strategy, objectives, and risks mitigation plan. It should also be noted that GIA makes the final decision on the audit plan.

Step VI: Prepare and issue audit engagement memo sharing the members of the audit team, scope, and timing of the audit.

Step VII: Conduct entrance meeting.

Step VIII: Commence fieldwork, including evaluating internal controls, validating, verifying, and confirming transactions.

Step IX: Share audit findings with stakeholders as they arise to ensure the validity and accuracy of the findings and collaborate on solutions and recommendations.

Step X: Draft the audit report and share it with stakeholders for review and feedback prior to or at the exit meeting.

Step XI: Conduct exit conference with stakeholders.

Step XII: Resolve open items and issue final audit report.

Step XIII: Follow up and report on the status of outstanding audit recommendations.

EXPECTED EFFECTIVENESS AND EFFICIENCY OF CSOPIA

The CSOPIA approach is expected to enhance the agility, effectiveness, efficiency, and value of GIA to the organization. It also improves and strengthens the quality of the assurance and advice, including insight and foresight, that GIA provides stakeholders. Drivers of the enhancements and improvements include the following:

- Understanding the current state and future direction of the business and operation, which enables the leaders and team members to anticipate and provide insight and foresight to assist stakeholders in making more informed decisions
- Performing more tailored or targeted audits based on risks
- Staying connected, current, and informed of stakeholders' business and operations
- Spending less time planning and documenting processes and procedures, and waiting for buy-in from stakeholders
- Streamlining the review of prior year workpapers and reports as the shelf life of audit findings and recommendations are often short-lived in a constantly changing environment

- Aligning GIA's audit plan and activities with the strategy, objectives, and risk mitigation plan and activities of the organization
- Reducing completion time of the audit by sharing audit findings as they arise and collaborating closely with stakeholders on value-added solutions
- Replacing detailed audit reports with a three-to-five-page summary report of significant or high risk audit findings, recommendations, resolutions, and status of outstanding recommendations
- Handling medium and low risk audit findings administratively with stakeholders
- Excluding audit findings and recommendations implemented during the audit from the audit report as there is no need to report findings that have been shared and addressed with stakeholders during the CSOPIA process
- Enhancing transparency, avoiding surprises, and reducing the prolong communication that often takes place at the end of fieldwork

ROLE OF CSOPIA IN BUILDING RELATIONSHIPS

The CSOPIA approach is expected to build and strengthen relationships and trust due to the engaging, and collaborative nature of the approach. It requires spending time listening to stakeholders' concerns and challenges, and empathizing when appropriate. This makes stakeholders feel more comfortable communicating with the leaders and team members of GIA. Sharing includes what is working well, what needs to be changed as well as their concerns and challenges. Stakeholders expect the leaders and team members of GIA to exercise due professional care in using the shared information.

The leaders and team members of GIA should not include audit finding(s) in the report to increase the number of audit findings reported as that will erode the confidence and trust in GIA. The situation is even more damaging when the stakeholder is the one who shared or brought the issue to GIA's attention. Using information shared by stakeholders for self-serving reasons degrades the integrity and reputation of GIA.

The CSOPIA approach will make the internal audit process a team approach and the notion of GIA being a member of the broader organizational team a reality. Stakeholders are invited to participate in the internal audit process from the beginning to the conclusion of the audit. This includes participating in the risk assessment and audit planning processes. They are also kept updated and informed of findings and recommendations as the audit progresses. Stakeholders will be provided with an opportunity to be proactive in addressing significant issues as they arise. Stakeholders usually feel more comfortable sharing with the leaders and team members of GIA when they are involved in the decision-making process. The inclusion and participation of stakeholders in the audit process promote a sense of ownership and interest in the outcome of the audit.

The CSOPIA approach is expected to enhance stakeholders' appreciation of GIA's work. This is by the leaders and team members' demonstration of interest in the well-being and success of stakeholders' business and operations. Demonstration may be by:

- Spending time understanding stakeholders' business and operations
- Listening, empathizing, and sharing with stakeholders who may be seeking advice on concerns that keeps them awake at night
- Focusing on the priorities of stakeholders

- Providing assurance and advice, including insight and foresight, on current, new, and emerging issues, and risks
- Focusing on assisting stakeholders find root cause and appropriate solutions for recurring issues

EXPECTED BENEFITS OF CSOPIA TO TEAM MEMBERS OF GIA

The CSOPIA approach is expected to enhance the agility of the leaders and team members of GIA. Agility is quickly becoming a must-have skill of leaders and managers to effectively lead and manage in a dynamic operating environment. The CSOPIA approach is expected to enhance the leaders and team members' ability to quickly pivot, respond, and adapt to change. This includes changes in the priorities of stakeholders and changes in the operating environment.

The CSOPIA approach is expected to position leaders and team members for a successful career within GIA and the organization from the following activities:

- Ongoing engagement and collaboration with stakeholders
- Building and maintaining effective relationships with stakeholders
- Reducing the planning and documentation phases of the audit process
- Aligning GIA's plan with the strategy, objectives, and risk mitigation plans of the organization
- Aligning GIA's resources with high-risk areas and what is most important to stakeholders and the organization
- Taking a team approach to performing audits
- Focusing on delivering timely and quality services to stakeholders
- Reducing the threat of GIA becoming irrelevant and less valuable to the organization

The CSOPIA approach enhances promotional opportunities for team members of GIA. It provides them an opportunity to demonstrate their soft skills and business acumen, including the knowledge, expertise, and understanding of the business and operations. The leaders and team members of GIA are in a unique position to learn and know more about the organization than most other leaders and staff in the organization. This is because of GIA's broad scope of audit coverage as well as the engaging, conversational, and collaborative nature of the CSOPIA approach. Leaders and team members of GIA who demonstrate knowledge, experience, and understanding of the business and operations are positioned well for consideration for promotional opportunities in other areas of the organization. It also serves as an incentive for the leaders and team members to remain with the organization.

CSOPIA AND THE IIA'S GLOBAL INTERNAL AUDIT STANDARDS

The CSOPIA approach is in alignment with the Institute of Internal Auditors (IIA) Global Internal Audit Standards. Concerns may be raised regarding the independence and objectivity of the engaging, and collaborative nature of the approach. However, the leaders and team members of GIA activities are still governed by the

Global Internal Audit Standards. They still retain the right to draw the line when their independence and/or objectivity are challenged or at risk. The key elements of an internal audit are still required, as follows:

- Independence and objectivity: Due professional care must be taken to ensure that the independence and objectivity of GIA are not impaired. The leaders and team members of GIA must not get involved with the management of the operations of the organization, except for its own operations. Also, decisions must be based on facts and free of bias or influence.
- Competence: GIA should not conduct a CSOPIA for which the skill or expertise does not exist within GIA or in the organization. Taking on such an assignment without the appropriate expertise and skill is contrary to the Global Internal Audit Standards. It also diminishes the meaningfulness of the engagement, conversation, collaboration, and value to stakeholders.
- Planning: While less time will be spent upfront planning for an audit, the planning of a CSOPIA is more engaging, conversational, and collaborative with stakeholders. The leaders and team members of GIA still have the final say of what is included in the internal audit plan based on risk and what is most important to stakeholders and the organization.
- Documentation: The audit plan and traceability of the fieldwork and supporting evidence of findings and recommendations must be streamlined and retained. There should be enough evidence in the workpapers for an independent party to review and arrive at a similar conclusion as GIA.
- Supervision and fieldwork: A competent and experienced team lead is required to supervise, review the workpapers, provide constructive feedback, and guide the CSOPIA audit team.
- Reporting the audit results: Required three-to-five-page summary audit report.
- Follow-up on the implementation of audit recommendations: Required to periodically report on the status of outstanding audit recommendations.

CHAPTER SUMMARY

The CSOPIA approach requires the use of a clean sheet of paper or an electronic device to capture the conversation during meetings with stakeholders. It also ensures that there is no distraction to the flow of the conversation during the meeting. Time is limited and a precious commodity in a dynamic operating environment. The team members of GIA must be mindful of that and plan effectively to make the best use of stakeholders' time.

The CSOPIA approach makes the notion of GIA being a member of the broader organizational team a reality due to the engaging and collaborative nature of the approach. It is expected to build and strengthen relationships and enhance stakeholders' trust and appreciation of GIA's work.

The CSOPIA approach incorporates the best of the agile and RBIA approach in performing internal audits. It is strategic, transformational, and requires a change in the mindset of leaders, team members, and stakeholders. This requires the buy-in and support of senior management, and the audit committee for the initiative to be successful. The CAE and leaders of GIA must be fully engaged in promoting and driving support for the initiative.

Ongoing engagement and collaboration with stakeholders are not an option but a requirement of the approach. It requires a manager with strong soft skills, business acumen as well as change and project management skills. Soft skills and business acumen are essential for the successful implementation and sustainability of the CSOPIA approach. This is necessary to effectively use the approach and have meaningful engagement and collaboration with stakeholders.

The CSOPIA approach is expected to be a win-win approach for leaders, team members, and stakeholders. It will provide reasonable assurance that the focus of the audit will be on current, relevant, and important topics to stakeholders. It will improve and enhance the quality of assurance and advice, including insight and foresight, that leaders of GIA provide to stakeholders. There is also more focus on assisting stakeholders identify root-cause and sustainable solutions.

The approach is expected to enhance leaders and team members agility and the effectiveness, efficiency, and value of GIA to the organization. It is also expected to enhance their readiness, resilience, relevance and provides an opportunity for team members to demonstrate, build, and strengthen their business acumen and soft skills. Additionally, the approach is expected to position the leaders and team members of GIA for promotional opportunities in other areas of the organization.

The CSOPIA approach is in alignment with IIA's Global Internal Audit Standards. Concerns may be raised over the independence and objectivity of the engaging and collaborative nature of the approach. However, the leaders and team members' activities are still governed by the IIA's Global Internal Audit Standards. They still retain the right to draw the line when their independence and/or objectivity are challenged or at risk.

13 Enhancing the Effectiveness and Efficiency of Internal Audit

INTRODUCTION

The chief audit executive (CAE) and the leaders of global internal audit (GIA) must evolve and abandon the traditional approach of leading. It is one of the most important steps that they can take to enhance GIA's effectiveness and efficiency. They cannot do this with a business-as-usual mindset. It requires reimagining how GIA operates, which is necessary to be ready, resilient, and relevant. This also enables the CAE and team members to effectively address new and emerging issues and risks and capitalize on opportunities from changes in the operating environment.

Technological innovations, tools, and big data are among the key drivers of the rapid, constant, and disruptive changes in the operating environment. The CAE and leaders of GIA must embrace and quickly adapt to value-added technological innovations and tools. They are creating opportunities for organizations to significantly improve and enhance the effectiveness and efficiency of operations.

The purpose of this chapter is to provide advice and guidance on why it is important for CAEs and the leaders of GIA to evolve and transform GIA's operations. This is necessary to improve and enhance the effectiveness and efficiency of GIA. This requires reimagining, including revisiting, rethinking, and reshaping GIA's operations. The survival, sustainability, and success of GIA depend on it in an ever-changing operating environment. Topics covered include the following:

- Overview of effectiveness and efficiency
- Transformation of GIA's operations
- Agile GIA leadership
- Reimagining GIA's operations
- Senior management and audit committee support
- Relationships with stakeholders
- Diversity and inclusion
- Creativity and innovation

DOI: 10.1201/9781003207559-13

- Readiness, resilience, and relevance
- Leveraging technology
- Talent management
- GIA's services and work products
- Skills and expertise
- The internal audit charter
- Performance indicators and metrics

Key learnings from the chapter include the following:

- Value in adopting an agile leadership approach
- Revisiting, rethinking, and reshaping GIA's operations
- Value in building and maintaining effective relationships with stakeholders
- Importance of attracting, hiring, developing, and retaining team members
- Importance of delivering quality services and work products
- Role diversity, inclusion, creativity, and innovation play in the effectiveness and efficiency of GIA
- Leveraging information technology to improve and enhance GIA's effectiveness and efficiency
- Value in expanding GIA's skills and expertise
- Role of effective performance indicators

OVERVIEW OF EFFECTIVENESS AND EFFICIENCY

Improving and enhancing the effectiveness and efficiency of GIA's operations must be a top priority of the CAE and leaders of GIA. Their focus must be on pursuing the right objectives and doing them the right way. GIA's effectiveness and efficiency are determined by the ability of the CAE and leaders to quickly think, respond, and adapt to change and what is most important to the organization and its stakeholders.

The CAE and leaders of GIA must improve and enhance the effectiveness and efficiency of GIA's operations to survive and succeed in a dynamic operating environment. Improving and enhancing GIA's effectiveness and efficiency mean doing the right things and doing them the right way, respectively. Doing things effectively or right is doing what is planned or expected. Doing things efficiently or the right way is doing them timely or expeditiously at a reasonable cost. The objective is to deliver the best quality service or product at a reasonable cost. You usually get what you pay for as low cost often results in low quality. Enhancing GIA's effectiveness and doing the right things include the following:

- Aligning GIA's work and activities, including audit findings and recommendations, with the strategy and objectives of the organization
- Allocating GIA's resources to high-risk areas and what is most important to the organization and its stakeholders

Enhancing GIA's efficiency and doing things the right way include the following:

- Performing the work in less time and cost
- Timely delivery of quality work products, including internal audit reports, as delays can be costly in terms of missed opportunities and time wasted performing the work

The sustainability of GIA depends on the ability of the CAE and leaders of GIA to enhance and improve GIA's operations. They must evolve and transform GIA's operations to effectively navigate the rapid pace of change and disruption in the operating environment. This requires reimagining GIA's operations, including revisiting and rethinking GIA's mission, vision, strategy, objectives, structure, policies, processes, and procedures. In the age of technological innovation and big data, the CAE and team members must embrace and leverage technology to navigate the rapid pace of change. This is important in maintaining and enhancing the effectiveness and efficiency of GIA's operation.

TRANSFORMATION OF GIA'S OPERATIONS

The CAE and leaders of GIA must abandon the traditional approach of leading GIA. They must evolve, transform, and adopt an agile approach of leading GIA. This is one of the most important steps that a CAE and leaders of GIA can take to improve and enhance the effectiveness and efficiency of GIA's operations. The traditional or historical approach of leading GIA is reactive and backward thinking and looking. It is an ineffective approach to leading GIA in a fast-paced, constantly changing, and disruptive operating environment. The CAE and leaders of GIA cannot wait to be asked to act. They must place themselves in a position to be the first to know of any relevant major activities and changes in the internal and external environments. This will enable them to be proactive in advising team members and stakeholders so they, in turn, can be proactive in taking any required action.

The CAE and leaders of GIA cannot improve and enhance the effectiveness and efficiency of GIA's operations with a business-as-usual mindset. It is a mindset of doing things the same way as done in the past. The results are likely to be irrelevant or of little or no value to the organization and its stakeholders in a constantly changing operating environment. GIA needs to provide team members and stakeholders with actionable and useful information to survive and remain relevant and valuable to the organization. What worked well today may not work well tomorrow in an ever-changing operating environment.

The CAE and leaders of GIA must build a welcoming, positive, and safe work environment for team members to be successful. The operating environment must be one where team members enjoy coming to work, learn, grow, and advance their career. The key elements of a welcoming, positive, and safe operating environment include the following:

- Embraces diversity, equity, and inclusion
- Provides competitive compensation package

- Provides team members with the necessary resources to be effective and efficient
- Cares for the well-being of team members, including their safety and security
- Invests in training and continuing professional education of team members
- Empowers team members to act on behalf of the organization within the scope of their knowledge and expertise
- Provides mentoring opportunities for team members
- Provides career development opportunities for team members to grow and advance their career

This is important in retaining team members, particularly high performers. High turnover of team members is a major risk to maintaining and enhancing the effectiveness and efficiency of GIA. This is due in part to the gap in the time it takes to hire and get a new team member up and running.

A competent, experienced, and high-performing team is required to improve and enhance GIA's operations. This includes a qualified and knowledgeable CAE and team members. They also need the required expertise and resources to meet the challenges and demands of a dynamic operating environment. A competent and experienced GIA team is an invaluable asset to an organization. Stakeholders rely on the team to provide them with independent and objective information. It includes assurance and advice, including insight and foresight, into the effectiveness of internal controls to mitigate risks to the objectives of the organization. This is to assist stakeholders in making more informed decisions. The organization and the CAE must also invest in training and continuing professional education to ensure that team members are up to date with the changes and activities in the operating environment.

The CAE must ensure that GIA is provided with the necessary resources to be effective and efficient. It includes the right fit and mix of staff, skills, expertise, and technological tools. The organization must invest in technological tools that will enable the CAE and team members to quickly respond to the rapid speed of change, and remain ready, resilient, and relevant. The investment is necessary for GIA to effectively address what is most important to team members and stakeholders. This will also assist in ensuring the timely delivery of quality services and work products that provide impactful advice, including insight and foresight, to team members and stakeholders.

AGILE LEADERSHIP

The CAE and leaders of GIA must adopt the agile methodology to lead, improve, and enhance the effectiveness and efficiency of GIA's operations. Agile leadership requires the CAE and team members to engage and work collaboratively to deliver what GIA and team members need most to be successful. It includes listening, empathizing where appropriate, and sharing with team members as the work progresses. This paves the way for the CAE and team members to timely arrive at workable solutions and results by leveraging the team's unique knowledge of the organization's business and operations. Agile leadership enables the CAE and leaders of GIA to quickly think, pivot, respond, and adapt to change and deliver what is most important to team members and the organization. This is vital to the readiness, resilience, and relevance of GIA and team members in a fast-paced, constantly changing, and disruptive operating environment. It also enables the CAE and leaders of GIA to effectively address existing, new, and emerging risks and opportunities.

The CAE and leaders of GIA must understand the characteristics of agile leadership to appreciate how it can improve and enhance the effectiveness and efficiency of GIA's operations. The characteristics include the following:

- Stakeholder focus
- Flexible and adaptable
- Quick decision-making process
- Engaging and collaborative
- Problem solver instead of fault finder
- Embraces and quick to adapt relevant change
- Supports continuous learning and improvement
- Learns and grow from failure
- Empowers team members
- Encourages creativity and innovation

The CAE and team members of GIA must be flexible, adaptable, and embrace change to improve and enhance GIA's operations effectiveness and efficiency. They must be in a ready mode to quickly respond, adjust, and adapt to change or do things differently. It requires engaging, listening, empathizing when appropriate, and the timely sharing of information. This will enable the CAE and team members to quickly think, pivot, respond, and adapt to change and what is most important to GIA, team members, and stakeholders. It also enables them to gain a better and deeper understanding and appreciation of the business, operation, and stakeholders' needs. The CAE and leaders of GIA must ensure that team members get the necessary training and have the required skills to assist in becoming more stakeholder-focused, adaptable, and flexible. It includes soft skills and business acumen.

REIMAGINING GIA'S OPERATIONS

The CAE and leaders must reimagine GIA's operations to address the challenges and demands of a dynamic operating environment. It requires revisiting, rethinking, and reshaping GIA's operations, including its mission, vision, strategy, objectives, and structure. The survival, sustainability, and success of GIA and the team depend on it. It is also necessary to improve and enhance GIA's effectiveness, efficiency, and value to the organization.

Revisiting GIA's operations requires obtaining an understanding of the past, current, and the expected future state of its operations. It includes revisiting existing standards, policies, processes, and procedures, staffing, systems, and applications to determine what is working well and what needs to be changed or be eliminated. This is to ensure that the focus of GIA going forward is on maximizing its value to team members and stakeholders.

Rethinking GIA's operations requires evaluating the various options that are available to enhance GIA's effectiveness and efficiency. This includes stepping outside of GIA's comfort zone and challenging existing standards, policies, processes, and procedures. It also includes taking risks, failing fast, and recovering quickly. The focus must be on what is most important to team members of GIA and stakeholders. This requires visualizing the future state of GIA operating in a dynamic operating environment. It includes considering the following:

- Big data
- Business and operations
- Competition
- Cybersecurity
- Geopolitical issues
- Global pandemics
- Global supply chain
- Integration
- Organizational structure
- Paperless operating environment
- Policies, processes, and procedures
- Profile of team members
- Regulatory requirements
- Required skills and expertise
- Required training
- Stakeholders and customers
- Technological innovations
- Terrorism
- The Cloud
- The economy
- Trends
- Use of technological tools
- Virtual office and working remotely

The reshaping of GIA's operation must take into consideration technological innovations and tools. Technological innovation and tools are key drivers of effectiveness and efficiency. They are driving the revisiting, rethinking, and reshaping of organizations' structures, policies, processes, and procedures. As mentioned before, this requires stepping outside of GIA's comfort zone and challenging existing standards, policies, processes, and procedures, taking risks, failing fast, and recovering quickly. The CAE and leaders of GIA must reshape GIA's operations by determining what changes must be made to align GIA's plans and activities with what is most important to the team members and stakeholders. The CAE and leaders of GIA must also take into consideration the following in reshaping GIA's operations:

- Top priorities of team members, stakeholders, and the organization
- Current and expected future state of the business and operations, industry, regulatory requirements, technological innovations, trends, technical and professional requirements

- Gaps and differences between the current and future state of GIA's operations
- Identifying and sharing potential solutions for gaps

Reshaping GIA's operations may require reinventing or restructuring GIA in order to quickly pivot, respond, and adapt to change. The structure must be designed to align and meet the changing needs of team members, the organization, and its stakeholders. A vertical or tall organizational structure is usually bureaucratic and not effective in a rapidly changing and disruptive operating environment. It will also limit GIA's team members' agility and ability to respond and act quickly to change.

SENIOR MANAGEMENT AND AUDIT COMMITTEE'S SUPPORT

Enhancing the effectiveness and efficiency of GIA's operations depends on the level of support the CAE receives from senior management, particularly the chief executive officer (CEO), and the audit committee. Their support set the tone at the top of the organization of their commitment, importance, and value of the CAE and GIA to the organization. Their support tends to cascade down the organization's chain of command, which enhances the cooperation with GIA by stakeholders across the organization. The CAE must develop an effective relationship with senior management and the audit committee in order to maintain their support. The CEO and senior management play a key role in the operational effectiveness, efficiency, and success of GIA. The audit committee is a valuable resource for the CAE should there be a major disagreement with senior management and/or any wrongdoing, malfeasance, or fraud by management. Their support also makes it somewhat easier for the CAE to obtain senior management support and cooperation, and the resources needed for GIA to be effective, efficient, relevant, and successful.

Senior management and the audit committee must ensure that the CAE has a seat at the c-suite table. This includes an effective reporting line in the hierarchy of the organization. A seat at the c-suite table enables the CAE to build and maintain an effective relationship with senior management. This also enables the CAE to stay connected and timely inform senior management on significant issues and activities.

An effective reporting line of the CAE and GIA is to highest level possible in the hierarchy of the organization. The higher the reporting line and visibility of the CAE and GIA in the organization, the higher the likelihood of a creative, innovative, agile, and effective CAE and GIA. The lower the reporting line of the CAE and GIA in the organization the likelihood that the function will be less effective. The function is likely to be slower in responding, acting, and adapting to change. This is because of the bureaucracy and the levels of reviews and approvals that may be required before an issue is shared and reported to senior management, the CEO, and the audit committee. Bureaucracy usually delays or extends the review process that is required to get major decisions approved. It is also a risk to creativity, innovation, agility, effectiveness, and efficiency of GIA in an ever-changing operating environment.

Senior management and the audit committee must ensure that GIA is provided with the necessary resources for the CAE and team to be successful. It includes the necessary funding to acquire and equip GIA with the right team, expertise, and technological tools. This will enhance GIA's ability to address existing, new, and emerging risks, and opportunities. The organization must not be penny wise and pound foolish. It could result in a pay now or pay later scenario. A pay later scenario often has a negative impact on the financial statements and the bottom line of an organization.

RELATIONSHIPS WITH STAKEHOLDERS

The CAE and leaders of GIA must build and maintain effective relationships with team members and stakeholders to improve and enhance the effectiveness and efficiency of GIA's operations. Stakeholders include members of the audit committee, senior management, peers, colleagues, professional organizations, and other parties of interest. This is necessary for the CAE and leaders to stay connected, current, and informed of changes in the operating environment. These are key elements in enhancing the effectiveness and efficiency of GIA's operations. This requires ongoing engagement, collaboration, networking, and attendance at professional training and educational events. The activities enhance the CAE and team members of GIA awareness of early warning signs of new and emerging trends, issues, risks, and improvement opportunities. The activities also enable the CAE and leaders of GIA to be proactive in providing advice, including insight and foresight, to team members and stakeholders. Additionally, it enables the CAE, team members, and stakeholders to be proactive in addressing change. This includes new and emerging issues and risks as well as capitalizing on opportunities that usually come along with change.

DIVERSITY AND INCLUSION

Diversity is a valuable resource of a global organization that the CAE and leaders of GIA must leverage to improve and enhance the effectiveness and efficiency of GIA's operation. The value is a result of the multicultural staff that usually exists in a global organization. They are usually from different countries, cultures, and backgrounds. They bring different perspectives to the table that enriches the decision-making process.

The CAE and leaders of GIA must embrace and create a diverse GIA-working environment to improve and enhance the effectiveness and efficiency of GIA's operations. A diverse working environment includes a diverse team, expertise, and tools. It provides the CAE and leaders of GIA with an opportunity to obtain input from a cross section of team members and stakeholders from diverse cultures and levels of society. It gives the CAE and leaders an opportunity to listen and become aware of alternative solutions to issues. Additionally, the inclusion of different perspectives, ideas, and opinions in the decision-making process usually results in quicker and more informed decisions.

Diversity and inclusion are usually the fountain of creativity and innovation in organizations operating in different countries. The creativity and innovation are from the different cultures, perspectives, and ideas that exist in such organizations. The CAE and leaders of GIA must capitalize on this opportunity to harness the benefits of diversity and inclusion. They must embrace, encourage, and respect different perspectives and opinions. That will drive creativity, innovation, and enhance the effectiveness and efficiency of GIA's operations. It will also lead to a more robust decision-making process that results in more impactful and influential decisions.

The inclusion and participation of team members and stakeholders in the decision-making process play a key role in the buy-in and support of GIA's plans and activities. It is particularly important for team members in the field. They are usually ready and eager to participate and contribute to the achievement of GIA's objectives. They at times feel excluded from the decision-making process. Their voices must be heard. The CAE and leaders of GIA must ensure that team members in the field are invited to participate in the decision-making process, especially those that are impacted by the decision. Team members' participation in the decision-making process gives them a sense of ownership of the decisions and increases the buy-in, support, and the likelihood of success of the decision and required action.

There are going to be instances where the CAE and leaders of GIA must act quickly. This is to be expected in a fast-paced, constantly changing, and disruptive operating environment. The CAE must ensure that a process exists to timely inform GIA's team members of such quick decisions. It is to ensure that team members do not feel left out of the decision-making process.

The CAE and leaders of GIA must diversify GIA's tool kit and value basket to enhance its effectiveness and efficiency. These are tools that will enable GIA to meet the demands and challenges of an ever-changing operating environment. This includes new and emerging trends, issues, risks, and improvement opportunities. A diversified tool kit must include technological tools such as data analytics, artificial intelligence, machine learning, robotics, and ChatGPT.

CREATIVITY AND INNOVATION

The CAE and leaders of GIA must be creative and innovative in navigating the rapid pace of change in the operating environment. They must engage in thinking out of the box and get comfortable with the uncomfortable to improve and enhance GIA's operations effectiveness and efficiency. It includes challenging existing standards, structures, policies, processes, and procedures. This is because those that work effectively and efficiently today may not work effectively and efficiently tomorrow. The CAE and leaders of GIA must evolve and transform GIA's operations to continue to effectively manage existing, new, and emerging risks and opportunities. This requires being creative and innovative in the development of strategies, structures, policies, processes, and procedures. This will enable GIA to remain relevant and continue to add value to the organization.

READINESS, RESILIENCE, AND RELEVANCE

Readiness is being prepared, ready to respond, and act at a moment's notice to a situation. It is the ability to quickly recognize, acknowledge, and address change. The CAE and team members of GIA must be in a ready mode to quickly think, pivot, respond, and adapt to change. This requires staying connected, current, and informed of activities and changes in the operating environment. This also requires ongoing engagement and collaboration with team members and stakeholders internal and external to the organization.

Resilience is the ability to quickly pivot and recover from a failure. It requires quickly recognizing, acknowledging, and addressing failure. This includes setbacks, errors, missed deadlines, and deliverables. Failure is a part of the journey to success so there is no time to fixate on failure in a fast-paced, constantly changing, and disruptive operating environment. The experience must be used as an opportunity to learn, improve, grow, and become more effective and efficient. It is also an opportunity to share with stakeholders who can benefit from the experience. The timely sharing of lessons learned from failures can be of significant value to an organization. This is because a problem in one country or region of the global organization often manifests itself in other countries and regions of the organization.

Relevance is the ability of GIA to continue to add value to the organization in a dynamic operating environment. Remaining ready, resilient, and relevant is critical to the survival, sustainability, and success of GIA. It requires building and maintaining effective relationships with team members and stakeholders. It includes networking with peers and colleagues internal and external to the organization. Additionally, it requires engaging, listening, learning, sharing, and discussing matters of mutual interest with stakeholders, peers, colleagues within and outside of the organization. Networking helps the CAE and team members to stay connected, current, and informed of activities and changes in the operating environment. This includes keeping current and informed of activities in the industry and profession.

LEVERAGING TECHNOLOGY

The CAE and leaders of GIA must embrace and leverage technology to improve and enhance GIA's operations. This is because embracing and leveraging technological innovations and tools play a key role in improving and enhancing GIA's effectiveness and efficiency. They are primarily responsible for the rapid and constant change, and disruption in the operating environment. They are also creating opportunities for organizations to improve and become more effective and efficient. This is by improving the speed and quality of their services and products to team members and stakeholders. Technological innovations and tools are breaking down barriers, eliminating silos, bureaucracy, redundant and duplicate activities, and streamlining policies, processes, and procedures. Processes and activities that took hours, days, weeks, and months to perform are now being done in seconds and minutes. Timeliness and quickness are valuable assets of an organization in a fast-paced, constantly changing, and disruptive operating environment.

Doing things manually that can be done electronically is a risk to the effectiveness and efficiency of GIA's operations. The CAE and leaders of GIA will not be able to meet the needs of GIA and stakeholders by doing things manually that can be done electronically. This includes manual activities such as sample selection, testing of internal controls and compliance, data analytics, and trend analysis. The team members of GIA time will be better spent interpreting the results of data and trend analysis and assisting stakeholders in identifying root cause and sustainable solutions. The CAE and leaders of GIA must be able to quickly abandon old best practices and tools and adopt more current, effective, and efficient ones. They must identify and seek funding for technological tools to take over routine and voluminous tasks that can be done electronically instead of manually. The tools must assist in enhancing GIA's agility, flexibility, and adaptability. The tools must also enhance GIA's readiness, resilience, relevance, and value to team members, the organization, and its stakeholders.

Digitalization is a revolutionary force that is driving organizations, including GIA, to revisit and rethink their strategy. This is because digitalization integrates the information and data of an organization's business and operations to make them more effective and efficient. The integration makes it easier for information to be collected and readily available to team members and stakeholders to do their work. The information is available to authorized users regardless of where they are located or reside in the organization. This enables the CAE and team members to quickly access, analyze, and use the digital information to make timelier and quality-driven and informed decisions. Activities that usually take days, weeks, or months to get done are now being done in seconds and minutes.

Digitalization converts information into digits and requires the consolidation, standardization of processes, and procedures, and integration of systems to realize its true value. This enables organizations to establish a single source of information that is more likely to be reliable, accurate, consistent, verifiable, and available 24/7. The CAE and leaders of GIA must ensure that the internal controls over digital information are effective and can be relied on for decision making by team members and stakeholders. The value of digitalization to the organization and GIA's operations includes the following:

- Converts and unlocks and makes available information once kept in silos
- Simplifies access to and availability of the organization's information
- Maximizes the use of big data for making more informed decisions
- Improves the quality of information, including the timeliness, reliability, accuracy, and consistency of the information
- Speeds up the processing and delivery of quality services and products
- Contributes to more robust data mining, analytics, and connecting the dots, including easier to identify the root cause of issues and sustainable solutions
- Enhances the transparency and sharing of the organization's information

The automation of GIA's operations paves the way for enhancing GIA's effectiveness and efficiency by capturing and storing administrative and operational information in a centralized database. This is an invaluable asset to GIA and the organization. A centralized database enables team members to effectively and efficiently mine and analyze the information. It is done to identify trends, anomalies, unusual transactions and activities, and new and emerging issues, risks, and improvement opportunities. This enhances the quality of GIA's services and work products and provides insight into the root cause of issues. It also leads to more sustainable solutions. Additionally, it enables the CAE, leaders, and team members to gain a deeper understanding of issues, including the following:

- What is working well
- What needs to be changed or eliminated

- Location of the issues
- Insight into responsibility and accountability

This enables the CAE, leaders, and team members and stakeholders to be proactive in mitigating new and emerging risks, and making more informed decisions.

Data analytics and artificial intelligence play a key role in enhancing the efficiency and effectiveness of GIA's operations. They provide a key source of advice, including insight and foresight, for GIA and the organizations in an ever-changing operating environment. Data analytics and artificial intelligence enable team members of GIA and stakeholders to perform more effective and robust data mining and analysis. They also play a key role in connecting the dots and identifying trends, anomalies, and unusual transactions and activities. This enables the CAE and leaders of GIA to make more informed decisions. It also enables them to be more proactive in quickly responding, acting, and adapting to change to remain ready, resilient, and relevant. The CAE and team members also have more time available to focus on interpreting the results of data analysis, connecting the dots, strategy, and core activities. It includes following up on exceptions and identifying the root cause and sustainable solutions.

Technological tools, such as machine learning and robotics, are playing a key role in enhancing the effectiveness and efficiency of GIA's operations. They are rapidly taking over tasks normally performed by humans. This includes recurring, routine, voluminous, and tedious tasks. It also includes internal audit tasks such as transactions and compliance tests, authorization limit and verification check that are normally performed by auditors. Technological tools are less prone to errors and pave the way for continuous auditing and monitoring, 24/7. This also makes it possible to evaluate 100% of a population or transactions instead of a sample. The tools enable the CAE and team members to focus more on interpreting the results of data analysis and connecting the dots. This enhances the timeliness and quality of the advice, including insight and foresight, that they provide stakeholders to assist them in making more informed decisions. They are also better able to apply their training, knowledge, and experience to things that are important to stakeholders such as strategy and core business activities.

TALENT MANAGEMENT

The CAE and leaders of GIA must attract, hire, and retain a diverse and high-performing team to improve and enhance the effectiveness and efficiency of GIA's operations. This requires investing in the hiring and development of a diverse and high-performing GIA team. It includes investing in the training and continuing professional education of the team members. Additionally, it requires the existence of effective policies, processes, and procedures to attract and hire the right candidates to join the team. The turnover of team members is a high risk to the effectiveness and efficiency of GIA's operation. As mentioned earlier, the CAE and leaders of GIA must build a welcoming, positive, and safe operating environment for the team to be successful. It must be an environment where team members enjoy coming to work, grow, develop, and advance their career within GIA or other areas of the organization. It is a loss to the organization for high-performing or talented GIA team members to leave the organization after investing in their career development. The team members of GIA are an invaluable asset and must be effectively managed.

GIA'S SERVICES AND WORK PRODUCTS

An effective and efficient GIA is one that can consistently deliver timely and quality services and work products to its internal and external stakeholders. The timely delivery of quality services is one of the greatest values that a CAE and leaders of GIA can provide its team members and stakeholders in an ever-changing operating environment. They need timely and quality information to effectively respond and adapt to change. Timely and quality information will assist team members and stakeholders in making more informed decisions. The decision could be a matter of survival at times.

Enhancing the quality of GIA's services and work products requires the implementation of effective structures and smart systems and tools. This includes policies, processes, procedures, and integrated systems as well as the use of technological tools. The structures and systems must be designed to ensure the consistent delivery of timely and quality services and work products that are useful and impactful. There is no time for perfection or delays in a fast-paced, constantly changing, and disruptive operating environment. The CAE and leaders of GIA must aim for reasonable, cost-effective, and not perfect assurance. They must also assess the risks and rewards of findings and recommendations, and exercise good judgment in arriving at reasonable, cost-effective, and sustainable solutions. Impactful advice, including insight and foresight, are those that are in alignment with what is most important to team members and stakeholders.

The provision of quality, including timely and consistent, services and work products is not always guaranteed in a fast-paced, constantly changing, and disruptive operating environment. There will be failures along the way. The important thing is to quickly recognize, acknowledge, and address failures. The lessons learned from failures must be timely shared with team members and others in the organization who can benefit from the experience. Team members and stakeholders' awareness of the issue will assist in mitigating the risk of the issue spreading to other areas of the organization.

SKILLS AND EXPERTISE

Experience and expertise only in technical or hard skills are not adequate to enhance the effectiveness and efficiency of GIA in a dynamic operating environment. The technical or hard skills include accounting, finance, and internal audit. The CAE and leaders of GIA must ensure that GIA has the current and required hard and soft skills to enhance the effectiveness and efficiency of GIA's operations. The skills and expertise must align with the current needs of the organization and its stakeholders, including GIA's team. This includes aligning with relevant and value-added technology, and industry, technical, and professional trends, and innovations.

A CAE must consider investing in and adding non-traditional skills and expertise to GIA's value basket. This will enhance GIA's effectiveness and efficiency in addressing the constant and disruptive changes in the operating environment. This will also enhance GIA's readiness, resilience, and relevance in addressing new, emerging, and unprecedented issues, risks, and opportunities that come along with change. The non-traditional skills and expertise include the following:

- Data Science
- Diversity, equity, and inclusion
- Environmental, social, and governance
- Data security and privacy
- Social work

Soft skills and business acumen play a key role in enhancing the effectiveness and efficiency of GIA's operations. They enrich the engagement, collaboration, and conversation with team members of GIA and stakeholders. Soft skills include effectively communicating, listening, empathizing when appropriate, sharing, and showing interest in team members and stakeholders' concerns and issues. Business acumen enables GIA leaders and team members to have meaningful discussions with team members and stakeholders. Soft skills and business acumen play a key role in assisting and supporting team members and stakeholders in navigating the fast-paced, constant change, which are at times unprecedented, and the disruption in the operating environment.

The CAE must strengthen and expand the soft skills and business acumen of team members of GIA. Soft skills and business acumen play a key role in enhancing GIA's effectiveness and efficiency in an ever-changing operating environment where ongoing engagement and collaboration are critical to survival. The CAE must ensure that the team members receive the required soft skills and business acumen training to capitalize on the opportunity to enhance GIA's effectiveness and efficiency. The training is also necessary for the team to have more meaningful engagement, conversation, and collaboration with stakeholders.

THE INTERNAL AUDIT CHARTER

An effective and efficient GIA operation is one that is guided by an internal audit charter (hereinafter the charter). The charter describes the purpose, role, responsibilities, and authority of the CAE and GIA. The charter must be supported by a policy and procedures manual. The policy and procedures manual provides the roadmap for standardizing and driving the effectiveness and efficiency of GIA's operations. It supports compliance with the guidelines of the charter. Standardization drives the consistent application of policies, processes, procedures, and performance of activities.

The CAE must ensure that GIA's policies, processes, and procedures are effective and efficient in enhancing GIA's operation. They must be dynamic, flexible, streamlined, and easy to understand to be effective and efficient. They must also ensure that the charter, policies, processes, and procedures are reviewed at least annually or as needed. This is to ensure that they are still relevant and effective to address the risks that come along with change.

PERFORMANCE INDICATORS AND METRICS

The CAE must adopt effective performance indicators and metrics to obtain timely and valuable feedback on the performance of team members of GIA. The tools that are available to assist in this effort include the following:

- Project-based performance evaluations
- Stakeholder survey
- 360 evaluations of the leaders and team members of GIA
- Project management tracking system and tools

Indicators of positive performance include the following:

- Good reputation and known for the following:
  - Integrity and credibility
  - Independence and objectivity
  - Professionalism
- Positive stakeholders' audit survey results
- Timely delivery of GIA's services and work products
- Increase requests for internal audits and advisory services
- Invitations to senior management meetings
- Continuous learning and improvement

CHAPTER SUMMARY

Improving and enhancing the effectiveness and efficiency of GIA's operations must be a top priority of the CAE and leaders of GIA. The survival, sustainability, and success of GIA depend on it. The CAE and leaders of GIA must build a welcoming, positive, and safe operating environment for team members to be successful. They cannot enhance the effectiveness and efficiency of GIA's operations with a business-as-usual mindset in a dynamic operating environment.

The CAE and leaders of GIA must evolve, transform, and adopt an agile leadership approach to improve and enhance the effectiveness and efficiency of GIA's operations. Agile leadership requires the CAE and team members to engage and collaborate with team members and stakeholders. The CAE and leaders of GIA must understand the characteristics of agile leadership to appreciate how it can improve and enhance GIA's effectiveness and efficiency. They must be flexible, adaptable, and embrace technology and change.

The CAE and leaders of GIA must reimagine GIA's operations to meet the demands of a dynamic operating environment. Reimagining GIA's operations requires revisiting, rethinking, and reshaping how GIA operates. Reshaping GIA's operations may require reinventing or restructuring GIA. This will require the support of senior management and the audit committee. They must ensure that the CAE has a seat at the c-suite table and an effective reporting line in the hierarchy of the organization. They must also ensure that the CAE is provided with the necessary resources to enable GIA to perform effectively and efficiently. An effective and efficient GIA begins with a competent and high-performing GIA team.

Diversity is a valuable resource of a global organization. The CAE and leaders of GIA must capitalize on this valuable resource to enhance the effectiveness and efficiency of GIA's operation. This valuable resource is the diversity of GIA's team that usually exists in a global organization. The team is usually from different countries, cultures, and backgrounds. They bring different perspectives, ideas, and opinions to the table and the decision-making process. That enriches GIA's decision-making process and results in better decisions. It also increases the buy-in, support, and success of the decision across the organization. Team members in the field, for the most part, welcome the opportunity to participate and contribute to the objectives of the organization and GIA. Participation gives them a sense of ownership of the decision and increases the likelihood of success of the decision or course of action.

The CAE and leaders of GIA must be creative and innovative. This is necessary to navigate the fast pace of change and disruption in the operating environment. This requires being creative and innovative in the development of strategies, structures, policies, processes, and procedures. Those, including tools, which worked well today may not work well tomorrow in an ever-changing operating environment.

The CAE and leaders of GIA must embrace and leverage technology to improve and enhance the effectiveness and efficiency of GIA's operations. Digitalization is a revolutionary force that is driving organizations, including GIA, to revisit and rethink their strategy. Doing things manually that can be done electronically is a risk to the effectiveness and efficiency of GIA's operations. The automation and digitalization of GIA's operations pave the way for doing things electronically. Digitalization, data analytics, artificial intelligence, machine learning, and robotics are key drivers in improving and enhancing the effectiveness and efficiency of GIA's operations.

The leaders and team members of GIA must remain ready, resilient, and relevant to improve and enhance the effectiveness and efficiency of GI's operations. This requires attracting, hiring, developing, and retaining a diverse and high-performing team and investing in continuous learning and improvement. Continuous improvement is not an option but a requirement in a fast-paced, constantly changing, and disruptive operating environment. This is also required for the consistent and timely delivery of quality services and work products. Enhancing the quality of GIA's services and work products requires the implementation of effective structures, systems, processes, procedures, and technological tools. The provision of quality, including timely and consistent, services and work products is not always guaranteed in an ever-changing operating environment.

Experience and expertise only in technical or hard skills are not adequate to enhance the effectiveness and efficiency of GIA. CAE's and the leaders of GIA must consider investing in and adding non-traditional skills and expertise to GIA's value basket. Soft skills and business acumen play a key role in improving and enhancing the effectiveness and efficiency of GIA's operations. CAEs and the leaders of GIA must strengthen and expand team members of GIA' soft skills and business acumen.

An effective and efficient GIA operation is one that is guided by an internal audit charter. The charter describes the purpose, role, responsibilities, and authority of the CAE and GIA. The charter must be supported by a policy and procedures manual. Additionally, the CAE and leaders of GIA must adopt effective performance indicators and metrics to obtain timely and valuable feedback on the performance of the leaders and team members of GIA.

14 Enhancing Internal Audit's Value to the Organization

INTRODUCTION

The chief audit executive (CAE) and leaders of GIA must go beyond providing assurance to enhance GIA's value to the organization. They must also proactively engage in providing advice, including insight and foresight. This will assist stakeholders in making more informed decisions in an ever-changing operating environment.

Enhancing GIA's value to the organization and its stakeholders depends on the team members' knowledge and understanding of the business and operations. There is no value to add if there is no understanding. This includes obtaining an understanding of the organization's internal and external operating environments. Understanding what is most important to the organization and its stakeholders is critical in enhancing GIA value to the organization.

The purpose of this chapter is to provide advice and guidance to the leaders of GIA on how to enhance GIA's value to the organization in a fast-paced, constantly changing, and disruptive operating environment. Topics covered include the following:

- Understanding the organization
- Engagement and collaboration
- Ready, resilient, and relevant
- Agile leadership and operating environment
- Continuous learning and improvement
- Alignment with strategy, objectives, and risk mitigation plans of the organization
- Relationships with stakeholders
- Going beyond assurance
- Solution-driven
- Leverage GIA's knowledge of the organization
- Service and work products
- Training ground for future managers and leaders

Key learnings from the chapter include the following:

- Importance of understanding the business and operations of the organization
- Benefits of continuous engagement and collaboration
- Value in adopting the agile methodology for leading GIA

DOI: 10.1201/9781003207559-14

- Importance of aligning GIA plans and activities with the strategy, objectives, and risk mitigation plans of the organization
- Value of building and maintaining effective relationships with stakeholders
- Importance of being ready, resilient, and relevant
- Importance of going beyond assurance to enhance GIA value to the organization
- Value in leveraging GIA's unique knowledge and understanding of the organization
- Value of providing stakeholders with quality information, including internal audit reports

UNDERSTANDING THE ORGANIZATION

The team members of GIA must understand and get comfortable with the fact that GIA is a support function. A key responsibility of GIA is to support and assist stakeholders achieve the objectives of the organization. This must be at the forefront of team members' thinking and activities. The CAE and leaders of GIA must also understand the nature and impact of an ever-changing operating environment on the effectiveness and efficiency of GIA. There is nothing stable anymore in the operating environment except for constant change. Stability is a thing of the past.

Enhancing GIA's value to the organization and its stakeholders depends on the team members' understanding of the business and operations of the organization. There is no value to the organization if there is no understanding. Team members must also have knowledge and understanding of the external operating environment to be effective and valuable to the organization. This will play a key role in the quality of the assurance and advice, including insight and foresight, that GIA provides stakeholders.

There are certain internal and external factors that must be considered in obtaining an understanding of the organization's business and operations. The internal factors include the following:

- Culture and language
- Mission, vision, and strategy
- Core business
- Business, operating, reporting, and compliance objectives
- Control environment
- Risks, including inherent risk, and mitigation plan
- Policies and procedures
- Systems and applications

The external factors include the following:

- Industry and profession
- Competition
- Regulations
- Economy
- Supply chain

- Government regulations
- Political, including geopolitical, environmental, social, and governance

The team members of GIA must regularly refresh their understanding of the needs of the organization and its stakeholders. It is necessary to ensure that their understanding of what is most important to the organization and its stakeholders remains intact. What is most important to the organization and its stakeholders can easily get lost in the fast-paced, constantly changing, and disruptive operating environment. Refreshing the understanding will ensure that team members of GIA keep the needs of the organization at the forefront of their thinking, planning, and activities. This will minimize deviation from what is most important to the organization and its stakeholders. It is also important in an ever-changing operating environment where deviation from the objectives of the organization can be costly.

ENGAGEMENT AND COLLABORATION

Enhancing GIA's value to the organization requires continuous engagement and collaboration with stakeholders. This is because change is continuous and so should be engagement and collaboration. Continuous engagement and collaboration are necessary for team members of GIA to stay connected, current, and informed of changes in the operating environment. What worked well yesterday may not work well today, and what worked well today may not work well tomorrow in an ever-changing operating environment. Continuous engagement and collaboration also enable team members to be more proactive in addressing change. They can timely connect the dots, share, and advise stakeholders of changes in the operating environment. This enables stakeholders to be proactive in mitigating new and emerging risks to their objectives as well as capitalizing on the opportunities that come along with change.

READY, RESILIENT, AND RELEVANT

A key role of a CAE is to build and maintain a ready, resilient, and relevant GIA team. The success, sustainability, and value of GIA to the organization depend on it. This requires obtaining and having a thorough and current understanding of the organization's business and operations. Readiness is being prepared to respond and act at a moment's notice to a situation. It is the ability to quickly recognize, acknowledge, and address change. The CAE and team members of GIA must be in a ready mode to quickly think, pivot, respond, and adapt to change or do things differently. This requires staying connected, current, and informed of activities and changes in the operating environment. This also requires ongoing engagement and collaboration with team members and stakeholders internal and external to the organization.

Resilience is the ability to quickly recover from a failure. To quickly recover from a failure is to timely recognize and acknowledge failure. This includes setbacks, errors, missed deadlines, and deliverables. Failure is a part of the journey to success. There is no time to fixate on failure in a fast-paced, constantly changing, and disruptive operating environment. The experience must be used as an opportunity to learn, improve, grow, and become more effective and efficient. It is also an opportunity to share with stakeholders who can benefit from the experience. Timely sharing of lessons learned from failures can be of significant value to an organization. This is because a problem in one country or region where the global organization operates often manifests itself in other countries and regions of the organization.

Relevance is the ability to focus and deliver on what is most important to the organization and its stakeholders. The team members of GIA must be proactive and agile to remain ready, resilient, relevant, and valuable to the organization and its stakeholders. They cannot wait to be asked to respond and adapt to change. They must also be flexible and adaptable to keep up with the fast pace and demands of the ever-changing operating environment.

AGILE LEADERSHIP AND OPERATING ENVIRONMENT

The CAE must adopt the agile methodology for leading GIA. An agile GIA leadership and operating environment will make it easier to engage, communicate, and collaborate more effectively with stakeholders. Agility enhances team members' ability to quickly think, pivot, respond, and adapt to change and what is most important to the organization and its stakeholders. The adoption of an agile leadership and operating environment enhances the survival, success, sustainability, and value of GIA to the organization. Agile leadership and operating environment will improve and enhance the CAE and team members' readiness, resilience, and relevance. It will require team members to adopt the methodology in performing their responsibilities.

Adopting the agile methodology for leading GIA paves the way for improving and enhancing the effectiveness, efficiency, and value of GIA to the organization and its stakeholders. This is because of the inclusive, engaging, collaborative, and stakeholder focus nature of agile. It enables stakeholders to breakdown complex projects into smaller and more manageable units and tasks. This usually expedites the completion and delivery of tasks and projects as well as the following:

- Building and strengthening relationships
- Breaking down barriers and hierarchies
- Simplifying and streamlining tasks and activities
- Eliminating silos, redundancies, and duplications

The simplification and streamlining of tasks and activities include work plans, flows, policies, processes, and procedures.

Agility requires team members of GIA to be proactive in assisting stakeholders. They cannot sit and wait to be asked to respond and adapt to change in an ever-changing operating environment. This requires timely analyzing, interpreting, summarizing, and sharing the results of information and data collected from team members and stakeholders across the organization. This enables team members to timely connect the dots and identify red flags, gaps, trends, and unusual transactions and activities. It also enables them to anticipate and timely share the information with impacted stakeholders.

CONTINUOUS LEARNING AND IMPROVEMENT

Continuous learning and improvement are essential in enhancing GIA's value to the organization. This is necessary to keep current, informed, and ready to quickly respond and adapt to change. Continuous learning and improvement are also fundamental to an agile GIA leadership and operating environment. An organization must invest in the training, continuing professional education, and development of the members of GIA's team. It enables them to timely provide advice, including insight and foresight, to stakeholders on new and emerging risks and opportunities. This assists stakeholders in proactively responding to rapid change and making more informed decisions. Additionally, continuous learning and improvement enhance the readiness, resilience, and relevance of team members. Readiness, resilience, and relevance are key elements to the survival, sustainability, and success of an agile GIA leadership.

ALIGNMENT WITH THE STRATEGY AND OBJECTIVES OF THE ORGANIZATION

Alignment of GIA's plans and activities with the strategy and objectives of the organization is a key factor in enhancing GIA's value to the organization and its stakeholders. This includes alignment with the business, operating, reporting, and compliance objectives, and risk mitigation plan and activities. Alignment is achieved through engaging and collaborating closely with stakeholders to determine what is most important in achieving the objectives of the organization. This is necessary for team members to stay connected, current, and informed of the activities in the operating environment. Additionally, engaging and collaborating closely with stakeholders enhance team members' readiness to quickly respond and adapt to change. There must be a mutual understanding and agreement between the leaders of GIA and stakeholders on what is most important to ensure that the alignment is effective.

Alignment of GIA's audit findings and recommendations with the objectives of the organization is critical in enhancing GIA value to the organization. This includes aligning the audit findings and recommendations with the risk mitigation plans and activities of the organization. The alignment is likely to attract the attention and interest of stakeholders because the focus is on what is most important to them.

Alignment requires keeping the objectives of the organization and its stakeholders at the forefront of the mindset of team members of GIA. This includes their thinking and activities. It is critical for the team members to stay focused on the objectives and the risk mitigation plan and activities of the organization. As mentioned earlier, deviation from the objectives or what is most important to the organization and its stakeholders can be costly. The alignment will enable team members to play a key role in proactively assisting stakeholders in mitigating risks to the achievement of the objectives of the organization. It will also assist stakeholders in capitalizing on opportunities that come along with change.

RELATIONSHIP WITH STAKEHOLDERS

The leaders of GIA must build and maintain effective relationships with stakeholders to improve and enhance GIA value to the organization. This requires ongoing engagement and collaboration, including meeting periodically or as needed, listening, empathizing, and sharing with stakeholders. It enables and enhances the leaders of GIA's ability to set and manage expectations and minimize surprises. Building and maintaining effective relationships with stakeholders also assist in enhancing the alignment of GIA plans and activities with the strategy, business, objectives, and risk mitigation plans and activities of the organization. This is because building and maintaining effective relationships play a key role in focusing on the objectives and what is most important to stakeholders. It also builds trust and paves the way for developing a trusted advisor relationship.

There are mutual benefits to GIA and the organization and its stakeholders from building and maintaining effective relationships. The key benefits include the following:

- Enhanced engagement and collaboration
- Enhanced clarity and understanding of roles and expectations
- Better understanding of the services that GIA provides
- Enhanced appreciation of GIA value to the organization
- Opportunity for staying connected, current, and informed
- Enhanced transparency and avoid surprises
- Early awareness of new and emerging trends, issues, risks, and opportunities
- Paves the way for partnering and developing a trusted advisor relationship
- Provides the leaders of GIA with an opportunity to promote and market GIA's services

Building and maintaining effective relationships enhance the readiness, resilience, and relevance of the leaders of GIA and stakeholders by the awareness and timely sharing of changes in the operating environment. This includes red flags and early warning signs of new and emerging risks, issues, trends, and opportunities as well as lessons learned from failures. This also makes it easier for the leaders of GIA and stakeholders to connect the dots and avoid surprises.

GOING BEYOND ASSURANCE

The leaders of GIA must go beyond assurance to enhance GIA value to the organization and its stakeholders. Assurance is more focused on the testing of historical or past transactions and activities. While the testing of past transactions and activities plays a key role in providing assurance, the value is at times less useful and short-lived in an ever-changing operating environment. As mentioned previously, what worked well yesterday may not work well today, and what worked well today may not work well tomorrow in an ever-changing operating environment. Going beyond assurance requires putting more emphasis on timeliness and quality of the advice, including insight and foresight, GIA provides stakeholders. This is particularly important in a fast-paced, constantly changing, and disruptive operating environment where the changes and disruption are unprecedented at times. The demand for timely and quality advice is usually high at such times. Stakeholders do not usually have the time to effectively manage the core business and navigate the changes and disruption in the operating environment.

The leaders of GIA must increase the level of their engagement and collaboration to go beyond assurance. It requires becoming proactive engaging with stakeholders. It also requires building and maintaining effective relationships with stakeholders and networking with peers and colleagues within and outside of the organization. Ongoing training and continuing professional education play a key role in going beyond assurance. It enables team members to stay connected, current, and informed of the activities in the internal and external operating environments. This also enables the CAE and team members to anticipate and be at the forefront of changes in the operating environment.

Going beyond assurance includes engaging and collaborating closely with assurance functions service providers. This includes compliance, risk management, information security and internal investigation as well as the organization's external auditor. Assurance functions service providers usually possess valuable information. The information can provide additional knowledge and intelligence when shared to improve and enhance the efficiency and effectiveness of the organization. Engaging and collaborating closely with assurance functions service providers in sharing and exchanging information enhance awareness. This includes awareness of red flags and early warning signs of new and emerging risks, trends, issues, and opportunities. It also enables team members of GIA to timely connect the dots, minimize surprises, anticipate, and provide value-added advice, including insight and foresight, to stakeholders on matters of importance to them.

Going beyond assurance will assist stakeholders who are faced with the challenge of having to make quick decisions in a fast-paced, constantly changing, and disruptive operating environment. Stakeholders are forced at times to make quick decisions without having all the "Is" dotted and "Ts" crossed. The decision could be a matter of survival of the organization or a missed opportunity. The CAE and leaders of GIA are in a unique position to go beyond assurance and assist stakeholders in making more informed decisions in such situations. This is due in part to the usual presence of team members in the field at the regional and local offices. They are often aware of red flags and early warning signs of new and emerging risks, trends, issues, and opportunities before headquarters or home office. The CAE, leaders, and team members' relationship with stakeholders, networking with peers within and outside of the organization, and continuous learning also enables them to assist stakeholders in making timely and informed decisions.

SOLUTION-DRIVEN

GIA must be a solution-driven operation to enhance its value to the organization and its stakeholders. This requires them to become problem solvers instead of fault finders. Problem solvers play a key role in assisting stakeholders achieve the objectives of the organization. Fault finders distract and often cause tension and conflict with stakeholders. They are at times alarmists creating fires where there is no smoke. Becoming problem solvers includes focusing on what is most important to stakeholders for them to achieve the business, operating, reporting, and compliance objectives of the organization. This also requires collaborating closely with stakeholders to identify the root cause of issues such as weaknesses and/or deficiencies in internal controls. Identifying the root cause of issues is key in finding sustainable solutions. This minimizes the risk of recurrence and the need for stakeholders to revisit issues.

There are going to be gaps and failures in an ever-changing operating environment. The CAE and leaders of GIA must ensure that time is not spent trying to find fault and reporting an issue if it was or is being effectively managed by stakeholders. This includes sharing and being transparent with other stakeholders who need to know. Team members must assess the situation to determine if lessons have been learned, corrective actions have been taken, and the experience shared with others in the organization who can learn and benefit from it. One of the worst things that an auditor can do is to report issues that stakeholders already know, corrected or are effectively addressing and shared with stakeholders who need to know. However, there is no harm done in following up during discussions with stakeholders on the status of the issue.

The leaders of GIA must exercise care in ignoring low-risk issues in a constantly changing operating environment. A low-risk issue yesterday is not necessarily going to be a low-risk issue today in an ever-changing operating environment. The leaders of GIA must review low-risk issues to determine if the risks have changed. The change may be an increase or a decrease in risk. The leaders of GIA must also determine if management has taken appropriate action to mitigate any increase in the risk levels or ratings and remove irrelevant risks from the risk register. They must also evaluate and prioritize risk areas and issues for action by stakeholders. There is no value in adding low-risk areas and issues to the workload of stakeholders. This is because stakeholders do not have the time or resources to address every risk that is identified or comes along with changes in the operating environment. Stakeholders must prioritize the risks and allocate the organization's resources accordingly. Additionally, stakeholders usually view spending time on low-risk issues as a waste of their time and a distraction from the core business of the organization. However, this should not distract the leaders of GIA from sharing and reporting low-risk issues where the risk has changed, especially if the risk has increased or grown.

LEVERAGE GIA'S KNOWLEDGE OF THE ORGANIZATION

The team members of GIA must leverage their unique knowledge and understanding of the business and operations to enhance GIA's value to the organization. The broad scope of GIA work and presence in the field at regional and/or local offices give the team members a unique knowledge and understanding of the business and operations of the organization. This enables and enhances their ability to provide stakeholders with timely and valuable advice, insight, foresight, and improvement opportunities. It also enables stakeholders to make more timely and informed decisions in an ever-changing operating environment. The unique knowledge and understanding enable team members to also do the following:

- Timely learn and share red flags and early warning signs
- Effectively connect the dots across the organization
- Enhance transparency and reduce surprises

- Educate stakeholders on new and emerging trends, issues, risks, and mitigation controls
- Provide advice on the relevance and effectiveness of existing governance structures, processes, policies, and procedures

The team members of GIA must leverage their unique knowledge and understanding of the organization to assist in improving and enhancing the control environment. This includes assisting in improving and enhancing the effectiveness of the organization system of internal control. An effective control environment plays a key role in mitigating risk to the achievement of the objectives of the organization. A key responsibility of a CAE is to provide reasonable assurance that the organization system of internal control is operating effectively and efficiently to mitigate risk to the organization. This includes governance structures, policies, processes, and procedures. Stakeholders internal and external to the organization rely on the assurance and advice that leaders of GIA provide to assist them in making informed decisions.

The team members of GIA must assist stakeholders with addressing the risks to their system of internal control from rapid changes in the operating environment. Stakeholders usually do not have the time to keep up with the fast pace of change. As a result, the review and update of existing internal controls usually lag in times of rapid change. This includes a delay in developing and implementing new measures to address the changes in the operating environment as well as eliminating irrelevant and/or outdated internal controls. The delay makes the organization vulnerable to fraudsters seeking to take advantage of the risk. The leaders of GIA must prioritize assisting stakeholders in addressing the internal controls needs of the organization in times of rapid change. This includes providing information on the following:

- Effectiveness and efficiency of the design of internal controls
- Effectiveness and efficiency of governance structures, policies, processes, and procedures
- Clarity, relevance, and reasonableness of the policies, processes, and procedures
- Cost effectiveness of the system of internal control
- Compliance with laws, regulations, policies, and procedures

SERVICE AND WORK PRODUCT

The leaders and team members of GIA must unleash their unique knowledge and understanding of the organization to enhance the quality of their service and work product. The unique knowledge and understanding are primarily due to the broad scope of GIA's work that covers every aspect of the organization. It is also due to GIA having boots on the ground or staff in the field at the regional and local office levels of the organization. They are usually privy to firsthand knowledge of activities and events in the field. This includes early warning signs, red flags, gaps in internal controls, and new and emerging trends, issues, and risks. GIA's unique knowledge and understanding of the business and operations of the organization is an asset. Stakeholders should utilize this asset to assist them in proactively mitigating risks and capitalize on opportunities emerging from a constantly changing operating environment.

The CAE and leaders of GIA must improve and enhance GIA's value to the organization by providing stakeholders with quality information and reports. The information and reports must be timely, actionable, and useful to enhance GIA's value to the organization and its stakeholders. The information must also be easy to understand, accurate, reliable, and relevant for it to be actionable and useful. Stakeholders usually do not have the time in a constantly changing and disruptive operating environment to read lengthy reports. They often must act quickly as it might be a matter of survival or a missed opportunity. The leaders of GIA must ensure that audit reports are clear, easy to read, understand, and the recommendations are relevant, reasonable, and actionable. This includes the following:

- Keeping audit report to a maximum of five pages with a one-page high-level executive summary highlighting significant matters and issues. The report usually includes items such as the following:
  - Significant matters, including current, new, and emerging issues, trends, red flags, gaps, and risks
  - Significant improvement opportunities
  - Status of the implementation of significant audit recommendations, including stakeholders' achievements
  - Disagreement with management
  - Management misconduct
  - Fraudulent transactions and activities
- Linking internal audit results to the strategy, objectives, and risk mitigation plan and activities
- Providing sustainable recommendations based on root cause analysis
- Utilizing bullets where applicable
- Making the information or message telegraphic
- Utilizing visualization tools such as graphics, tables, and charts

The CAE and leaders of GIA must provide stakeholders with impactful information and reports to improve and enhance GIA's value to the organization. The information and reports usually center around the provision of assurance and advice, including insight and foresight. The information must be in alignment with what is most important to the organization and its stakeholders to be impactful. This includes linking the information to the strategy, objectives and risk mitigation plan and activities of the organization. This will assist stakeholders in effectively mitigating risks to the strategy and objectives and making more informed decisions. It will also assist stakeholders in capitalizing on the opportunities that come along with change.

The information and reports the CAE and leaders provide stakeholders must contribute to the effectiveness and efficiency of the organization. The focus must be on what is most important to stakeholders and the organization. This includes the following:

- Making it easy for stakeholders to navigate and manage change in an ever-changing operating environment by:
  - Delivery of timely, high-quality and impactful service and work products
  - Timely sharing of assurance and advice, including insight and foresight
  - Keeping stakeholders informed of new and emerging risks and opportunities

- Identifying and sharing opportunities for leveraging information technology to automate and streamline policies, processes, and procedures
- Assisting in mitigating the risks of technological innovations and the explosions of big data

TRAINING GROUND FOR FUTURE MANAGERS AND LEADERS

GIA can be an excellent training ground for developing future managers and leaders of the organization. This is usually an underutilized or overlooked value of a matured GIA function to serve the organization. A mature GIA function is ideal for the role because it is one of, if not the only, functions in an organization where staff is exposed to the inner workings of every aspect of the organization. Staff can see and learn about most if not all aspects of the organization. This is more than what any other staff will learn in a lifetime as a member of the organization. Rotating future managers and leaders through GIA as part of their career development program is a win-win option for the candidates, GIA, and the organization.

The benefits to the organization and its staff for utilizing GIA as a training ground for future managers and leaders are unique to GIA. The learnings and experience will remain valuable to staff for the rest of their career. The learnings and experience include the following:

- Exposure to a broad scope of the organization operations
- Better understanding of risk assessment
- Deeper understanding and appreciation of how the different departments and functions in the organization operate
- Enhanced understanding of the value, importance, and appreciation of internal controls
- Enables and enhances participants ability to connect the dots
- Greater appreciation and understanding of the value of GIA work

It takes a mature GIA to be recognized as a valuable training ground for the organization's future managers and leaders. This includes a competent, experienced, and respected CAE and leadership team and a well-established GIA. GIA must also be recognized as a valuable function of the organization where all or most of the following are in place:

- Internal audit charter
- Internal Audit Manual containing GIA's policies and procedures covering its administrative and functional (technical) activities
- Competent and experienced managers and supervisors to guide and support team members
- Team approach
- Forward-thinking team
- Dynamic audit plan
- Risk-based audit approach
- Stakeholder focus

- Welcome creative and innovative thinking
- Embraces and values diversity, equity, and inclusion
- Respects and open to different perspectives and points of views
- Mentorship program

The benefits to GIA for serving as a training ground for future managers and leaders is an opportunity for the leaders to receive fresh and constructive feedback on GIA's operation. It is also an opportunity to build relationship and trust with other departments and expands team members' knowledge and expertise including the following:

- Inflow of fresh ideas that drive and stimulate creativity and innovation
- Fresh look at GIA's operations
- Builds and strengthens relationships and trust
- Enhanced appreciation of GIA's work
- Learning from experts
- Open the door for secondment and guest auditor opportunities

CHAPTER SUMMARY

Enhancing GIA value to the organization and its stakeholders depends on the team members understanding of the business and operations of the organization. There is no value to add if there is no understanding. The team members of GIA must regularly refresh their understanding of the needs of the organization and its stakeholders. Understanding will assist in keeping the objectives of the organization at the forefront of team members' thinking, planning, and activities.

Enhancing GIA value to the organization requires continuous engagement and collaboration with stakeholders, peers, and colleagues within and outside of the organization. Continuous engagement and collaboration enable stakeholders to be more proactive in addressing change. This is required for team members to stay connected, current, informed, and ready to quickly respond, and adapt to change. Continuous learning and improvement also enhance the team members' readiness, resilience, and relevance. A key role of CAE is to build and maintain a ready, resilient, and relevant GIA team.

The CAE must adopt the agile methodology for leading GIA. The methodology assists in paving the way for enhancing GIA's effectiveness, efficiency and value to the organization and its stakeholders. This will require team members to adopt the methodology in performing their responsibilities. It includes focusing on continuous learning and improvement, which are fundamental to an agile GIA leadership and operating environment. The focus is necessary to keep current and ready to quickly respond and adapt to change. Continuous learning and improvement also enhance the team members' readiness, resilience, and relevance.

A key factor in enhancing GIA's value to the organization and its stakeholders is the alignment of GIA's plans and activities with the objectives of the organization. This includes alignment with the strategy, objectives, and risk mitigation plans and activities of the organization. The alignment of findings and recommendations with the objectives of the organization is one of the most important elements of enhancing GIA's value to the organization. Alignment requires keeping the objectives of the organization and its stakeholders at the forefront of the mindset of the leaders and team members of GIA.

The leaders of GIA must build and maintain effective relationships with stakeholders to improve and enhance their value to the organization. There are mutual benefits to GIA and the organization from building and maintaining effective relationships. It builds trust and enhances the alignment of GIA's plans and activities with the strategy and objectives of the organization and its stakeholders. It also enhances the readiness, resilience, and relevance of the leaders of GIA.

The leaders of GIA must go beyond assurance to enhance their value to the organization and its stakeholders. They must increase the level of their engagement and collaboration to go beyond assurance, which requires becoming proactive engaging with stakeholders. They must become proactive to raise the level of their engagement and collaboration with stakeholders. Going beyond assurance also includes collaborating closely with assurance functions service providers. It will also assist stakeholders who are faced with the challenge of having to make quick decisions in an ever-changing operating environment. The leaders must also be solution-driven to enhance their value to the organization and its stakeholders.

The CAE and team members of GIA must leverage their unique knowledge and understanding of the business and operations to enhance GIA's value to the organization. This includes assisting with improving and enhancing the organization's control environment to effectively mitigate risks from the rapid pace of change. They must also unleash their unique knowledge and understanding of the organization to enhance the quality of their work product. The information and reports provided to stakeholders must be impactful and contribute to the effectiveness and efficiency of the organization.

GIA can be an excellent training ground for developing future managers and leaders of the organization. This includes secondment and rotation opportunities. The benefits to the organization and its staff are unique to GIA because of its broad scope of work. It takes a mature GIA to be recognized as a valuable training ground for future managers and leaders of the organization. The benefits to GIA for serving as a training ground for future managers and leaders is a win-win option for the candidates, GIA, and the organization.

15 Scaling Up Advisory Review Services

INTRODUCTION

There is no better time for a chief audit executive (CAE) to scale up global internal audit (GIA) advisory review services than in times of rapid change and disruption in the operating environment. The demand for advisory review services is usually high at such times. The changes and disruption in the operating environment are often driven by technological innovations, government regulations, global health crises, geopolitical, and societal issues. Organizations are often forced to change their plans and transform their operations during these dynamic times. This is necessary for organizations to remain competitive, and profitable. The COVID-19 pandemic, for example, forced organizations across the globe to accelerate their plans and initiatives to survive by shifting from in-person to virtual and digital processes to remain in business. The other option is to become obsolete and go out of business, which all organizations try to avoid.

Organizations often do not have the resources to address the disruption in the operating environment. This includes new and emerging risks, some of which are unprecedented, and opportunities that come along with change. Organizations often seek advice from advisory service providers or consultants to navigate the changes and disruption.

The purpose of this chapter is to provide advice and guidance on why it is important for CAEs to scale up GIA's advisory review services in times of rapid change and disruption in the operating environment. Topics covered include the following:

- The nature of advisory reviews
- Scaling up advisory reviews
- Support for advisory review services
- Advisory review policy
- Bridging gaps in skills and expertise
- Handling request for an advisory review
- Advisory review process
- Key differences between advisory reviews and internal audit
- Disposition of the results of the advisory review
- Comparison of in-sourcing and out-sourcing of advisory reviews
- Value of advisory reviews to the organization and GIA

Key learnings from the chapter include the following:

- Understanding the nature of advisory reviews
- Value of scaling up or adding advisory review services to GIA's value basket

DOI: 10.1201/9781003207559-15

- Importance of having an advisory review policy
- Partnering with others to bridge the gaps in skills and expertise
- Risk in undertaking an advisory review without the required skills or expertise
- Important steps in the advisory review process
- Key differences between internal audit and advisory reviews
- Sharing advisory review report with others
- The pros and cons of in-sourcing and out-sourcing of advisory reviews
- Value of advisory reviews to the organization and GIA

THE NATURE OF ADVISORY REVIEWS

The demand for advisory reviews is usually high during times of rapid change and disruption in the operating environment. It is a time where there is a rise in new, emerging, and, at times, unprecedented risks, and opportunities. The new risks and opportunities usually require the assistance and advice of professionals with specialized skills and expertise. This is to assist stakeholders with effectively managing the risks and capitalize on the opportunities that come along with change. Stakeholders are usually not able to effectively perform their regular responsibilities and navigate the rapid changes in the operating environment. Advisory reviews are usually to provide assurance and advice, including insight and foresight, to assist stakeholders in making informed and critical decisions.

Stakeholders at times engage GIA to perform advisory reviews to quickly obtain information and results. The information is to assist in making more informed decisions in mitigating risks and capitalizing on the opportunities that come along with change. The CAE and leaders of GIA must assign a mature team with the required skills and expertise to perform the advisory review. The team leader must be agile, competent, and experienced.

Advisory review requests usually come with high visibility, risks, and rewards. The request for an advisory review is usually time sensitive and from a key stakeholder, including the board, audit committee, or a member of the senior management team. A request to GIA for an advisory review is a sign of the maturity and value of GIA to the organization. However, advisory reviews are often demanding, requires specialized skills and expertise that may not exist in GIA or the organization, and may conflict with GIA's approved audit plan.

Advisory reviews are based on procedures agreed to by GIA and the requestor of the review. The requestor usually shares and discusses with GIA the objective of the review and the procedures they want GIA to perform. Engaging and collaborating closely with the requestor is required to ensure that the requestor's needs are met. This is also to ensure that the review process and procedures are in alignment with the needs of the requestor. As the review progresses, reviewing and discussing findings and incorporating feedback from the requestor into the review process will assist in ensuring that the objective of the review is met.

Advisory review requests are either planned or unplanned. GIA's annual expense budget and audit plan may include funding for advisory reviews. This is usually based on known or expected activities and agreement with stakeholders. The types and scope of advisory review vary from organization to organization, and industry to industry. Requests for advisory reviews are usually driven either by a specific event or change in the internal and/or external operating environment. The types of advisory reviews that GIA may be requested to perform include the following:

- Cyberattack
- Contract agreements
- Change management process
- Data protection and security breach
- Efficiency and effectiveness of operations
- Geopolitical-related issues
- Global pandemics related issues
- Incident response and recovery process
- Information systems implementation
- Merger and acquisitions related matters
- New and emerging issues and risks
- Compliance with new regulations
- Pre- and post-award of grants
- Supply chain and third party
- Waste and abuse

Unplanned advisory review requests are often a disruption to GIA's approved audit plan as the review is often triggered by changes in the internal and/or external operating environment. The CAE and leaders of GIA must at times reassign team members and obtain funding to cover the additional cost of undertaking the advisory review. This often requires the CAE negotiating with stakeholders for the funding of unplanned advisory reviews. There are stakeholders who have no problem covering the costs and others that are not as keen to provide the funding. They consider the in-house advisory review a free service, and it is a challenge at times obtaining reimbursement for performing the review. It is best to secure the funding for the unplanned advisory reviews upfront.

SCALING UP ADVISORY REVIEWS

There is no better time for a CAE to scale up GIA advisory review services than in times of rapid change and disruption in the operating environment. As mentioned above, the demand for advisory review services is usually high at such times. It is a time where there is a rise in new, emerging, and, at times, unprecedented risks, and opportunities. Organizations must quickly address the risks that come along with change to survive, remain competitive, and successful. Technological innovations, global pandemic, government regulations, geopolitical issues are among the key drivers of the rapid change and disruption. The reasons why there is no better time for the CAE to scale up GIA's advisory review services include the following:

- Management usually need assistance navigating the new and emerging risks and capitalize on the opportunities that come along with change
- Organizations are often forced to change their plans in times of rapid change and disruption in the operating

- Stakeholders are usually overwhelmed balancing their regular job and effectively manage change
- Organizations are not likely to have the expertise to effectively address new and emerging risks
- Everyone is in a learning mode

Organizations and stakeholders must become creative and innovative in addressing the constant changes and disruption in the operating environment. A good example are the changes that organizations, stakeholders, and individuals made during the COVID-19 pandemic to survive, remain competitive, and profitable. The changes included the following:

- Cutting back on office rental costs
- Employees worked remotely
- Reduction in business travel
- Remote project management
- Remote observation of inventories
- Virtual meetings, interviewing, and recruiting

The increase in demand for advisory review services is an opportunity for the CAE to demonstrate GIA's value to stakeholders and the organization. Management is not usually able to perform their regular work and keep up with the rapid, constant, and unprecedented changes, and disruption in the operating environment. This paves the way for the CAE to engage and scale up GIA's advisory review services for the organization. The CAE and team members have unique knowledge of the organization's business and operations and the ability to quickly mobilize staff. The unique knowledge of the business and operations and relationships with stakeholders across the organization make GIA a valuable resource for advisory reviews. The reviews can play a key role assisting stakeholders in mitigating risks and capitalizing on the opportunities from the changes in the operating environment.

The CAE must be proactive in finding out what type of advisory review services is most important to stakeholders. This requires engaging with stakeholders to determine what their current and expected advisory review needs are. Once the stakeholders' needs are identified, the CAE must be proactive and engage in securing the necessary resources to address the needs. Knowing what is most important to stakeholders coupled with the necessary resources will enhance GIA's readiness to provide advisory review services to the organization in times of rapid change and disruption. It will also enable the organization to be more proactive in responding to new, emerging, and unprecedented risks and opportunities.

The Chief executive officer (CEO) and senior management must seriously consider providing the CAE with the necessary resources to enhance GIA's ability to effectively perform advisory reviews. The ability of GIA to effectively perform advisory reviews is a valuable resource and service to an organization and its stakeholders. GIA's advisory reviews will assist in reducing the organization's dependency on consulting firms for advisory review services in times of rapid and constant change in the operating environment. Effectively performing advisory reviews will require a competent and experienced team with the required skills and expertise. This will also require investing in continuous learning, training, and technological tools. The skills and expertise include the following:

- Agility
- Business acumen
- Communication
- Change management
- Critical thinking
- Cybersecurity
- Data protection and security
- Data analytics
- Diversity, equity, and inclusion
- Environmental, societal, and governance
- Information technology
- Soft or interpersonal
- Problem solving
- Project management

Risks to the reputation and assets of an organization are high during times of rapid change and disruption in the operating environment. This is because the implementation of internal controls tends to lag in such times. As a result, things could go wrong quickly in an organization from the delay in implementing internal controls, including financial loss, waste, abuse, and fraud. The root cause of these issues includes the following:

- Lack of segregation of duties
- Lack of policies, processes, and procedures
- Outdated policies, processes, and procedures
- Inexperienced or incompetent staff

The CAE and leaders of GIA can play a proactive role assisting stakeholders mitigate new and emerging risks to the organization's business, operating, reporting, and compliance objectives. This requires the inclusion and participation of GIA up front in an advisory role in the planning and discussion phases of strategic or major initiatives. It is particularly important during risk identification, assessment, and mitigation plan phases of the planning and discussion of major strategic, organizational, operational, and systems changes.

SUPPORT FOR ADVISORY REVIEW SERVICES

The value of GIA's advisory review services to the organization and its stakeholders depends on the buy-in and support of the CEO and senior management. This is because the effectiveness of advisory review services usually requires investment in specialized skills, expertise, and technological tools. The CEO and senior management must also be willing to invest in and utilize GIA's advisory review services when the need arises instead of engaging a consulting firm. The value of GIA's advisory review to the organization and its stakeholders includes the following:

- Cost savings to the organization
- Immediate mobilization of staff
- Little or no learning curve understanding the business and operations
- Easy access and availability of GIA's team to stakeholders for advice and to respond to follow-up questions

ADVISORY REVIEW POLICY

The development of an advisory review policy is a key element of scaling up GIA's advisory review services. The CAE must take the lead in developing the advisory review policy. The CEO and the audit committee as well as senior management's buy-in and support are required for the effective performance of advisory reviews by GIA. The CAE must also collaborate, share, and solicit input and buy-in from stakeholders within and outside of GIA. This must be done before submitting the policy to the CAE's manager, the CEO, and the audit committee for review and approval.

The advisory review policy is designed to provide guidance and clarity to all staff regarding the performance of advisory reviews by GIA. The content of the policy usually includes the purpose, authority, roles, responsibilities, scope, and applicability. The following is a description of each:

- Purpose: Explains why an advisory review policy is needed and provides guidance on what must be done
- Authority: Covers the authority of GIA, including access to staff, systems, documents, records, and reports
- Role: Provides clarity of roles, responsibility, and accountability
- Scope: Covers the type of advisory reviews GIA will undertake
- Applicability: Covers who the policy applies to and the effective date

The advisory review policy sets the tone at the top of the organization for the activity. This requires the buy-in and support of the CEO, including members of the senior management team, and the audit committee. Their buy-in and support are an indication of the organization's commitment and the importance of GIA's advisory reviews to the organization. This also enhances management and staff cooperation and support across the organization for the activity.

The advisory review policy enhances the effectiveness of GIA's advisory review services. Key factors that enhance the effectiveness include the following:

- Formality: Recognized as the organization's official guidance for the performance of advisory reviews by GIA.
- Clarity: Minimizes confusion and misunderstandings regarding the purpose of the activity.
- Order: Brings order to the process and the activity.
- Consistency: Ensures advisory review guidelines are applied consistently across the organization.

- Exception: Ensures exceptions to the advisory review policy are reviewed and approved before implementation.

BRIDGING THE GAPS IN SKILLS AND EXPERTISE

The CAE and leaders of GIA must get comfortable partnering with experts internal or external to the organization. This is to assist in areas where the required skills and expertise to perform an advisory review is lacking. The fact is that there are going to be areas where GIA either lacks the required skills and expertise or is not fully capable of performing an advisory review. The reasons include the following:

- Traditional and unapplicable skills and expertise
- Required skills and expertise may not be needed on an ongoing basis to warrant the investment
- Costs outweigh the benefits

The CAE must engage and seek assistance from internal experts in areas where GIA lacks the required skills and expertise to perform advisory reviews. This is usually a good option for the organization because of the following:

- Quick mobilization and deployment of staff to perform the advisory review
- Internal knowledge and understanding of the business and operations of the organization
- Little or no learning curve as the staff will be familiar with the operations and business
- Cost savings to the organization compared to engaging a consulting firm

Areas within the organization that the CAE can engage for assistance include the following:

- Finance and accounting
- Information technology
- Data protection and security
- Operations
- Human resources

The senior leader of the entity within the organization with specialized skills or expertise must approve the sharing of staff with GIA. The CAE may encounter challenges with the request for in-house assistance as leaders are often reluctant to loan their staff for special projects. This is often because of limited resources and conflicting priorities. It can also become stressful for the staff with specialized skills or expertise with pressure from two leaders competing for his or her time. The CAE has the option of seeking senior management or the CEO's support for the request, but that may damage the relationship with the leader of the entity with the expertise. The other viable option for the CAE is to partner with an outside service provider to assist GIA in areas where it lacks required skills or expertise.

The CAE should consider partnering with an external service provider to assist GIA in areas where it is not fully capable of performing an advisory review. This can be a valuable option to the organization and GIA's operation. An evaluation of potential partners is necessary to ensure that the right fit is selected to assist GIA. Key factors to consider in the evaluation process include the following:

- Competence and experience with the subject matter
- Qualifications, including education, training, and certifications
- Business acumen
- Communications skills
- Problem-solving methodology, including identifying root cause and solutions
- Knowledge and experience with information technology and tools
- Cost

The value that the organization and GIA can gain from partnering with an external service provider includes the following:

- Enhanced knowledge of the subject matter
- Exposure to specialized skills, expertise, and experience
- Knowledge of current activities and trends in the industry

A key concern with this option is the cost. However, cost may not be an issue for the organization as it may be a matter of survival and remaining relevant, competitive, and profitable.

HANDLING THE REQUEST FOR AN ADVISORY REVIEW

A CAE must confirm the objective(s), agreed upon procedures, deliverables, and timing of the review with the requestor and perform a risk assessment before undertaking the advisory review. The risks to GIA of undertaking the review are high but so are the rewards. The risk assessment will assist the CAE in determining the following:

- Whether the skills and expertise exist in GIA or other areas of the organization to assist GIA in undertaking the review
- Whether the deliverables and timelines are reasonable and realistic
- Whether the CAE will need external assistance in performing the review
- Impact of the review on the approved internal audit plan and whether audit committee approval is required
- Cost and responsibility for funding the review
- Whether to accept or decline the request

A CAE has four key options to consider deciding whether to undertake or decline a request for an in-house advisory review. The four key options are as follows:

- Accept the request because GIA has the required skills and expertise to perform the review

- Accept the request by partnering with expert(s) in other areas of the organization to assist GIA in areas where it is not fully capable of performing the review
- Accept the request by partnering with an external service provider to assist GIA in areas where there are no in-house skills and expertise
- Decline the request if GIA does not have the required resources, including skills, expertise, and funding to perform the review

If GIA is unable to perform the review, the CAE should explain to the requestor the reason(s) for declining the request and provide alternative solutions, including outsourcing the review.

The CAE and GIA's integrity, credibility, and reputation are at risk by undertaking an advisory review where GIA is not fully capable of performing. The CAE must get comfortable with the fact that GIA will not always have the required skills and expertise to address stakeholders' needs. The required skills and expertise are being driven by the rapid and constant pace of change and disruption in the operating environment. The risks of undertaking an advisory review that GIA is not fully capable of performing include the following:

- Over-promising and underdelivering
- Cancelation, delay, and/or deferral of planned internal audits
- Deviation from the approved audit plan
- Loss of future advisory review work

THE ADVISORY REVIEW PROCESS

The CAE must ensure that the advisory review process is effective and efficient. This includes adopting a collaborative and agile approach for providing advisory review services. The focus is on quickly obtaining an understanding of what is most important to the requestor and required for the timely delivery of valuable results. The advisory review process must be flexible and easy to follow to maximize the benefits to stakeholders. Key steps in the advisory review process include the following:

Step I: Confirm agreed upon procedures and timing of engagement with requestor.
Step II: Select advisory review team lead.
Step III: Select team members.
Step IV: Conduct advisory review planning meeting.
Step V: Prepare and issue engagement memo.
Step VI: Conduct kick-off meeting.
Step VII: Commence the review.
Step IIX: Share findings and recommendations with the requestor as they arise.
Step IX: Update requestor periodically on progress.
Step X: Prepare and share draft report with requestor for feedback.
Step XI: Update and issue final report.
Step XII: Conduct stakeholder satisfaction survey.
Step XIII: Follow-up on interdepartmental recommendations.

KEY DIFFERENCES BETWEEN ADVISORY REVIEW AND INTERNAL AUDIT

As mentioned earlier, advisory review is based on procedures agreed to by GIA and the requestor. The agreed-on procedures are designed to address the specific needs of the requestor. The objective of an advisory review is usually to provide advice, including insight and foresight, on either a specific topic, event, or an activity. It may also include providing assurance on the effectiveness of the organization's governance programs and processes. The timeliness in the delivery of actionable and valuable results is usually what is most important to stakeholders. A comparison of advisory reviews and internal audits is shown in Table 15.1.

TABLE 15.1
Comparison of Advisory Review and Internal Audit

Subject	Advisory Review	Internal Audit
Key driver	Planned and unplanned requests	Approved audit plan
Primary objective	Provide advice, including insight and foresight, on either a specific topic, activity, or a significant change in the internal and/or external operating environment of the organization. It may also include providing assurance on the effectiveness of governance, risk, compliance, and internal controls	Provide assurance, advice, including insight and foresight, into the effectiveness of governance, risk, compliance, and internal controls
Planning and supervision	Required	Required
Scope	Based on the needs of the requestor	Based on audit plan and program
Testing procedures	Agreed on procedures	Outlined in audit program
Test selection method	Usually non-statistical or haphazard	Usually statistical, random, or non-statistical
Compliance with IIA's Global Internal Audit Standards	Only those related to advisory reviews or consulting services	Required
Exercise of due professional care	Required	Required
Sharing of the results of findings and recommendations	Controlled by the requestor except for significant and interdepartmental findings and recommendations	Predetermined distribution list and impacted stakeholders
Distribution of the report	Controlled by the requestor	Predetermined distribution list
Response to findings and recommendations	Optional	Required
Implementation of recommendations	Optional	Required or agree to disagree by the CAE and the stakeholder
Follow up on the implementation of audit recommendations	Optional except for significant and interdepartmental findings and recommendations	Required
Rating of the results	Not required	Required in some cases

Advisory review is based on procedures agreed designed to address the specific needs of the requestor.

DISPOSITION OF THE RESULTS OF THE ADVISORY REVIEW

The requestor of the advisory review owns and controls the sharing and distribution of the advisory review report. The sharing and distribution of the advisory review report must be in accordance with the wishes of the requestor and the advisory review policy. It is customary for the requestor to share the results of the advisory review and the report with the requestor's manager. The CAE must advise and collaborate with the requestor on the timely sharing of significant and cross cutting findings and recommendations with impacted stakeholders. The sharing must include the CEO and senior management. If the requestor refuses to share significant findings and recommendations with impacted stakeholders and senior management, the CAE must escalate the matter to key stakeholders. This includes the requestor's manager, the CEO, and the chairpersons of the board and/or the audit committee. This is done to enhance the transparency and minimize surprises. It also enables impacted stakeholders to be proactive in taking action to mitigate risks to their operations.

The requestor and impacted stakeholders are not obligated to implement recommendations resulting from the advisory review. They may use the results to either make informed decisions and/or confirm compliance or their understanding of the issue or matter. However, it is good business practice and policy to require the sharing of significant advisory review findings and recommendations with senior management and the CEO. This includes the periodic sharing of the implementation status of interdepartmental recommendations. In addition, the CAE must follow-up and report periodically on the status of the implementation of advisory review recommendations aimed at mitigating significant and cross-cutting risks to the organization.

COMPARISON OF IN-SOURCING AND OUT-SOURCING OF ADVISORY REVIEWS

There are areas where GIA will have an advantage over a consulting firm and others where it will not. The areas include the following:

- Deeper knowledge and understanding of the operations and business of the organization
- Deeper knowledge and understanding of the culture of the organization
- Ability to quickly assign and deploy GIA staff to perform the advisory review
- Shorter learning curve of the organization's business and operations
- Readily available in-house support
- Potential cost savings

Consulting firms usually want to be the leaders in providing solutions on new and emerging issues, risks, and opportunities to their clients. The firms typically have the resources and dedicated staff to quickly conduct research and offer solutions to their clients. However, consulting firms are not immune to the change and disruption in the operating environment. They too must embrace and adapt to the changes in the operating environment to survive and remain competitive, and profitable. The challenges of consulting firms are no different than other organizations operating in an ever-changing operating environment. The areas where a consulting firm usually has an advantage over GIA in providing advisory review services to an organization include the following:

- In-house specialists and experts
- Dedicated staff to perform research
- More current on matters of interest, including the following:
  - Technological innovations and tools
  - New and emerging risks and opportunities
  - New and/or pending laws and regulations
- Independence

VALUE OF ADVISORY REVIEWS TO THE ORGANIZATION AND GIA

The value of GIA's advisory reviews to stakeholders and the organization is enhanced when GIA is involved early in the process of strategic or major initiatives. The value to the organization and its stakeholders from the early involvement of GIA includes the following:

- Pre-award or pre-implementation reviews: These reviews are performed before a formal agreement is made or a major project is initiated or undertaken. This includes the award of a contract or a grant, and the undertaking of a major project. Reviews are usually performed to verify or validate supporting information or to determine that necessary steps have been taken, such as risk assessment and development of a plan, before undertaking a major project.
- Follow-up or post-implementation reviews: The reviews are performed to ensure that the implementation is operating as planned as well as effectively and efficiently. It is best to perform reviews within the first three months of a major undertaking. The benefits of performing such a review include the following:
  - Objectives of the undertaking are being achieved
  - Provides reasonable assurance whether mitigation controls identified and agreed to in the planning phase, particularly for high-risk areas, are operating as planned as well as effectively and efficiently
  - Assist in minimizing surprises and significant audit findings and risks, including financial loss, in subsequent months and years
  - Assist in identifying major new or emerging risks and opportunities on the ground not considered in the planning phase

The value of GIA's advisory reviews to GIA's operations and team includes the following:

- Indication and recognition of GIA's maturity
- Recognition of GIA as a relevant partner and advisor

- Improves GIA's image as a problem solver instead of a fault finder
- Development of new skills, expertise, and opportunities for team members
- Increase in knowledge and understanding from an advisory review makes the audit of the area more efficient and effective
- Enhances the value of the CAE as a trusted strategic advisor
- Supports GIA having a seat at the table of a major initiative
- Supports proactive internal auditing

CHAPTER SUMMARY

Stakeholders at times engage GIA to perform advisory reviews to assist in mitigating risks and capitalizing on the opportunities that come along with change. The requests usually come with high visibility, risks, and rewards. It requires engaging and collaborating closely with the requestor to ensure that the objective of the review is met. The types and scope of an in-house advisory review varies from organization to organization, and industry to industry. The reviews are based on procedures agreed to by GIA and the requestor of the advisory review. The reviews are either planned or unplanned. Unplanned advisory review requests are often a disruption to GIA's approved audit plan. Also the performance of advisory reviews often requires specialized skills and expertise.

There is no better time for a CAE to scale up GIA's advisory review services than in an ever-changing operating environment. Organizations are often forced to change their plans and transform their operations in such times. The changes and disruption usually drive the increase in demand for advisory review services and is an opportunity for the CAE to demonstrate GIA's value to the organization and its stakeholders. The CAE must be proactive in finding out what type of advisory review services is most important to stakeholders. The risk of loss is high during times of rapid change and disruption in the operating environment. The CAE and leaders of GIA can play a proactive role in assisting stakeholders to mitigate new and emerging risks to the organization's business, operating, reporting, and compliance objectives.

The development of an advisory review policy is a key element of scaling up GIA's advisory review services. The advisory review policy sets the tone at the top of the organization for the activity. It also enhances the effectiveness of GIA's advisory review services. It is designed to provide guidance and clarity to all staff regarding the performance of advisory reviews by GIA.

A CAE must not undertake an advisory review where GIA lacks the required skills and expertise or is not fully capable of performing. It is a risk to the integrity and reputation of the CAE and GIA. The CAE must get comfortable partnering with experts internal or external to the organization to assist in bridging gaps in specialized skills and expertise.

The CAE must ensure that the advisory review process is effective and efficient. It includes adopting a collaborative and agile approach for providing advisory review services. This approach enables team members to respond and act quickly. The focus is on quickly obtaining an understanding of what is most important to stakeholders by engaging and collaborating closely on the timely delivery of valuable results. This includes listening, understanding, empathizing, sharing, and aligning with their needs. The advisory review process must be in alignment with what is most important to the organization and its stakeholders.

The advisory review is based on procedures agreed to by GIA and the requestor. The agreed-on procedures are designed to address the specific needs of the requestor. The objective of an advisory review is usually to provide assurance or advice on either a specific topic or activity. It may also include providing assurance and advice, including insight and foresight, into the effectiveness of the organization's governance programs and processes. This includes risk management, compliance, and internal controls. The timeliness in the delivery of actionable and valuable results is usually what is most important to stakeholders. This is particularly important to stakeholders in times of rapid and constant change and disruption in the operating environment.

The requestor of the advisory review owns and controls the sharing and distribution of the advisory review report. The CAE must advise and collaborate with the requestor on the timely sharing of significant and interdepartmental findings and recommendations with impacted stakeholders. The requestor is not obligated to implement the recommendations of the advisory review. However, the CAE must follow-up and periodically report on the implementation status of significant advisory review findings and recommendations.

The demand for advisory review services is usually higher in times of rapid change and disruption in the operating environment. There are areas where GIA will have an advantage over a consulting firm and others where it will not. Consulting firms are usually better prepared to meet the specialized needs of their clients in an ever-changing operating environment. They usually want to be the first out the gate providing solutions on new and emerging issues, risks, and opportunities to their clients.

The organization's senior management must consider providing the necessary resources to enhance GIA's ability to effectively perform advisory reviews. The value of the review services to the organization depends on the buy-in and support of the CEO and senior management. The value of the reviews to stakeholders and the organization is enhanced when GIA is involved early in the process of strategic or major initiatives.

16 Establishing a Proactive Fraud Investigation Function

INTRODUCTION

The journey of establishing a proactive fraud investigation function begins with the creation of an antifraud policy. The policy sets the tone at the top and must contain a strong statement regarding retaliation, frivolous allegations, and disciplinary actions. While the ultimate responsibility for fraud risk rests with the board of directors (hereinafter the board), and senior management, fraud prevention is the responsibility of everyone affiliated with the organization. The Association of Certified Fraud Examiners (ACFE) defines fraud, based on Black's Law Dictionary, as any activity that relies on deception in order to achieve a gain. Fraud becomes a crime when it is a "knowing misrepresentation of the truth or concealment of a material fact to induce another to act to his or her detriment."[1] "In other words, if you lie in order to deprive a person or organization of their money or property, you're committing fraud."[2]

The mission of a proactive fraud investigation function is to effectively support the organization's fraud risk mitigation program. The leader of the function must act proactively to assist in minimizing the risk of fraud to the organization. The operating environment is constantly changing and disruptive and so too is fraud and the schemes under which it is perpetrated. A proactive fraud investigation function is a key element of the organization's governance structure and system of internal control. The leader of the function must play a key role in providing fraud awareness training to stakeholders. This keeps stakeholders informed of the threat of fraud to the organization and mitigating activities. Promoting the value of a proactive fraud investigation function paves the way for enhanced engagement and collaboration with stakeholders.

Fraud investigation is an expensive and highly technical area and activity. It requires specialized knowledge, expertise, and technological tools to investigate effectively and efficiently. A proactive fraud investigation function must have the support of senior management and the board to be successful. A separate department or entity of fraud investigation assists in preserving the integrity, credibility, independence, and objectivity of the function.

The purpose of this chapter is to provide advice and guidance on how a proactive fraud investigation function plays a key role in minimizing fraud risks. This includes

DOI: 10.1201/9781003207559-16

minimizing the risk of financial loss and reputational damage to the organization. Topics include the following:

- Antifraud policy
- Responsibility for fraud prevention
- Mission of a proactive fraud investigation function
- Building and maintaining effective relationships
- Support of key stakeholders
- Key requirements of a proactive fraud investigation function
- Managing fraud investigations
- Managing challenges, resistance, and expectations
- Proactive fraud investigation processes and procedures
- Proactive fraud investigation report
- Reporting of alleged fraudulent activities
- Cyber-fraud
- Leveraging technology
- Antifraud controls
- Whistleblower hotline
- Fraud awareness training

Key learnings from the chapter include the following:

- Importance of having an antifraud policy
- Reason fraud prevention is everybody's business
- Reason fraud investigation function must be proactive
- Pros and cons of in-sourcing, co-sourcing, and out-sourcing of fraud investigations
- Importance of promoting the values of a proactive fraud investigation function
- Key requirements of a proactive fraud investigation function
- Value of the following:
    - Building and maintaining effective relationship with other leaders of assurance functions
    - Leader of the function reporting to the highest possible level in the organization
    - Antifraud controls and a whistleblower hotline to an organization
    - Embracing and leveraging technology
    - Providing fraud awareness training

ANTIFRAUD POLICY

The journey of establishing a proactive fraud investigation function begins with the creation of an antifraud policy. The policy sets the tone at the top regarding the organization's fraud investigation function. Setting the tone at the top signifies the importance and value of the fraud investigation function to the organization. The policy must be shared with everyone affiliated with the organization, including board members, employees, contractors, vendors, and volunteers. The policy should be part of new board members, employees, and volunteer orientation program and reshared at least annually. The policy must also be displayed conspicuously in all communal areas of the organization and provided to consultants and vendors.

The board's oversight role for fraud risks includes overseeing the organization's antifraud policy in collaboration with senior management. Senior management usually includes the chief executive officer (CEO) and his or her direct reports. Senior management or consultants usually draft the policy for review and approval by the board. The policy must be reviewed at least annually and as needed to ensure that it is still relevant to address the risk of fraud in the operating environment. Senior management is responsible for overseeing the implementation, monitoring, and periodically reporting to the board on the effectiveness and compliance with the organization's antifraud policy. They are also responsible for ensuring that processes and procedures are implemented to support compliance with the policy.

The organization's antifraud policy must contain a strong statement regarding retaliation, frivolous allegations, and disciplinary actions. Retaliation is a malicious act against an individual, group, or organization for reporting and/or taking disciplinary action for alleged fraudulent activities. Malicious act is to either intend to or inflict harm to someone without a cause or for no reason. It includes threat of physical harm, sabotage, and defamation of character. A frivolous allegation is a baseless or inaccurate claim made against an individual, group, or organization. This is usually because of a grudge or revenge by a disgruntled person. Retaliation and frivolous allegations are disruptive and a distraction in the organization. The antifraud policy must prohibit misconduct against anyone for reporting alleged or suspicious fraudulent activities. This behavior must be subjected to disciplinary action up to and including termination. Disciplinary action is the action taken to correct, prevent, and deter unacceptable and bad behaviors such as retaliation and frivolous activities from recurring. Disciplinary actions may be in the form of a verbal or written warning, suspension, unpaid leave, termination, or referral to law enforcement for prosecution, as well as pursuing the recovery of losses.

The ACFE defines fraud, based on Black's Law Dictionary, as any activity that relies on deception in order to achieve a gain. Fraud becomes a crime when it is a "knowing misrepresentation of the truth or concealment of a material fact to induce another to act to his or her detriment."[3] "In other words, if you lie in order to deprive a person or organization of their money or property, you're committing fraud."[4] There are internal and external fraudulent activities that are committed against organizations. Internal or occupational fraud is committed by those within the organization, including board members, senior management, managers, supervisors, employees, and volunteers. Fraudulent activities include conflict of interest, misstatement of financial statements, misappropriation of assets, embezzlement, and falsification of documents, among others. Falsification of documents includes signatures, checks, inventory receiving documents, invoices, sales cut-off, and alteration to citation. External fraud is committed by individuals operating outside of the organization. The type of fraud includes bribery, kickbacks, falsification of documents, extortion, and bid rigging. Falsification of documents includes but is not limited to signatures, checks, and invoices.

Organizations get credit for having an effective antifraud policy and a proactive fraud investigation function. This includes a proactive fraud investigation program and effective processes, and procedures. It is expected and welcomed by external stakeholders, including investors, donors, creditors, regulators, insurance companies, prospective board members, and employees. An antifraud policy, processes, procedures, and an effective investigation program are key areas of focus of external stakeholders' assessing the governance of an organization.

RESPONSIBILITY FOR FRAUD RISK

Fraud prevention is everyone's business. While the ultimate responsibility for fraud risk rests with the board and senior management fraud prevention is the responsibility of everyone affiliated with the organization. It includes employees, consultants, contractors, vendors, and volunteers. They have an obligation and responsibility to immediately report alleged or suspected incident of fraud observed against the organization. Senior management must ensure that everyone affiliated with the organization is aware of the organization's antifraud policy. This can be done when they join or do business with the organization as part of new board members and employee orientation programs. An organization that is afflicted by a significant fraud affects everyone who is affiliated with the organization. The impact and fallout are more damaging and disruptive if the fraud is perpetrated by senior management. Fallout includes any of or a combination of the following:

- Damage to the image and reputation of the organization
- Loss of monetary assets
- Loss of current investors, donors, and creditors
- Increase interest of new investors seizing the opportunity to capitalize on a vulnerable organization
- Decrease in the organization's credit rating
- Disruption of the organization operation
- Change in the leadership of the organization
- Demise or dissolution of the organization

The oversight of fraud risks is a key element of an organization's governance program. The board and senior management are responsible for the organization's governance and fraud risk management program. The board fraud risk oversight role is often delegated to a subcommittee of the board such as the audit or risk committee. A key element of the board's fraud risk oversight responsibility is to periodically meet with senior management and the leader of fraud investigation. The periodic meetings are to inform the board of new fraudulent activities and the status of ongoing fraud investigations. The meetings are also for the board to discuss and obtain assurance on the effectiveness of internal controls to mitigate the risk of fraud to the organization. The periodic meetings may be restricted to a limited number of attendees on a need-to-know basis. This is because of the sensitivity and confidential nature of fraud investigations.

A fraud investigation function is a key element of the governance of an organization. A member of the senior management team should be assigned to oversee and/or manage the function. This is due to the usual sensitivity of matters requiring investigation. It is critical in preserving the integrity, credibility, and confidentiality of the function. Additionally, it contributes to the independence, objectivity, and effectiveness of the function. The function can be managed either in-house, outsourced, or co-sourced to a professional investigation firm.

Fraud risk assessment and mitigation are key elements of an organization's fraud risk management program. Each manager must be required to prepare a risk assessment for their area(s) of responsibility. This includes identifying risks to their areas of operation and the achievement of the objectives of the organization. They must also update their fraud risk assessment regularly to address the changing nature of risk in the operating environment.

A fraud risk mitigation plan is required to address fraud risks identified in the fraud risk assessment process. It plays a key role in preventing, detecting, and deterring fraudulent activities. The mitigation plan contains activities and measures that are being taken to minimize the opportunity for fraud to take place. Fraudsters will think twice about committing a fraudulent act where the opportunity does not exist. Opportunity is one of the three drivers of fraud along with the justification and the need. A fraud mitigation plan ensures that internal controls are in place to minimize the opportunity for fraud to take place. This includes holding fraudsters accountable, reporting fraudulent activities to law enforcement, and publicizing fraudulent activities, if legal, in the organization's newsletter.

Senior management is responsible for developing and implementing the organization's fraud risk management program. However, they usually delegate this responsibility to managers. This includes developing and implementing processes and procedures to ensure compliance with the fraud policy. Senior management also at times establishes management policies as a source of guidance for managers to effectively manage and ensure compliance with the organization's antifraud policy. The policies and procedures are usually standardized. A standardized, automated fraud risk management system, processes, and procedures are the most effective and efficient means of managing and accomplishing this responsibility.

Managers are responsible for managing risks in their area(s) of responsibility. As mentioned earlier, senior management usually delegates the implementation of policies to their managers. Managers, in turn, must develop and implement processes and procedures to effectively manage the risks. This requires identifying, assessing, including evaluating and prioritizing, and documenting fraud risks in their area(s) of responsibility. They are also responsible for mitigating, tracking, updating, monitoring, and reporting periodically on the effectiveness of their fraud risk management program. The periodic reporting is usually to their supervisor, the fraud risk coordinator, if applicable, and senior management.

A proactive fraud investigation function is a valuable resource for managers to tap into for guidance on assessing and managing fraud risk. Managers do need assistance at times in performing their fraud risk assessment. This is an opportunity for the leader of a proactive fraud investigation function and internal audit (IA) to enhance their value to the organization. This includes advising, providing awareness training, sharing experiences, and emerging fraud risks to assist senior management and managers proactively address potential fraud in the organization.

Organizations that do not have a fraud investigation function often turn to internal audit (IA) to perform investigations of allegations of fraud. This is a valuable service to the organization when it does not have a fraud investigation function. However, this could be a double edge sword for IA since fraud investigation is an expensive and highly specialized area. It requires a team member with investigative knowledge, experience, and expertise to lead and/or perform the investigation. IA taking on that role also plays into the policeman perception often held regarding internal auditors. The reputation of IA could implode or disappear in a minute from a botched fraud investigation. The policing mindset is also a risk to the value of IA as a collaborative and trusted partner.

MISSION OF A PROACTIVE FRAUD INVESTIGATION FUNCTION

The mission of a proactive fraud investigation function is to effectively support the organization's fraud risk management program. The strategy of the program is to mitigate the risk of fraud to the organization's assets and reputation from internal and external fraudulent activities. This includes fraudulent activities such as misappropriation of assets, embezzlement, bribery, kickback, material misstatement of financial statements, falsification of documents, and extortion. These activities often result in s financial loss and reputational damage to an organization. Damage may include the demise, or dissolution of organizations such as in the case with MCI, WorldCom, Enron, Computer Associates, and Compaq.

The strategy of the fraud investigation function is to proactively assist stakeholders in mitigating risk of fraud to the organization. This is by proactively assisting in preventing, detecting, and deterring fraudulent activities against the organization before they materialize or in the early stages. While the approach should lessen the number of traditional fraud investigations, it does not eliminate the performance of traditional investigations. Traditional investigations activities will continue to be an important element of a proactive fraud investigation function.

Key difference between a proactive and a traditional fraud investigation approach lies in the strategy. The former is more forward-thinking and -looking, while the latter is reactive, backward-looking, and -thinking. However, the responsibilities and activities of both are similar, including the following:

- Maintaining the integrity and credibility of the function
- Sharing allegations of fraud in a timely manner with stakeholders on a need-to-know basis
- Conducing preliminary review of all fraud allegations to determine if an investigation is warranted
- Notifying key stakeholders of the disposition of fraud allegations
- Developing a detailed plan for each investigation
- Obtaining and documenting sufficient evidence to support the conclusion of the investigation
- Sharing the draft report with the legal department and update as needed before it is finalized
- Sharing the results of the investigation with key stakeholders before the issuance of the final report on a need-to-know basis

- Updating draft investigation report as needed with feedback from key stakeholders
- Delivering objective, unbiased, factual, and evidential investigation reports that can withstand scrutiny in a court of law
- Reviewing, tracking, and periodically reporting on the status of fraud allegations and investigations
- Completing investigations within a reasonable time
- Managing expectations
- Sharing improvement opportunities in a timely manner with stakeholders who can benefit from the lessons learned

Leaders of fraud investigation functions must evolve from the traditional and adopt a proactive approach to effectively support their organization's fraud risk mitigation program. They cannot sit and wait for allegations of fraud to be reported to act. The traditional approach is usually reactive and backward-looking with a policeman stigma attached to it. Investigators show up after the damage is done and at times make things worse. Additionally, the traditional approach contributes to the fear and the isolation of the function in the organization. A proactive approach to internal fraud investigations will minimize fear and isolation thereby enhancing the value to the organization.

Proactively assisting in mitigating the risk of fraud to the organization is one of the most important roles of a fraud investigation function. This is because change in the operating environment is constant and so too is fraud. Fraudsters know that organizations are most vulnerable in times of constant change in the operating environment. They know that internal controls, including structures, policies, processes, procedures, lag at such times and usually take advantage of the situation. The leaders of proactive fraud investigation functions can assist in minimizing the risk of fraud by doing the following:

- Advocate for the preparation of a fraud risk assessment by all managers
- Conduct periodic fraud awareness training for stakeholders
- Remind stakeholders of fraud risks, inherent and otherwise, that the organization encounters in pursuit of its mission, vision, and objectives
- Leverage technology to mine, analyze, connect the dots, and identify fraud red flags
- Share early warning signs of fraud red flags in a timely manner with stakeholders
- Invest in continuing training and education of team members
- Keep current on activities in the fraud space
- Collaborate with counterparts in other organizations

Additionally, the lessons learned, including the root cause and remedies, from investigations must be timely shared with stakeholders on a need-to-know basis. This will assist in mitigating fraud risks in other areas of the organization. Fraudulent activities will recur if suppressed, covered up, sugar coated, or ignored. The root cause of fraud must be identified and effectively addressed instead of a short-term fix.

The presence of a proactive fraud investigation function is a key element of the organization's governance structure and system of internal control. The function plays a key role in safeguarding the assets of the organization and preventing fraud, waste and abuse. Perpetrators will think twice before committing fraud if they are aware that there are controls in place to detect and investigate their illicit activities.

BUILDING AND MAINTAINING EFFECTIVE RELATIONSHIPS

The leader of a proactive fraud investigation function must build relationships with stakeholders. This includes the board, senior management, managers, and other assurance functions leaders. It enhances the engagement and understanding of stakeholders' fraud risk concerns thus enabling the leader to collaboratively assist in proactively mitigating fraud risks. It also enables the leader to better manage expectations, including the timing and confidentiality of the sharing of information on a need-to-know basis.

Building and maintaining effective relationships with the other leaders of assurance functions is essential in preventing, detecting, and deterring fraud risks. Other leaders of assurance functions include global internal audit or IA, risk management, compliance, and information security. The leaders of assurance functions are usually involved in gathering, analyzing, validating, tracking, monitoring, and reporting activities across the organization. The proactive fraud investigation function leader should meet periodically or as needed with the other leaders of assurance functions. This is to collaborate, share, and exchange information and intelligence on fraud risk to the extent possible. Sharing includes status updates on existing, new, and emerging fraud risks, and opportunities to mitigate them. The knowledge and intelligence gained from the meetings enable the leaders of assurance fuctions to leverage the information to connect the dots and provide stakeholders with insight and foresight regarding fraud risk. It also enables stakeholders to anticipate and proactively address fraud risks before they materialize or in the early stages of the fraud.

Confidentiality is a key factor in collaborating and sharing information with stakeholders. There will always be information that the leader of fraud investigation can only share on a need-to-know basis. This includes the nature, source of allegations, and the details of ongoing investigations. Confidentiality preserves the integrity and credibility of the investigation and protects witnesses. It also minimizes and prevents exposure to fraud schemes, which could be shared and perpetrated elsewhere in the organization. The sharing of certain information could also compromise the investigation. This could result in the loss of confidentiality, trust, and confidence in the function and the outcome of its investigation.

The leaders of a proactive fraud investigation function must actively promote the value of the function across the organization. The contribution of the function at times is overlooked and unappreciated usually by those motivated by self-interest instead of the mission and objectives of the organization. The self-interest activities may include defrauding the organization, conflict of interest, and misstatement of financial statements. The leaders of a proactive fraud investigation function must be able to share how the role supports and contributes to the objectives and the fraud risk mitigation plan and activities of the organization. This includes assisting in protecting the reputation and assets of the organization. Additionally, it is an opportunity for the leader to educate stakeholders on the intrinsic value of the function, including serving as a deterrent to those who may be contemplating committing fraud. These activities also reduce the policeman perception, fear, and isolation of the function.

The leader of a proactive fraud investigation function must capitalize on the benefits of building and maintaining effective relationships with stakeholders. Benefits include the following:

- Enhance the engagement, collaboration, and timely sharing of information
- Enable the leader to stay connected and timely informed of early warning signals and red flags
- Provide an opportunity to promote the role and value of the function to the organization
- Fast track connecting the dots and the prevention, detection, and deterrence of fraud
- Pave the way for a trusted advisor relationship with stakeholders
- Pave the way for quicker and easier access to employees and information
- Contribute to the agility of a proactive fraud investigation function
- Reduce and minimize the policeman perception and isolation of the function

SUPPORT OF KEY STAKEHOLDERS

A proactive fraud investigation function must have the support of senior management and the board to be successful. Their support set the tone at the top regarding the importance and value of a proactive fraud investigation function to the organization. This is particularly important in an operating environment where fraud risk is constantly changing. It also contributes to the support and cooperation of stakeholders and employees across the organization.

Integrity, credibility, confidentiality, fairness, independence, and objectivity are the pillars of a proactive fraud investigation function. Sustainability of the pillars and the effectiveness of the function depend on the level of support the function receives from senior management and the board, including support of the following:

- Establishing antifraud policy and procedures
- Setting the reporting line of the leader of the function to the highest feasible level of management
- Hiring or appointing a competent, knowledgeable, and experienced leader and team
- Providing the necessary resources for the function to be proactive, effective, and efficient, including funding for continuing training and professional education, expertise, and technological tools

KEY REQUIREMENTS OF A PROACTIVE FRAUD INVESTIGATION FUNCTION

Fraud investigation is an expensive and highly technical area and activity. It requires specialized knowledge, expertise, and technological tools, which often do not exist within the organization. The organization may not need specialized knowledge, experience, expertise, and technological tools full-time. A lean fraud investigation team, which comprises a competent and experienced leader, such as a certified Fraud Examiner (CFE), and a couple senior investigators may be all that is needed. Additional resources and/or expertise can be provided by a co-source partner. This may be a more cost-effective alternative than a large internal fraud investigation function. Out-sourcing the function outright to a firm that provides fraud investigation services is also an option. The cost benefit of an in-house investigation function varies due to many factors that must be considered before a decision is made whether to have the function in-house, co-sourced, or out-sourced.

The reporting line of the leader of a proactive fraud investigation function in the hierarchy of the organization matters. This includes direct access to the board. Reporting is most effective when the leader of the function reports administratively to the highest possible level in the organization and functionally to the board. The reporting can be either to the chairperson of the board or a subcommittee such as the audit or risk committee. A member of the senior management team must be assigned the responsibility to oversee and/or lead the organization's fraud investigation function and/or program. This is required regardless of which option, in-sourcing, co-sourcing, out-sourcing, is selected. A competent, knowledgeable, and experienced professional such as a CFE should lead the function due to the usual sensitivity and confidential nature of issues requiring investigation.

The leader of the function reporting to the highest possible senior management level in the organization signals the importance of the function to the organization. It is critical in preserving the integrity and credibility of the function. The formation of a separate department or entity of fraud investigations enhances the independence and objectivity of the function. The benefits to the organization of having the leader report to the highest possible level of senior management in the organization include the following:

- Gives the function the power that it needs to get management's cooperation and support in conducting investigations
- Enhances the independence, objectivity, and authority of the function
- Enhances the support and cooperation of senior management and managers

There are pros and cons of in-sourcing, co-sourcing, and out-sourcing of fraud investigations. Each has its merits depending on the size and complexity of the organization, the frequency of fraud, and the availability of resources. This includes funding, skills, expertise, technological tools, and time.

In a co-sourced or out-sourced fraud investigations program, the leader overseeing the program must have fraud investigation knowledge and experience. With co-sourcing, the leader of the fraud investigation function engages a co-sourcing partner to provide expertise for areas where the function lacks the expertise. With out-sourcing, the out-source partner does all the work. This includes planning, staffing, performing, preparing, and delivering the investigation reports to the leader of the fraud investigation program. This usually includes the presentation of the investigative findings and a report by the out-source partner to senior management and the board on a need-to-know basis. At the end of the day, responsibility for fraud risks rests with senior management and the board of the organization.

MANAGING FRAUD INVESTIGATIONS

The leader of a proactive fraud investigation function must obtain an understanding of fraud allegations before assigning the case to a team. This is to ensure that a competent, knowledgeable, and experienced leader and team, including specialists and subject matter experts, are assigned to perform the investigation. Consideration should be given to out or co-sourcing segments of the investigation if specialized knowledge or expertise does not exist within the organization.

A proactive fraud investigation must be well planned before it is launched. A key element of the planning is securing to the extent possible evidential matters before announcing and launching the investigation. Once the word gets out that there is or will be an investigation, the perpetrator(s) may destroy evidential items such as mobile phones, computer hardware, software, files, emails, documents, and accounting records. This includes procurement documents, such as contracts, purchase orders, receiving documents, and invoices. Implicated employee(s) should be placed on leave until cleared or the investigation is completed. This ensures that they do not interrupt, compromise, or try to influence the investigation. The investigator or investigating team must prioritize interviewing suspected employee(s) before they go on leave, suspended, resigned, or terminated. Employee(s) may resign and/or disappear once the word gets out that there is an investigation. Terminating the employment of a suspected employee before an interview with the investigator could result in the loss of valuable information on a deeper issue in the organization.

It is in the best interest of the organization for implicated employee(s) to be placed on leave of absence or modified duties until cleared by the investigation. This will prevent tampering and/or destruction of evidence, intimidation, retaliation, and threats of physical harm to employees and witnesses. There will be justifiable pushback at times from employees named in frivolous allegations. The allegation could be from a disgruntled person who may want to cause trouble. This is where a covert preliminary review of the allegation by a CFE or a trained investigator becomes invaluable to an organization. It minimizes the risk of taking unnecessary actions. Special care, including risk and reward, must be taken in sharing the names of those mentioned in the allegations. There is a risk of defamation of character, monetary damages, and disruption to operations from such disclosures. Allegations must be kept secured preferably in a database, for future reference and data analysis.

Confidentiality is a key element of the integrity and credibility of fraud investigations. Confidentiality of the investigation process is strengthened and preserved when allegations and investigations are shared on a need-to-know basis. Stakeholders normally informed of fraud allegations include the chief audit executive (CAE), manager and senior leader of the impacted area, the CEO, chief legal officer, chief people officer, and the chairperson of the board. It is important to keep the list to a bare minimum.

MANAGING CHALLENGES, RESISTANCE, AND EXPECTATIONS

Fraud investigations can be disruptive and a major distraction in an organization. The disruption and distraction often come from hostility generated by anger, feeling of betrayal, finger-pointing, and blame games that take place in such an environment. Fraud investigations have the potential of bringing an organization to a halt and/or its demise. Impact of results of investigation may also include the following:

- Damage to the image and reputation of the organization
- Loss of investors, donors, creditors, suppliers, and customers
- Loss of revenues
- Loss of key leaders and staff

Management and stakeholders often complain about the delays and the amount of time it takes to complete a fraud investigation. The complaints are understandable at times due to the length of time it takes to complete and deliver the investigation results. Investigations are often very disruptive, take time away from the core business, and can bring operations to a halt. However, the delays are often caused by an increase in the scope of the investigation due either to the pervasiveness of the fraud or the discovery of other fraudulent activities. This is often unknown at the outset of the investigation.

It is important to share upfront with stakeholders the possibility of delays and to keep them informed of changes in the expected completion date of the investigation. A reasonable time estimate of the completion can be given to stakeholders with the caveat that it is subject to change. An increase in scope usually requires additional time to gather sufficient evidence. In some cases, the evidence is clear-cut, but it must still be properly corroborated, substantiated, documented, and able to withstand scrutiny in a court of law. The reputation of the organization is at risk of legal liability, claims, and damages if the evidence is unsupported or false.

One way of minimizing the delays of investigation is to covertly do as much work as feasible before officially announcing and/or launching the investigation. This includes immediately taking control of all pertinent documents, including emails and text messages. It also allows the investigation team to interview and collect pertinent assets of the organization before an employee is either temporarily or permanently separated from the organization. This is to minimize the risk of the implicated employee engaging in destroying documents, intimidating, retaliating, and issuing threats to those who cooperate with the investigation. In some instances, the implicated employee immediately resigns and disappears once the investigation is announced.

Fraud investigations must be overseen and conducted by an independent, competent, and experienced fraud professional who must be independent of the entity being investigated. However, there are managers who want to direct or conduct their own fraud investigations even though they do not have the skills or expertise to conduct investigations. This includes fraud investigations of their operations and/or area(s) of responsibility, employees, and even themselves. They are also, in most cases, not capable of gathering sufficient convincing evidence to produce a fraud investigation report that will withstand scrutiny in a court of law. The motive of these managers is usually for self-serving reasons such as fear of discovering their malfeasance.

The leaders of fraud investigation functions are usually the bearers of bad news. This is because investigators are usually engaged to investigate what went wrong, how it happened, who is responsible, and the impact and fallout. The investigations results are often contested by perpetrator(s) as they are always looking for opportunities to discredit the results of the investigation and the investigators. Usual comments include there is no fraud here, and the investigation is a waste of resources. It is imperative that there is factual and sufficient evidence gathered to support the conclusion that fraud has been committed. The supporting evidence must be able to withstand scrutiny in a court of law. Investigators also provide advice on how to prevent the fraud from happening again.

There are stakeholders at times who would prefer not to address the bad news and pretend that they did not know about the situation, hoping that it will go away. They may also engage in retaliatory actions against the investigator and team members. Retaliation and frivolous allegations against investigators, team members and witnesses distract and disrupt an organization's operations. Responding to those activities takes away time and attention from the organization's core business and must be promptly addressed. There must be consequences for retaliation and frivolous allegations as ignoring them opens the door for the continuation of fraudulent activities. It is also a risk to the reputation, financial position, and stability of the organization. This could be from lawsuits, penalties, fines, and cease-and-desist orders for non-compliance with laws and regulations.

Employees are at times reluctant to report their awareness or observations of fraudulent activities. Reasons include fear of retaliation, frivolous allegations against them and their families, and/or becoming an outcast in some cultures and organizations. This is usually the case in authoritarian societies, cultures, and organizations. The customs and norms in such societies, cultures, and organizations often bound employees to the power and authority of the leader or seniority whose decisions are uncontestable. The fear of retaliation is also an issue in cultures and organizations where reporting fraudulent activities and wrongdoings is forbidden. It is viewed as going against the customs and norms of the culture. An employee or a family member may be at risk of becoming an outcast in such cultures and organizations for reporting fraudulent activities. Also, fraud and wrongdoings usually go unreported in cultures where there is a "my time now mentality." This is also the situation in cultures where defrauding an organization or government signifies strength and achievement. There are also organizational stakeholders who would prefer to disregard fraud allegations instead of reporting or addressing them. Addressing fraud allegations and the results of an investigation is time-consuming and hard work. It usually takes stakeholders out of their comfort zone and distracts them from the core mission and objectives of the organization.

PROACTIVE FRAUD INVESTIGATION PROCESSES AND PROCEDURES

A proactive fraud investigation function must have documented processes and procedures to be effective. The processes and procedures must be clear and easy to follow.

Complex processes and procedures are a risk that can result in misunderstanding, confusion, ambiguity, and inconsistencies. The processes and procedures must also be communicated and understood by everyone affiliated with the organization. The following is an overview of the processes and procedures:

- Intake of reports of allegation(s) of fraudulent activities: All allegations must be taken seriously.
- Preliminary review of allegations: A preliminary review must be performed of all allegations to determine the veracity of the allegation and whether a fraud investigation is warranted.
- Disposition of fraud allegations: If an investigation is warranted, the case is assigned to an investigator. If the allegation is not warranted, the case is closed, and the information is stored in the fraud database in accordance with the organization's retention policy.
- Notification: Stakeholders are notified of the disposition of the allegation on a need-to-know basis.
- Preparation of investigation planning memo: The key contents of the memo include the investigation team, objectives, scope, and expected timing of the investigation.
- Performance of the fraud investigation: This is the evidence-gathering phase. It includes investigative activities such as interviews, reviews of hard copy and computer files, emails, and documents. This is done to obtain evidence to either confirm, refute, or render the results inconclusive.
- Supervisory review and approval of the evidence: This must be done by at least one level above the investigator performing the investigation.
- Prepare and share the draft investigation report with legal for comments: This is to identify and discuss the disposition of any information in the report that may expose the organization to damages and liabilities. The leader of the fraud investigation function is not obligated to change the report if there is a disagreement with legal.
- Share and discuss the investigation results with key stakeholders for input on a need-to-know basis.
- Update the draft investigation report with input from stakeholders as deemed necessary.
- Finalize and issue the investigation report: The report must be issued to stakeholders on a need-to-know basis and in accordance with the organization's antifraud policy.
- Disciplinary action and reporting fraud to law enforcement: It is a senior management and/or board decision as to what disciplinary action to take. This is usually done in consultation with human resources and legal departments.
- Sharing of improvement opportunities: This is a value-added service to share lessons learned and improvement opportunities observed during the investigation. The sharing is with stakeholders who can benefit from the experience, including other assurance functions leaders.

PROACTIVE FRAUD INVESTIGATION REPORT

A proactive fraud investigation report must be credible and objective. Integrity and confidence in the services of a fraud investigation function depends on it. A credible and objective fraud investigation report includes the following:

- Supported by sufficiently documented factual and evidential matter
- Free of influence and bias
- Able to withstand scrutiny in a court of law

Any hint or sense that the result of an investigation is not credible, and objective is a risk to the reputation of the investigation function. It is also a risk to the integrity and confidence in the organization's fraud investigation function and its reports.

The investigation report should be shared on a need-to-know basis. This is to preserve confidentiality and protect witnesses and those providing evidence from retaliation and frivolous allegations. The report should be shared at least one level above the accused reporting line once it is reasonably and clearly determined that the level above the accused is not implicated. The sharing includes opportunities to improve internal controls deficiencies or weaknesses observed during the investigation. This must be done in a timely manner with stakeholders whose operations can benefit from the lessons learned. The observed weaknesses and deficiencies are better shared in a separate report. The separate report minimizes delays in the completion and issuance of the investigation report. This is because sharing and obtaining an agreement on the improvement opportunities from stakeholders often takes time. The timely sharing of the results of investigations with key stakeholders is a key element of a proactive fraud investigation function. Key stakeholders are usually a small group that includes the following:

- The chairperson of the board
- CEO
- Members of the senior management team, including the manager(s) of the impacted area(s) of operations
- Chief legal officer or general counsel
- CAE
- Chief human resource officer or chief people officer

The leaders of a proactive fraud investigation function must minimize the risks of claims and liabilities by sharing the report with legal before it is finalized and issued. This is to highlight and discuss any disclosures that may expose the organization to claims and liabilities. This could include wrongful termination, defamation of character, and damage to the reputation of the organization. The leader of fraud investigation is not obligated to change the report if there is a disagreement with legal.

The investigation report should contain an executive summary and a detail section. The executive summary of an investigation report usually contains an overview of the background, scope, allegations, key findings, impact, and conclusions. The detail section of the report contains the supporting information of the investigation, including the following:

- Background
- Scope
- Allegation(s)
- Findings and impact
- Evidentiary exhibits cited
- Conclusion as follows:
    - Confirmed since there is sufficient evidential matter to support the allegations
    - Partially confirmed since evidence was found to support some of the allegations
    - Unfounded since there is no evidence found to confirm the allegations
    - Inconclusive as the evidence is insufficient to either confirm, disprove, or refute the allegations

A proactive fraud investigation report must be able to withstand scrutiny in a court of law. The investigation report must only contain evidence that is relevant to the investigation. The report must be supported with sufficient evidence that is factual, reliable, relevant, and accurate. The report must also be clear, concise, easy to read, and understand. A lay person should be able to read and understand the report. This is particularly important in a global organization where there are language barriers.

REPORTING OF ALLEGED FRAUDULENT ACTIVITIES

The best practice for reporting alleged fraudulent activities is directly to the leader of fraud investigation. The reporting includes fraudulent activities that an employee or anyone affiliated with the organization suspects, aware of, or observed against the organization. The reporting of fraudulent activities directly to the leader of fraud investigation enhances the confidentiality of the investigation. It also helps to protect the reporter from retaliation and frivolous allegations. Additionally, it mitigates the risk of a staff altering, suppressing, attenuating, or ignoring fraud allegations and activities. This includes a manager conducting the fraud investigation or disregarding such activities as a low priority item.

The direct reporting of alleged fraudulent activities to the leader of fraud investigation is likely to speed up the investigation process. The practice in some organizations is for employees to report fraudulent activities to his/her manager. The reporting must be at least one level above those implicated in the fraudulent activity. For example, an employee must report fraudulent activities by his or her manager to at least one level above the manager or, better yet, directly to the leader of fraud investigation. The reporting of such activities must be in accordance with the anti-fraud policy. Reporting of fraudulent activities to the leader of fraud investigation is the preferred practice, as the reporter may not know the scope of the activity.

Reporting of fraudulent activities to law enforcement is a deterrent to fraud. The reporting is a senior management and/or board decision. Reporting fraudulent activities to law enforcement sends a strong message to employees of the organization's position on such activities. Public knowledge of fraudulent activities is a deterrent to employees and assists in mitigating future occurrences. Perpetrators of fraudulent activities will think twice about committing fraud because of the fear of prosecution and/or incarceration. Some form of disciplinary action is required whenever there is fraud in an organization. The action taken by management should be in accordance with the organization's antifraud policy and commensurate with the severity of the malfeasance.

The governance of the organization is weakened when disciplinary action is not taken against perpetrators and enablers of fraudulent activities. This includes those who are engaged in suppressing and covering up fraudulent activities. These activities are signs of poor governance and encourage perpetrators to continue their illicit activities.

Reporting of fraudulent activities to law enforcement is at times a risk versus reward or cost benefit decision. This is because the cost of reporting fraudulent activities to law enforcement at times outweighs the benefits. As is the case in countries where the local law enforcement is either corrupt, lacks resources, and/or takes forever for the case to be investigated and prosecuted. The following are some of the reasons why fraudulent activities are not aggressively pursued in some organizations:

- Reputational damage and potential financial loss to the organization
- Low monetary value of the fraud
- Lack of resources, including time and money, to refer the case to law enforcement for prosecution
- Low priority due to lack of resources and high local law enforcement caseload
- Corrupt local law enforcement

The decision to refrain from reporting fraudulent activities to law enforcement is a potential risk to an organization as the organization and perpetrators could subsequently be investigated and prosecuted for failure to report activities that violate laws.

CYBER-FRAUD

Cyber-fraud is a type of modern-day piracy. Pirates used ships to get to their targets, attack them, and take and share the bounty. Cyber-fraud is easy work, comparatively speaking, as there are no traveling or physical battles involved. There are often no early warning indicators or safeguards to timely detect and prevent cyber-fraud attacks. Cyber-fraudsters can initiate an attack from the comfort of their home thousands of miles away from the target. They use the World Wide Web (WWW) or the internet to get to their target, hack, and hold them hostage for ransom or other clandestine purposes.

Cyber-fraud attacks are not a matter of if they will occur, but when. Organizations information technology (IT) professionals are up against experts when it comes to cyber-fraud. Fraudsters can attack or hack any organization that they choose. This is because they have the expertise and tools and are just as sophisticated as the top IT companies in the world. Cyber-fraud is their business and they have formed groups to operate the illicit business. The levels of sophistication and confidence in launching and getting away with their criminal activities have escalated. It is to the point where they are now offering ransomware and malware as a service, RAAS and MAAS, respectively. Some are rogue government-sponsored operators holding major organizations hostage and disrupting their operations until a ransom is paid. For example, several global IT companies have been hacked at least once by cyber-criminals. This includes Facebook, Microsoft, Adobe, and FireEye to name a few.

Cyber-fraud attack is the nightmare of an organization's board. The threat of a cyber-fraud attack is at the top or forefront of most organizations' governing bodies and risk management. Most governing bodies realize there is not much they can do to prevent an attack. The focus is on quick and early detection and response to minimize the damage and fallout of a cyber-attack. A business continuity and an incident response plan play a key role in minimizing the damage that can be caused from a major incident or disaster such as a cyber-attack. The growing increase in cyber-attacks are issues that will keep senior management and board members awake at night. This includes ransomware, malware phishing, vishing, smishing attacks, data security, and privacy breaches. Organizations must invest in technological tools and highly skilled IT professionals to monitor, quickly detect, and address attacks when they occur as it is not a matter of if but when.

There are organizations that are fearful of publicly disclosing cyber-attacks due to the following:

- Embarrassment regarding the perception of lack of basic internal controls to detect and timely address cyber-attack against their organization
- Reputational damage and financial impact the attack will have on the organization, including the following:
  - Payout out of thousands and millions of dollars to cyber-criminals
  - Loss of customers
  - Decrease in revenues from the disruption of being held hostage

LEVERAGING TECHNOLOGY

The leader of a proactive fraud investigation function must embrace and leverage technology. Information is one of the most valuable assets of an organization. However, this asset is of little or no value to an organization if it is not shared or is in an unusable form. Embracing and leveraging technology have enabled leaders of fraud investigation functions to maximize the utilization of the abundance of information (big data) that is available to the organization. For example, digitalization converts and unlocks the organization's information into a usable form. Information is more transparent, accessible, consistent, accurate, reliable, and verifiable. Organizations can now unlock and maximize the use of one of its most valuable assets. Stakeholders across the organization can now make more informed and quality decisions.

Digitalization will enhance the quality of a proactive fraud investigation function's intelligence and evidence-gathering process. Gathering quality evidence is one of the most important activities of a fraud investigation function. The availability of usable big data in the operating environment enhances the quality of the intelligence and evidence-gathering process. Additionally, the information is accessible anywhere in the organization where the internet is available. Digitalization improves the following:

- Agility of the fraud investigation function
- Data mining and analytical capabilities of fraud investigation
- Identification of root cause and prevention of future incidents
- Credibility, including accuracy, reliability, and verifiability of evidence
- Standardization and consistency of information across the organization

Automation of a proactive fraud investigation function enhances its effectiveness, efficiency, and value to the organization. A key element of the automation process is the establishment of a fraud investigation database. The database enhances the proactiveness and agility of the function. The value of a fraud investigation database to the organization includes the following:

- Restricts access to sensitive and confidential information on a need-to-know basis
- Enhances the security and privacy of sensitive and confidential information
- Serves as a single source of information for fraud allegations and investigations
- Provides quick access to fraud allegations and investigation information
- Allows for more robust data mining and analysis
- Allows for interface and continuous monitoring of transactions and activities
- Assists and contributes to the early detection, prevention, deterrence, and correction of fraud
- Provides information on where, how, trends, potential actors/suspects, and the type of fraudulent activities that are being perpetrated against the organization
- Assists in preventing the spread of fraud in other areas and entities of the organization

Digitalization and automation enable the leader of a proactive fraud investigation to leverage other technological tools, including the following:

- Data mining and analytics
- Robotics
- Robotic process automation
- Machine learning
- Artificial intelligence
- Internet of things

Technological tools enable the leader of the fraud investigation function to enhance and improve the effectiveness, efficiency, and value of the function to the organization. The tools make it easier and quicker for the investigation team to obtain information from across the organization to analyze and connect the dots.

Leveraging technology enhances the fraud investigation team's ability to timely identify fraud red flags. This enables the investigation team to identify who, where, when, how, and the type of fraudulent activities that are being perpetrated against the organization. It also enables the leader and team members to be proactive in anticipating, preventing, detecting, and stopping fraudulent activities before they spread and become a disaster. Red flags are valuable indicators of potential fraud that should not be ignored. Red flags include new and/or ongoing unusual and suspicious behaviors and activities. The behaviors and activities include the following:

- Bullying
- Autocratic, illusive, and abusive managers
- Disrespectful and unprofessional behaviors
- Refusal and/or delay in providing requested information or documents
- Attacks and discredits the results of investigations
- Intimidates or threatens the investigators and witnesses

Digitalization, automation, and other technological tools make information readily available, accessible, consistent, accurate, reliable, and verifiable. This enables the investigation team to effectively and efficiently mine, analyze, deduce, and connect the dots. It also enhances the leader of a proactive fraud investigation to provide more timely advice, including insight and foresight, to stakeholders in mitigating new and emerging fraud risks. Timely sharing of the lessons learned, and potential remedies enables stakeholders to be proactive in taking necessary precautions to prevent fraudulent activity in their area(s) of operation. The savings in resources, time, and money from avoiding such activities and the disruption to the organization are priceless.

ANTIFRAUD CONTROLS

Antifraud controls are essentials elements of fraud prevention, detection, and deterrence. As mentioned earlier, the leaders of fraud investigation cannot sit and wait for allegations of fraud to be reported to act. They must adopt a proactive, collaborative, and agile approach to effectively assist management in mitigating fraud risks in the organization. This includes working with the leaders of assurance functions to share emerging risks, trends, red flags, and unusual transactions and activities.

Fighting fraud is an ongoing battle. Antifraud controls can only minimize fraud risks as fraudsters are quickly adapting and finding new ways to defraud organizations. The ACFE Occupational Fraud 2022: A Report to the Nation indicated that the presence of antifraud controls is associated with lower fraud losses and quicker fraud detection, and that nearly half of losses occurred due to lack of internal controls or override of existing controls.[5] Antifraud controls include the following:

- Presence of effective tone at the top
- Existence of the following:
  - Antifraud policy and code of conduct
  - Effective system of internal control

    - Independent IA function
    - Whistleblower hotline
    - Physical security, including surveillance cameras, and access controls to sensitive areas of the organization such as entrances to buildings, IT hardware and software, inventory, stockrooms, and safes
- Performance of the following:
    - Background checks of employees
    - Ongoing fraud risk assessment by managers for their areas of operations
    - Surprise audits, including cash and stock counts and payroll distributions
    - Periodic fraud awareness training
    - Annual external audit
- Hold fraudsters accountable by taking appropriate disciplinary action and/or referral to law enforcement for investigation and prosecution
- Utilize data analytics and artificial intelligence for continuous monitoring of transactions and activities, analyzing big data, and identifying fraud red flags
- Reward whistleblowers

The 2022 Association of Certified Fraud Examiners (ACFE) Report to the Nation mentioned two controls – job rotation/mandatory vacation policies and surprise audits – that were associated with at least a 50% reduction in both median loss and median duration.[6] However, they were not among the eight controls considered common antifraud control by over 70% of CFEs responding to the survey. The two controls were among the least common controls implemented, with only 25% of organizations having a job rotation/mandatory vacation policy and 42% using surprise audits, indicating that numerous organizations have an opportunity to add these highly effective tools to their antifraud programs.[7] Other controls with notable reductions in median loss and median duration include proactive data monitoring/analysis and formal fraud risk assessments.[8]

WHISTLEBLOWER HOTLINE

A proactive fraud investigation function must have access to a whistleblower hotline. The whistleblower hotline provides a safe and secure channel for anyone within or outside the organization to report fraudulent activities anonymously and confidentially. The preference is for an independent third party to provide the whistleblower hotline service. This is to enhance the integrity, credibility, and confidence in the program. The value of the whistleblower hotline program is significantly diminished if there is an ounce of perception of the breach of confidentiality and trust in the program.

Clarity on what should be communicated through the whistleblower hotline is critical. It is at times inundated with human resource issues, including abusive conduct and harassment. A point person in the fraud investigation function or an outsource service should review and classify the allegations into different buckets. This includes a bucket for the office of fraud investigation, human resource, and legal. There may also be a bucket for the chief CEO and the chairperson of the board for certain allegations. This includes allegations involving senior management and/or board members.

The whistleblower hotline must be independent, anonymous, and confidential to be effective. This enhances the independence and objectivity of the fraud investigation function and minimizes the risk or perception of influence and bias of investigations. An independent fraud investigation function also minimizes the risk of distrust of an anonymous whistleblower hotline. Anonymity reduces the fear of employees or others from reporting actual or suspicious fraudulent activities. Confidentiality enhances trust in the investigation process and minimizes the fear of retaliation and frivolous allegations.

An anonymous and confidential whistleblower hotline allows anyone within or outside the organization to report suspicious, actual, or observed incidents of fraudulent activities without disclosing their identity. This provides a safe and secure channel for employees and others who fear reporting fraudulent activities to their managers or supervisors. Employees are sometimes reluctant to report their awareness or observations of fraudulent activities for fear of retaliation. They also fear the repercussions of going against the customs and norms of the culture. Implementing an independent, anonymous, and confidential whistleblower hotline minimizes the risk of retaliation, frivolous allegations, and unacceptable behaviors in an organization.

FRAUD AWARENESS TRAINING AND CHALLENGES

The leader of a proactive fraud investigation function must play a key role in providing fraud awareness training to stakeholders. Proactive fraud investigation is an ongoing process that plays a key role in keeping stakeholders current and informed of fraud risk. Additionally, the function is well equipped to effectively deliver the training to stakeholders. This is because of the team's knowledge, experience, expertise and understanding of the vulnerabilities of the organization and the operating environment. This enhances a proactive fraud investigation function's value to the organization.

Fraud awareness training should be provided periodically or as needed to keep stakeholders informed of the threat of fraud to the organization. This includes the board of directors, senior management, and managers. The training encompasses existing, new, and emerging fraud risks, red flags, trends, and mitigating activities. It assists stakeholders in the prevention, deterrence, and early detection of fraudulent activities. The training will also assist in minimizing the impact and fallout of fraudulent activities, including reputational damage, financial loss, loss of customers, and possible dissolution of the organization. Additionally, the training serves as a refresher and reminder to stakeholders of the ongoing threat of fraud risks, inherent and otherwise, that the organization faces in pursuit of its mission, vision, and objectives. It helps to ensure that stakeholders do not become complacent.

The nature, types, and schemes of fraudulent activities are usually universal. The schemes are usually similar. Fraud in one country, region, or location will likely resurface in other places where the organization operates. This enables the leaders of a proactive fraud investigation to anticipate and act quickly to identify, prevent, and deter new and emerging fraudulent activities across the organization. The following are examples of universal or common type of fraud:

- Cyber-fraud, including the following:
    - Hacking
    - Malware attacks, including ransomware, phishing, vishing, and smishing

- Misstatement of financial records and statements, including the following:
  - Over/under reporting of revenues and expenses
  - Dual sets of accounting records
  - Manipulation of cut-offs
  - Tax evasion and underreporting
  - Change in estimates
- Embezzlement
- Misappropriation of assets, including the following:
  - Cash
  - Inventory
  - Office supplies
- Procurement and construction fraud, including the following:
  - Conflict of interest
  - Bribery
  - Kickback
  - Bid rigging
  - Substandard work and materials
  - Over and double billings
- Accounts Receivable fraud, including the following:
  - Kiting
  - Lapping
- Inventory fraud, including the following:
  - Falsification of goods or receiving reports
  - Pilferage
  - Duplicate invoice
  - Over/under valuation
- Falsification of documents, including the following:
  - Inventory receiving documents
  - Expense reports
  - Ghost employees
  - Timekeeping records
  - Vacation and sick time records
  - Tax returns
- Extortion

Organizations are most vulnerable to fraud risk in an ever-changing operating environment. The operating environment is constantly changing and disruptive and so too is fraud risk. Mitigation plans and activities must also constantly adjust to combat fraud risk. However, mitigation plans and activities or internal controls tend to lag in an ever-changing operating environment. As mentioned earlier, fraudsters are aware of the vulnerabilities and are quick to take advantage of them before loopholes are closed. Additionally, fraudsters are often quick to adapt to enhanced antifraud controls and devised schemes to override them.

There are countries where a blind eye is turned toward bribery and kickbacks. In such countries, it is usually the custom and the norm. This is, for example, where the issuer of a purchase order or a contract expects to receive a kickback from the recipient of the purchase order or contract. This type of activity goes without saying as it is expected, and it is the custom and the norm. Bribery and kickbacks are not considered illegal in countries or cultures where it is customary or the norm. However, it is illegal for organizations operating in such countries to engage in bribery and kickbacks when it is illegal in the organization's home country. This includes countries such as the United States, Canada, the UK, France, Germany, and Australia to name a few. In the United States, such fraudulent activities are investigated and prosecuted under the Foreign Corrupt Practices Act ("FCPA").

Fraudsters who get away with fraud in one organization tend to continue the bad behavior in the next organization with which they are affiliated. This is because they know they can get away with it without any repercussions. Their fraudulent activity may not become known in a background check of the employee because there is no public record, and it was not reported to law enforcement. Additionally, it is illegal in some countries for organizations to share former employees' personal information. Actions often taken when fraudulent activities are not reported to law enforcement include the following:

- A slap on the wrist and/or transfer of the employee to another location
- A verbal or written warning
- Employee is asked to either resign or be terminated
- Recovery of the assets

CHAPTER SUMMARY

`The journey of adopting a proactive fraud investigation function begins with the creation of an antifraud policy. The organization's antifraud policy sets the tone at the top regarding the organization's fraud investigation function. The board's oversight role for fraud risk includes overseeing the organization's antifraud policy in collaboration with senior management. The antifraud policy must be supported with processes and procedures to effectively address allegations of fraudulent activities. The organization's antifraud policy must also contain a strong statement regarding retaliation, frivolous allegations, and disciplinary actions. Organizations get credit for having an effective antifraud policy and a proactive fraud investigation function.

Fraud prevention is everybody's business. This includes board members, employees, consultants, contractors, vendors, and volunteers. While the responsibility for fraud risk rests with the board and senior management, fraud prevention is the responsibility of everyone affiliated with the organization. Fraud awareness training plays a key role in keeping stakeholders informed and assisting them in mitigating fraud against the organization. Organizations are most vulnerable to fraud risk in a fast paced, constantly changing, and disruptive operating environment. The leader of a proactive fraud investigation function must play a key role in keeping stakeholders current on fraud risks.

The mission of a proactive fraud investigation function is to effectively support the organization's fraud risk mitigation program. The leaders of fraud investigation functions must act proactively to assist in minizing the risk of fraud to their organizations from a constantly changing and disruptive operating environment. They cannot sit and wait for allegations of fraud to be reported to act. They must evolve and adopt a proactive approach to investigating fraud. The presence of a proactive fraud investigation function is a key element of the organization's governance structure and system of internal control.

The leaders of a proactive fraud investigation function must build relationships with stakeholders. They must capitalize on the benefits of building and maintaining effective relationships. Building and maintaining effective relationships with the other leaders of assurance functions plays an important role in preventing, detecting, and deterring fraud risks. Also, the leader of fraud investigation must actively promote the value of the function across the organization since the contribution of the function is often overlooked and unappreciated.

The leader of a proactive fraud investigation function must play a key role in providing Fraud awareness training to stakeholders. The nature, types and schemes of fraudulent activities are usually universal. Organizations are most vulnerable to fraud risk in a fast paced, constantly changing, and disruptive operating environment. The leader of the function must play a key role keeping stakeholders current on fraud risk. There are countries where a blind eye is turned toward bribery and kickbacks. Fraudsters who get away with committing fraud without repercussion will continue their fraudulent activities.

A proactive fraud investigation function must have the support of senior management and the board to be successful. The reporting line of the leader of a proactive fraud investigation function matters in the hierarchy of the organization. It is important that whoever the leader of fraud investigation reports to has prior knowledge or experience of fraud investigations. A member of the senior management team must be assigned the responsibility to oversee and/or lead the organization's fraud investigation function and/or program. Organizations that do not have a fraud investigation function or program often turn to IA to perform investigations of allegations of fraud.

The management of a proactive fraud investigation begins with the assignment of a competent leader, such as a CFE, and team to perform the investigation. The investigation must be well planned before it is launched. It is in the best interest of the organization for employee(s) implicated in a fraud investigation to be placed on leave of absence or modify duties until cleared by the investigation. The integrity and credibility of fraud investigations rest on the confidentiality of the investigation processes and procedures. The processes and procedures must be clear and easy to follow. The processes and procedures must also be communicated and understood by everyone affiliated with the organization.

Fraud investigations can be disruptive and a major distraction in an organization. Management and stakeholders often complain about the delays and the amount of time it takes to complete a fraud investigation. One way of minimizing the delays of fraud investigation is to covertly do as much work as feasible before officially announcing and launching the investigation.

There are managers who want to direct or conduct their own fraud investigations. Their motive could be self-serving as at times they may engage in unethical behaviors. Leaders of fraud investigations are usually the bearers of bad news. The results of a fraud investigation are often contested by the perpetrator(s) of the fraud. Retaliation and frivolous allegations against investigators and witnesses of fraud distract and disrupt an organization's operations. As a result, employees are at times reluctant to report their awareness or observations of fraudulent activities.

A proactive fraud investigation function must have a whistleblower hotline. The whistleblower hotline must be independent, anonymous, and confidential for it to be effective. This allows anyone within or outside of the organization to report allegations of fraudulent activities without disclosing their identity. The best practice for reporting allegations of fraud should be directly to the leader of fraud investigation. The reporting of alleged fraudulent activities to law enforcement is a deterrent to those activities. The governance of the organization is weakened when disciplinary action is not taken against perpetrators of fraud. This includes not reporting the alleged fraudulent activities to law enforcement. Reporting of alleged fraudulent activities to law enforcement is at times a risk versus reward decision.

Confidentiality is a key factor in collaborating and sharing the results and report of investigation with stakeholders. Sharing the results must be on a need-to-know basis. The leaders of a proactive fraud investigation function must minimize the risks of claims and liabilities by sharing the report with legal before it is finalized and issued. The report must be credible, objective, clear, concise, and easy to read and understand. The report must also be able to withstand scrutiny in a court of law.

Embracing and leveraging technology enhances the agility, effectiveness, efficiency, and value of a proactive fraud investigation function to the organization. Digitalization and automation, for example, enhance the quality of the function's intelligence and evidence-gathering process. Digitalization and automation also enable the leader of fraud investigation to leverage other technological tools to enhance the effectiveness and efficiency of the investigation process. Embracing and leveraging technology enhances a proactive fraud investigation function's team ability to timely identify red flags and prevent and deter fraudulent activities. It also enables the investigation team to identify who, where, when, how, and the type of fraudulent activities that are being perpetrated against the organization.

NOTES

1 Fraud 101: What is Fraud? (acfe.com).
2 Ibid.
3 Ibid.
4 Ibid.
5 ACFE, Occupational Fraud 2022: A Report to the Nation.
6 Ibid.
7 Ibid.
8 Ibid.

17 Mindset and Skillset of the Next Generation of Leaders of Internal Audit

INTRODUCTION

Leaders of the next generation of internal audit (IA) or global internal audit (GIA) belong to those who are ready to evolve and embrace change, technological innovations, and build their soft skills and business acumen. This includes adapting an agile mindset and operating environment. The precedings are the key drivers of the survival, sustainability, and success of the next generation of leaders of GIA. The pendulum has swung from the heavy focus on technical or hard skills to a more balanced soft skills GIA-operating environment. This requires a dynamic mindset as technological innovations are constantly disrupting the operating environment. A traditional GIA cannot effectively address the complexity, constant changes, disruption, and demands of an ever-changing operating environment.

The purpose of this chapter is to provide advice and guidance on the type of mindset and skillset the next generation of leaders of GIA must have to survive and succeed in an ever-changing operating environment. Topics covered include the following:

- Dynamic mindset
- Agility
- Soft skills
- Business acumen
- Self-learning
- Assessment of skillset and expertise
- Stakeholder focus
- Relationships and trust
- Diversity, equity, and inclusion (DEI)
- Leveraging technology
- Investing in GIA

Key learnings from the chapter include the following:

- Reasons why the mindset of the next generation of the leaders of GIA must be dynamic
- Role of agility in the survival and success of the next generation of leaders of GIA

DOI: 10.1201/9781003207559-17

- Importance of soft skills and business acumen
- Value of periodic inventory of skillset and expertise, and self-learning
- Importance of stakeholder focus and building and maintaining relationships
- Value of DEI
- Value in leveraging technology and investing in training and continuing professional education
- Must-have skills and expertise of the next generation of internal auditors

DYNAMIC MINDSET

The next generation of leaders of GIA must have a dynamic mindset as technological innovations and change are constantly disrupting the operating environment. They are driving how organizations operate to survive and remain effective and efficient. The next generation of leaders of GIA must also change to remain effective and efficient by ensuring that their mindset and skillset are in alignment with the changes. Their survival and operating environment depend on it.

Leaders of the next generation of GIA belong to those who are ready to evolve, embrace change, technological innovations, and adopt an engaging, collaborative, and agile operating environment. This is required to effectively address new and emerging risks, demands, and opportunities that come along with change. The characteristic of a dynamic mindset includes the following:

- Adaptable
- Agile
- Creative
- Collaborative
- Empathetic
- Fearless
- Flexible
- Forward-thinking
- Proactive
- Inclusive
- Innovative
- Ready
- Relationship oriented
- Relevant
- Resilient
- Self-learning
- Stakeholder focused

AGILITY

Agility is a word that must be at the forefront of the mindset of the next generation of leaders of GIA. This is because agility is quickly becoming a must-have skill of leaders to effectively lead in an ever-changing operating environment. The next generation of leaders have no choice or other option than to adopt the agile methodology for leading GIA operations. This is necessary for them to survive, remain ready, resilient, relevant, and valuable to their organization. Adopting the agile methodology for leading is a strategic and transformational initiative. It requires the buy-in and support of key stakeholders. This includes the leaders of GIA, senior management, and the audit committee of the board of directors.

Agility enables and enhances the ability of the next generation of leaders of GIA to meet the demands and challenges of a fast-paced and continuously evolving operating environment. The following are some of the characteristics of what it takes to be agile:

- Embrace and welcome change
- Stakeholder and customer focused
- Engaging and collaborative
- Learn quickly, share, and grow from failure
- Creative and innovative
- Adaptable and flexible
- Open to new ideas
- Risk taker
- Proactive
- Forward thinker
- Empathetic
- Ready
- Relevant
- Resilient

There is often not as much time as desired to quickly learn, plan, respond, and adapt to rapid changes in an ever-changing operating environment. Agile methodology assists stakeholders in effectively navigating and adapting to change. It is a trial-and-error or learn as you go approach that is often used to address rapid and disruptive change. It requires an agile GIA leadership team and operating environment that is collaborative, innovative, and adaptable.

Agility is one of the key drivers of the survival, sustainability, and success of the next generation of leaders of GIA. Agility enables them to quickly think, pivot, respond, and adapt to change, including planned and unplanned events. This is because agility requires engaging and collaborating with stakeholders to generate relevant, actionable, and valuable results. Forward-thinking leaders are embracing the agile methodology to remain ready, resilient, and relevant. It is required to improve, grow, and preserve the value of their organization.

SOFT SKILLS

The focus of the scope of the work in a traditional GIA is primarily on finance and compliance. Now, there is more emphasis on soft skills than in the past as they are required to effectively engage and collaborate with stakeholders on an ongoing basis. They are also required to understand the nature of the changes, disruption, risks, and opportunities in the operating environment. Honing soft skills will help the next generation of leaders of GIA in determining how best to assist stakeholders navigate the risks, opportunities, and demands from the changes and disruption. Soft skills are also necessary for leaders to remain ready, resilient, relevant, and valuable to the organization. The leaders do this by being proactive and agile, and anticipating and providing timely advice to stakeholders on new and emerging risks and opportunities that come along with change. The next generation of leaders of GIA must be equipped with the necessary soft skills to effectively engage and collaborate with stakeholders.

Soft skills must be a key element of the mindset of the next generation of leaders of GIA. As mentioned above, soft skills are required to effectively engage and collaborate with stakeholders. The changes in the operating environment are occurring rapidly and so should the engagement, conversation, and collaboration with stakeholders. This enables and enhances the next generation of leaders to pivot, respond, and adapt quickly to the changes in the operating environment. Soft skills that will assist in responding and adapting quickly to change include the following:

- Agility
- Collaboration
- Engagement
- Listening
- Networking

BUSINESS ACUMEN

The mindset of the next generation of leaders of GIA must include business acumen. It is imperative that they obtain an understanding of the business and operation of the organization before engaging and collaborating with stakeholders. They must come to the table with knowledge and an understanding of the strategy, objectives, and risks to the organization and its stakeholders. This is necessary to have a productive conversation with stakeholders. It will also assist the next generation of leaders in focusing on what is most important to stakeholders. They will have a better understanding of strategy, objectives, and risks of stakeholders' business and operations. They will also have a better understanding of what is working well, what needs to change or improve. This will assist the next generation of leaders to determine how best to assist stakeholders achieve their business, operating, reporting, and compliance objectives.

SELF-LEARNING

The mindset of the next generation of GIAs' leaders must be one that believes in self-learning. They cannot rely solely on the organization or GIA for their career, professional development, and advancement. Organizations and GIA usually invest in career and professional development and support the advancement of staff and team members. GIA's budget usually has a line item for training and continuing professional education for the team. However, the investment, for the most part, must benefit the organization and GIA for it to receive budget approval. There are forward-thinking CAEs who see the benefit of expanding the diversity of the skillset of the team by investing early in emerging skills and expertise before they become the norm. However, it is not likely that the organization or GIA will invest in the training of all its staff to become experts.

The next generation of GIAs leaders must be proactive in keeping current on opportunities to develop and advance their professional careers. This is because technological innovations and tools are rapidly taking over activities that were normally performed by internal auditors. They must take an interest in their career development and invest in self-learning. It includes investing in skills and topics such as cybersecurity, payment card industry (PCI), data security and privacy, environmental, social, and governance (ESG), and DEI. This will enable and enhance their ability to meet the current and future demands and capitalize on the opportunities from the changes and disruption in the operating environment.

The next generation of internal auditors must take a periodic inventory of their skillset and expertise to determine if their professional career is at risk. As mentioned above, technological innovations and tools are taking over activities that were normally performed by internal auditors. The tools include automation, digitalization, robotics, machine learning, artificial intelligence, and internet of things. It is a continuing trend that internal audit professionals must be aware of and keep on their radar. Self-learning will enable them to plan and obtain the necessary training and/or adjustment to their skillset and expertise to survive and be successful. It will also enable them to remain resilient, relevant, and valuable to the organization, and advance their career.

The next generation of leaders of GIA must evolve and rise above technology-driven and other career ending disruptions and changes in the operating environment. They cannot be complacent as it is a risk to their career advancement and professional development. They must expand their skillset and expertise to ensure they remain valuable to their organization. Self-learning mitigates the risk of becoming complacent and enhances the agility and value of the next generation of leaders to their organization. This also enables them to embrace and quickly adapt to relevant changes, remain marketable, and advance their career.

ASSESSMENT OF SKILLSET AND EXPERTISE

The next generation of leaders of GIA must periodically assess their skillset and expertise. This is to ensure their skillset and expertise are relevant and in alignment with what is important to the organization and stakeholders. The skillset and expertise must evolve to effectively address the complexity, disruption, and demands that come along with change. There is no assurance that what worked well in the past is going to work well in the future. The periodic revisiting and assessment of skills will ensure that leaders have the requisite expertise and remain relevant to effectively address the needs of the organization, stakeholders, and the changes in the operating environment. Additionally, the periodic assessment is necessary for the next generation of leaders and team members of GIA to remain ready, resilient, relevant, and valuable to the organization.

Technological innovations and tools are the primary driver for the periodic assessment of skillset and expertise. They are the key to enhancing the effectiveness and efficiency of organizations as they are taking over many technical activities. This includes recurring and voluminous financial, accounting, compliance, monitoring, and reporting activities, including the following:

- Testing 100% or an entire population instead of a sample
- Testing of internal controls and compliance
- Processing of financial transactions and statements
- Continuous auditing and monitoring of compliance activities
- Providing periodic reports

Technological innovations and tools will allow the next generation of leaders of GIA to strengthen and enhance their soft skills and business acumen. Time saved in adopting and embracing technological innovations and tools can be used toward other activities. There is also more time to engage and collaborate with stakeholders on their priorities, including strategy and core business. Additionally, there is more time to effectively interpret, translate the results of data analysis, and connect the dots. This is a key source of information for anticipating and providing timely assurance and advice, including insight and foresight, to stakeholders to assist them in making more informed decisions.

The next generation of leaders of GIA must have access to technical skills and expertise that do not exist on the team. They must engage with experts to assist them in areas where technical skills or expertise are lacking. This can be accomplished by engaging with other areas of the organization or an external firm to provide the skills or expertise. In addition to audit, the most common must-have skills include the following:

- Business Acumen
- Change management
- Cloud computing
- Communications
- Critical thinking
- Cybersecurity
- Data analytics
- Data security and privacy
- DEI
- ESG
- Information technology (IT)
- Problem solving
- Project management
- PCI
- Relationships building
- Risk assessment
- Strategic thinking
- Supply chain management

STAKEHOLDER FOCUS

The next generation of leaders of GIA must be stakeholder focused. It is a mindset that focuses on what is most important to the organization and its stakeholders, including team members of GIA. The priorities of stakeholders must be at the forefront of their thinking and activities, which requires engaging and collaborating with stakeholders on a regular basis. This enables the leaders to stay connected, current, informed, and focused on the strategy and objectives of the organization and its stakeholders. The next generation of leaders' plans and activities must be in alignment with the strategy, business, operating, reporting, and compliance objectives of the organization.

The next generation of leaders of GIA must listen and provide stakeholders with what they need most to be successful in achieving the objectives of the organization. Change is constant and there will be changes to what is most important to stakeholders since nothing is static. It is important for the next generation of leaders to align with the priorities of stakeholders by obtaining an understanding of the following:

- What is most important to them
- What is working well, needs improvement, or should be eliminated
- Key challenges and/or risks
- Partnership needed from GIA to assist in achieving their objectives

Leaders of the next generation of GIA must put the organization and stakeholders' interest ahead of theirs. This is to ensure that what is most important to the organization and its stakeholders is at the forefront of team members' thinking. Putting the organization and its stakeholders' interest ahead of theirs is the essence of the role of GIA as a support function. It exists to assist stakeholders achieve the objectives of the organization by providing assurance and advice, including insight and foresight, into the effectiveness of operations. Additionally, the next generation of leaders will be expected to anticipate and provide insight and foresight to assist stakeholders in making more informed decisions.

RELATIONSHIPS AND TRUST

The mindset of the next generation of leaders of GIA must be one that believes in building relationships and trust. Relationship building plays a key role in keeping current and informed about what is most important to stakeholders. It enables and enhances the ability and agility of the next generation of leaders to quickly respond, adapt to change, and what is most important to stakeholders.

Networking plays a key role in building relationships and trust. The next generation of leaders of GIA must engage and network with peers and colleagues within and outside of the organization. Networking is an excellent way to stay connected, current, and informed of changes in the internal and external operating environments, including the profession and industry. The sharing of lessons learned, emerging risks, and issues of common interest help organizations to anticipate and be proactive in mitigating risk and minimizing reinventing the wheel. Time saved studying and researching an existing or emerging issue that a peer or colleague in another organization has experienced and resolved is a key benefit of networking. The information sharing enhances the readiness, resilience, relevance, and value of the next generation of leaders of GIA to the organization.

DIVERSITY, EQUITY, AND INCLUSION

The mindset of the next generation of leaders of GIA must be one that embraces dicersity, equity, and inclusion (DEI). DEI will enhance their ability to be more creative, innovative, and agile. Creativity, innovation, and agility are key drivers of survival, success, and value to the organization in an ever-changing operating environment. It has been reported that diverse organizations are more creative, innovative, and successful than those that are not.[1]

Diversity is a valuable resource of a global organization with a multicultural and diverse workforce. The next generation of leaders of GIA must leverage diversity to enhance the creativity, innovativeness, and agility of GIA. Diverse cultures, teams, skillsets, and expertise broaden the scope for innovative ideas, and solutions to issues. The inclusion of diverse team members at the decision-making table leads to more informed decisions based on the different perspectives they provide. They are likely to be the ones to enhance the value of the next generation of leaders to the organization. This is by anticipating and providing insight and foresight into the next big new or emerging issue, risks, and opportunities. Emerging issues, risks, and opportunities in a remote area or location in the organization could be the next big economic breakthrough or a global pandemic.

LEVERAGING TECHNOLOGY

The mindset of the next generation of leaders of GIA must be one that embraces and leverages information technology. Embracing and leveraging information technology mean the integration of technological tools into GIA's workflow. This will require organizations and the next generation of leaders to invest in technological innovation and tools. The investment is necessary to enhance the effectiveness, efficiency, and value of GIA to the organization.

Information technology is a key driver of change, disruption, and opportunities in an ever-changing operating environment. Information technology has forced organizations to transform their operations to survive and remain sustainable. Technological innovations have driven the success, profitability, and creation of new businesses and opportunities for organizations across the globe. It is also the cause of the demise of many organizations that were reluctant to embrace technological innovations and change. The transformation includes accelerating, and fast-forwarding business operations and plans. This was evident during the COVID-19 global pandemic and included from:

- Working in the organization's office to working from home or remotely
- Working within the organization's network to working in the Cloud
- Restricted to relaxed access controls to the organization's systems and network

- Face to face to virtual meetings
- Manual signature to electronic signatures
- In-person shopping to online shopping

The next generation of leaders of GIA has no choice other than to embrace and leverage information technology. They must embrace and leverage it to maintain and enhance their effectiveness, efficiency, and value to the organization. This includes being ready, resilient, and relevant. It is a matter of survival in some cases as technological innovation is rapidly changing and disrupting the operating environment. What was best practice and effective yesterday may not be effective today and what is effective today may not be effective tomorrow. Embracing and leveraging information technology means abandoning old habits, manual and traditional approaches, and utilize information technology to transform GIA into an electronically driven operating environment.

Information technology is revolutionizing organizations operations across the globe. It is the key driver of improved and enhanced effectiveness, efficiency, and success of organizations. Technological innovations and tools have enabled organizations to integrate activities, streamline policies, processes, and procedures, eliminate redundant and duplicate activities, and effectively mine and analyze big data. Tasks and activities that took hours, days, and weeks to complete are now done in seconds and minutes. This is by taking over many of the routine, recurring, and voluminous technical tasks of organizations and professions. It has made organizations more effective, efficient, and sustainable. It has also made more time available for the leaders and team members to engage and collaborate with stakeholders on strategic matters, core business, and risks. Technological tools include the following:

- AI
- Automation
- Digitalization
- IoT
- ML
- BOTs
- RPA
- ChatGPT

Technological tools will enhance and enable the next generation of leaders of GIA to separate the trees from the forest. It will enhance their ability to harness the value of big data, which is one of the most valuable assets of an organization. This is an opportunity for the next generation of leaders to use technological tools to effectively manage the data explosion in the operating environment. The availability and explosion of big data over the years have made it impossible to rely on manual processes or outdated technological tools to work effectively and efficiently. The next generation of leaders and team members can easily get sidetracked with the abundance of big data that is now available to assist organizations achieve their objectives. This also keeps the organization and the next generation of leaders from drowning in the global ocean of big data. It is easy to get lost and shift the focus from what is most important to the organization and its stakeholders in an ever-changing operating environment.

INVESTING IN GIA

Investing in information technology and training of team members must be a part of the mindset of the next generation of leaders of GIA. This is critical to the survival, sustainability, and success of GIA and team members. Knowledge and experience gained using technological tools will assist in timely identifying opportunities for improving the effectiveness and efficiency of GIA. The agility, effectiveness, and efficiency are derived from the easy access to data and information and the ease in maximizing the use of big data. Technological tools make it easier to mine, analyze, interpret, and connect the dots of big data. It also enhances the quality of assurance services, advice, including insight and foresight, which is provided to stakeholders to assist them make more informed decisions. The quality of the information and data is likely to be more timely, accurate, reliable, verifiable, and actionable. Technological tools also enhance the effectiveness of GIA's risk assessment processes and activities. They play a key role in providing insight and foresight on emerging issues gained from connecting the dots across the organization.

Technological innovation and tools are driver of effectiveness and efficiency in a dynamic operating environment. They will enable the next generation of leaders of GIA to respond and adapt to change much quicker by accelerating and fast forwarding the transformation of GIA to an agile operating environment. This includes the transformation from a traditional, hybrid, or manual to an automated, integrated, and digitalized operating environment. The transformation will also enable team members not to be buried in the sea of big data. Big data is now readily available 24/7 within and outside the organization and in the Cloud. This will also enable the next generation of leaders and team members to spend more time on strategy, core business, and what matters most to the organization.

The mindset of the next generation of leaders of GIA must include investing in training and continuing professional education of team members. This is necessary to build and maintain skills and expertise, which is also necessary for the team to remain ready, resilient, relevant, and valuable to the organization and its stakeholders. Investing in training and continuing professional education also contributes to the agility of the next generation of leaders and team members. Additionally, it is an alternative to outsourcing by developing in-house specialized skills and subject matter expertise. This includes cybersecurity, IT, advisory services, and PCI. The cost of these specialized services is generally high, and it may be more cost-effective to co-source or outsource the work. The decision must be based on a cost-benefit analysis as the need or demand for in-house specialized skills or subject matter experts may not justify the cost.

Investing in training and continuing professional education events enables the next generation of leaders and team members of GIA to keep current and informed of changes and innovations in the profession and industry. The events include seminars, workshops, and conferences. The events are a source of current knowledge, expertise, and an excellent opportunity for the next generation of leaders to network with peers and colleagues from other organizations. Networking enables them to engage, collaborate, and share to the extent possible experiences and lessons learned. The experiences and lessons learned help in avoiding reinventing the wheel or starting from scratch. The time saved from lessons learned from peers and colleagues who had a similar situation and are willing to share the experience is a key benefit of networking. It enhances the next generation of leaders' ability to anticipate, advise, and assist stakeholders in quickly adapting to changes in the operating environment. Additionally, investing in training and continuing professional education is attractive to potential candidates and regulators in their assessment of the governance and control environment of an organization.

Organizations and leaders of GIA usually invest in the training and continuing professional education that are beneficial primarily to the organization. This includes investing in new skills and expertise that the organization needs to remain competitive and successful. The next generation of leaders of GIA must ensure that they are in the loop of the skills and expertise that are most important to the organization and its stakeholders. This will enable them to be proactive and take advantage of obtaining the required skills and expertise that the organization needs to be successful. It will also enable them to be ready, resilient, relevant, successful, and valuable to the organization.

The investment in GIA by the organization plays a key role in the survival, sustainability, success, and value of the next generation of leaders to the organization. The investment is required to adequately equip them with the resources they need to be successful. The investment is necessary to attract, hire, and develop a high-performing, diverse, and multicultural team. This includes funding for ongoing training and continuing professional education for the team. It is also necessary for them to effectively address new and emerging risks, opportunities, and demands of the operating environment.

CHAPTER SUMMARY

The next generation of leaders of GIA must have a dynamic mindset as technological innovations are constantly disrupting the operating environment. Technological innovations and tools are driving how organizations operate to survive and remain effective and efficient. The next generations of leaders of GIA must also change to remain effective and efficient. This is by embracing, adapting, and ensuring that their mindset is in alignment with the changes. The sustainability and success of the next generation of GIA belongs to leaders who are ready to evolve, embrace change and technological innovations, and adopt an engaging, collaborative, and agile operating environment.

The pendulum has swung from the heavy focus on technical or hard skills to a more balanced soft skills operating environment. This requires spending more time engaging and collaborating with stakeholders to stay connected, current, and informed of what is most important to them and the organization. The next generation of leaders of GIA must be able to respond and adapt quickly to change and what is most important to stakeholders. This is because technological innovations are constantly changing and disrupting the operating environment.

The next generation of leaders of GIA must update and expand their skills and expertise as the skillset of a traditional GIA is not adequate or sufficient to address the complexity, constant changes, disruptions, and demands of an ever-changing operating environment.

NOTE

1 The Importance of Diversity and Inclusion for Today's Companies (forbes.com).

Notes

- Assurance functions: Include compliance, internal audit, internal investigation, information security, and risk management.
- Board: Refers to the board of directors of the organization.
- Ever-changing or dynamic operating environment is the same as fast paced, constantly changing, and disruptive operating environment.
- Global internal audit (GIA) and internal audit (IA) are used interchangeably.
- Leaders of GIA: Include the CAE and administrative and functional leaders.
- Management: Includes the CEO, senior management, and managers.
- Technological tools: Include artificial intelligence (AI), automation, digitalization, data analytics (DA), machine learning (ML), robotics (BOT), robotics process automation (RPA), and ChatGPT.
- Senior management: Includes the CEO and usually his/her direct reports.
- Stick, sustainable, and long-lasting are used interchangeably.
- Team members of GIA: Include the CAE, administrative and functional leaders, and staff

Index

D

E

F

G